Business in Society:
Consensus and Conflict

CW01066637

Other BEC Higher National Level core texts from Butterworths:

People and Employment
Organizations: Structure and Policy
Data Studies

Business in Society: Consensus and Conflict

Tom Burden
Reg Chapman
Richard Stead
School of Accounting and Applied Economics,
Leeds Polytechnic

Butterworths
London   Boston   Sydney   Wellington   Durban   Toronto

All rights reserved. No part of this publication may be
reproduced or transmitted in any form or by any means,
including photocopying and recording, without the written
permission of the copyright holder, application for which should
be addressed to the Publishers. Such written permission must also
be obtained before any part of this publication is stored in a
retrieval system of any nature.

This book is sold subject to the Standard Conditions of Sale of
Net Books and may not be re-sold in the UK below the net price
given by the Publishers in their current price list.

First published 1981

© **Butterworths & Co (Publishers) Ltd. 1981**

British Library Cataloguing in Publication Data

Burden, Tom
Business in Society.
1. Business
I. Title   II. Chapman, Reg   III. Stead, Richard
658   HF5351   80–42221

ISBN 0–408–10693–X
ISBN 0–408–10694–8 Pbk

Typeset by William Clowes (Beccles) Ltd
Printed and Bound in Great Britain by Mansell Bookbinders Ltd, Witham, Essex

Preface

This book is about business in modern society and is intended primarily for students and teachers on Business Education Council Higher Level courses. It is also suitable for those on other business studies and social science courses at certificate, diploma and undergraduate levels.

The book brings together material from economics, sociology, politics and law to provide an overall view of business and the environment in which it operates. Many perspectives on business reflect deeply held beliefs and values. The distinctive approach of this volume involves using two different perspectives, one which emphasizes Consensus and the other Conflict, to analyse business in modern society.

There are questions and exercises at the end of each chapter. A number of questions require only short answers and are set to test understanding of the main points of the chapter. Other questions are set to encourage further investigation and application, frequently involving a search for relevant information using the Appendix on official sources of data. Finally, a few projects are suggested to encourage further analysis and application.

Abbreviations

bn	billion (thousand million)
BL	British Leyland
BP	British Petroleum
CAP	Common Agricultural Policy
CBA	Cost benefit analysis
CBI	Confederation of British Industry
CCC	Competition and credit control
CEGB	Central Electricity Generating Board
DHSS	Department of Health and Social Security
EDC	Economic Development Council
EEC	European Economic Community
EFTA	European Free Trade Area
EIB	European Investment Bank
FIS	Family Income Supplement
GATT	General Agreement on Tariffs and Trade
GDP	Gross Domestic Product
GNP	Gross National Product
GP	General Practitioner
HP	Hire purchase
IMF	International Monetary Fund
IRC	Industrial Reorganization Corporation
JP	Justice of the Peace
LAFTA	Latin American Free Trade Area
£M3	Sterling M3
MLH	Minimum List Heading
MNC	Multinational corporation
MP	Member of Parliament
MSC	Manpower Services Commission
NATO	North Atlantic Treaty Organization
NCB	National Coal Board
NCWP	New Commonwealth and Pakistan
NEDC	National Economic Development Council
NEDO	National Economic Development Office
NEB	National Enterprise Board
NHS	National Health Service
NI	National Income
OECD	Organization for Economic Cooperation and Development
OPEC	Organization of Petroleum Exporting Countries
PSBR	Public Sector Borrowing Requirement
R & D	Research and Development
RSPCA	Royal Society for the Prevention of Cruelty to Animals
SEG	Socio-economic group
SIC	Standard Industrial Classification
TUC	Trades Union Congress
UN	United Nations
VAT	Value Added Tax

Contents

Business in society: Framework for analysis

Part A will provide the historical and analytical background for analysing business in Britain. In Chapter 1 the broad scope of the business world will be explained together with the wide range of economic, technological, political, legal and social factors affecting business. Chapter 2 will outline the major divisions of belief and ideology about the role of business in Britain. In addition, the contribution of social science to the understanding of business is described. In Chapter 3 the main changes which have taken place in business and economic activity in Britain over the last century will be outlined. The role of government in economic matters and the various strategies available to governments for managing the economy will also be indicated.

Chapter 1

Business and society

1.1 Introduction

Businesses both large and small face a rapidly changing society which continually presents them with new problems and opportunities. The changes which affect business include those in the economy, in technology, in the political and legal systems and in society at large.

Businessmen have always been concerned with changes in the economic system resulting from the behaviour of competitors, as well as in general economic conditions such as the rate of inflation or the level of demand for goods. They have likewise been concerned with the monitoring of technological changes which may transform methods of work and threaten markets for particular products. Today, however, those in business need also to take account of broader social and political factors. In recent years, for instance, there has been increasing public concern about pollution, conservation, discrimination on grounds of sex and race, health and safety at work and a range of other matters involving the social responsibilities of business. These are matters not only of public concern but also of government action.

This book will analyse the main economic, technological, political, legal and social changes that affect business. The main changes which have taken place will be described and possible future developments will be indicated. These matters are inevitably the subject of great controversy. Nor is this surprising, for any discussion of business in society should touch upon the issues of power and wealth in society—how they are distributed and how they ought to be distributed. In many discussions of business, however, these issues are largely ignored, or else the discussions are based on unstated economic, social and political judgements. It is a distinctive feature of this book that issues of power and wealth are seen as central to an understanding of business in society. Moreover, the book will make explicit the frequently unstated differences of belief and ideology about the role of business in British society.

1.2 The scope of the business world

In the nineteenth century a clear distinction existed between 'business' and 'government'. 'Business' was synonymous with commercial activities undertaken for profit. The benefits from business accrued directly to investors and indirectly to society by the creation of wealth. In contrast, 'government' was concerned with a very limited range of non-commercial functions such as defence, foreign relations and law and order. The prevailing ideology was one of *laissez-faire*, that is, a belief in a free enterprise economy with the minimum of government intervention. Although the government provided a stable framework for economic activity, for instance, by maintaining the value of the currency, on the whole business was left to businessmen.

Over the last century this distinction between business and government has become obscured. Government has become increasingly involved in the economic affairs of the private sector of business and there has grown up a large commercial public sector. Furthermore, the development of government social services is closely linked to economic and industrial developments. The growth of non-commercial private sector organizations also demonstrates that the private sector is no longer synonymous with organizations undertaking commercial activities for profit.

The increasing involvement of government in economic affairs over the last century has blurred the distinction between 'government decisions' and 'business decisions'. Governments need the cooperation of finance, industry and trade unions to implement policies. In turn, economic interests frequently consult governments and try to persuade them to adopt particular policies. Consequently, decisions by business on employment, wages, location and so on are often influenced by government pressures, whilst government decisions are similarly influenced by employers, unions and other business interests. This interpenetration of government and business decision-making creates a symbiotic relationship in which government and business become dependent on each other.

The growth of public enterprise has further obscured the boundary between government and business. The term 'public enterprise' is used to describe the commercial activities of organizations owned or controlled by the state. The term covers the nationalized industries, which are some of the largest businesses in Britain, government shareholdings in limited companies such as British Petroleum (BP) and British Leyland (BL), the promotional activities of such bodies as the National Enterprise Board, and the trading services of local authorities. Public enterprise organizations are not solely commercial enterprises for they have public service obligations. Nevertheless, they form a large and strategic part of the business world.

Social service organizations of government, which are not normally considered as businesses, are also closely bound up with the business world. The growth of social services, such as education, health and housing, has been profoundly influenced by changes arising from the economy. Such services emerged on a national scale following the industrial revolution and the consequent growth of towns. Continued pressure for such welfare services came from organized labour, often supported by businessmen who saw the advantages of a healthy, educated workforce. The pattern and level of social service provision today continue to be influenced by economic conditions. In addition, social service organizations are among the largest in Britain, managing resources greater than most companies and involved in complex planning and decision-making similar to that of most large organizations. Indeed, recent attempts to import more sophisticated planning methods borrowed from the commercial sector may increase the similarities between the social services and other sectors.

Within the private sector there has been a proliferation of non-commercial organizations. In cases such as churches and charities their involvement with business is peripheral to their main activities. They may, nevertheless, become involved in campaigns to influence business and government. For instance, many church bodies have campaigned to stop British investment in South Africa. More significant are those voluntary organizations set up as pressure groups to influence government and business. Trade unions and professional associations are the most important example of such groups operating from within the business world. An increasing number of groups have been formed outside business to influence the decisions of firms and governments. The environment lobby, for instance, has been active on such varied matters as nuclear energy, motorway building and recycling waste products. Similarly, the consumer movement is also now a force which government and business must take into account. Sometimes, as in housing and retailing, consumerism leads to self-help projects and cooperatives being formed as alternatives to traditional forms of business. Finally, there are many research and propaganda bodies that may influence government and business through their publications. Although not business enterprises themselves the activities of all these non-commercial organizations make them as much a part of the world of business as business itself.

1.3 Business sectors

1.3.1 Classifying business organizations

From the previous section it is clear that the scope of business extends beyond the commercial private sector and includes the commercial and many of the social activities of governments. In addition, there is need to take account of the non-commercial private organizations when analysing the scope of business. Within the business world, however, it is necessary to distinguish the major types of enterprise.

There is no shortage of classifications that highlight similarities and differences among business enterprises. They have been classified according to size, technology, ownership, function, structure and many other features. For the purposes of this book it is appropriate merely to identify a few broad categories, or sectors, of business organizations. This can be conveniently achieved by using two simple criteria for classifications: type of ownership and type of dominant orientation.

Type of ownership. This distinction is between public and private ownership. Although the boundaries are increasingly blurred there are still major differences between organizations in the public and private sectors according to the kind of services they provide, how they are financed, who the supposed beneficiaries of their operations are, how decisions are made and to whom, and for what, they are accountable.

Type of dominant orientation. This distinction is between those organizations which are predominantly economic and commercial, producing goods and services for sale at a profit, and those which are mainly concerned with social and public welfare.

Using these two criteria it is possible, as *Table 1.1* shows, to divide the business world into four main sectors and also to indicate the position of the non-commercial voluntary organizations.

Table 1.1   The main business sectors

Orientation	Ownership	
	Private	*Public*
Commercial	Industry and commerce Finance	Public enterprise
Social	Voluntary organizations	Social services

1.3.2 The main business sectors

The **industrial and commercial sector** includes all private sector commercial organizations except financial institutions. The sector includes the business enterprises that dominate agriculture, manufacturing, distribution and many service industries. The **financial sector** includes banks, insurance companies, pension funds and various markets such as the Stock Exchange and international money markets.

These two sectors share a common economic orientation, derive their resources from charges on users and the owners or investors are expected to be the prime beneficiaries. The structure and technologies of the industrial and commercial sector differ from those of the financial sector, which is smaller, less diverse and more centralized in its ownership and decision-making. Compared to the public enterprise sector, however, firms in these two sectors have more freedom in their operations. Although accountable to investors and dependent on clients and market conditions, there is generally less government involvement and less accountability to the public as a whole than in the other two sectors.

The **public enterprise sector** includes all the trading or commercial operations of the public sector whether by central or local government, nationalized industries or joint public–private enterprises. The services are provided for the benefit of the immediate consumers and society as a whole, and are financed by charges on consumers. Public enterprise organizations use general industrial technologies and their structures and powers are usually determined by Parliament. In order to safeguard the public interest they are held accountable to Parliament or to elected local authorities.

The **social services sector** includes government organizations operating at national, regional and local levels. The main services provided are health, education, housing, welfare or personal social services, and social security. The main beneficiaries are expected to be the clients who use the services, and in most cases resources come from taxation rather than charges on clients. The main methods of provision in many social services involve direct client–official contact. This also distinguishes them from the more impersonal technologies of the other sectors. The structures and powers of social service organizations are determined by Parliament and they are accountable to local councillors or Parliament.

Voluntary organizations are predominantly social and welfare oriented, but there are important differences in the degree of social orientation and in the methods they use. The differences have already been noted between churches and charities and research and propaganda bodies. There are also important differences between those organizations, such as the anti-smoking body ASH, which advance a cause, and those, such as trade unions and employer associations, which are primarily concerned to advance the material interests of their members.

Voluntary bodies derive their resources primarily from members or voluntary contributors. They often have a large membership and nominally democratic decision-making. Frequently, power rests only with an active minority, rather than with the rank and file or the public who are claimed to be the main beneficiaries of the organization.

Voluntary organizations are not business enterprises and do not form an identifiable business sector. They do, however, share many characteristics with organizations in the main business sectors and are an important part of the environment in which all the sectors operate. For these reasons they are included in *Table 1.1* and are given detailed treatment later in the book, especially in Part C.

All classifications obscure as well as illuminate; for instance, the distinction drawn between public and private ownership is often unclear as companies like BP and BL illustrate. There may also be problems of ascribing orientations to particular organizations. For instance, the pursuit of profit may be sacrificed to the interests of managers and workers in a company. Nevertheless, this simple classification provides a convenient way of describing major differences and similarities among business enterprises which are dealt with in more detail in later chapters. Moreover, the sectors broadly correspond with the classification used by the government.

For statistical purposes, the government uses the **Standard Industrial Classification** (SIC) to categorize business organizations according to the work they do. Broadly, these are industries; for instance, Order XIII represents textiles. The classification also includes a finer level of detail, the **Minimum List Heading** (MLH). Order XIII textiles is thus subdivided into 10 MLHs such as woollen and worsted, jute, lace and cotton spinning. Typically, any factory will be making more than one product, and it is classified according to its most important output.

This classification is used, for example, in the annual Census of Production, which is primarily an enquiry into the volume of work being done in the various industries, and in the annual Census of Employment, which looks at the changing way in which labour is distributed between industries. *Table 1.2* gives the results of this survey for 1977. The four business sectors correspond substantially to groups of SIC Orders. Private industrial and commercial organizations cover mainly Orders I, III–XX, XXII and XXIII. The financial sector covers Order XXIV, while public enterprise dominates Orders II (mining), VI (metal manufacture), XXI (gas, water and electricity) and XXII (transport and communication). The remaining Orders (XXV and XXVII), namely, professional and scientific services and public administration, cover the social services sector.

1.4 The environment of business

Those involved with business have long sought to explain why one business organization is more successful than another. In particular,

Table 1.2 Employees in employment (Great Britain, 1977)

SIC Order	Industry	Employees ($\times 10^3$)	
I	Agriculture, forestry and fishing	378	
II	Mining and quarrying	348	
III–XIX	Manufacturing industries	7 150	
III	Food, drink, tobacco		689
VI	Metal manufacture		483
VII–XII	Engineering and allied industries		3 252
XIII–XV	Textiles, leather and clothing		890
XX	Construction	1 232	
XXI	Gas, water and electricity	337	
XXII	Transport and communication	1 447	
XXIII	Distributive trades	2 700	
XXIV	Insurance, banking and finance	1 128	
XXV	Professional and scientific services	3 546	
XXVI	Miscellaneous services	2 294	
XXVII	Public administration	1 564	
	Total	22 126	

Source: *Department of Employment Gazette*, February 1980

there have been attempts to discover features of organizations which produce success. Many of the earliest writers on organizations suggested that there were universal or 'classical' principles of sound management which gave rise to organizational success. These principles stressed the importance of the structure of the organization, particularly the way work was divided up and coordinated. It was claimed that the principles could be applied equally in the private and public sectors, as well as in voluntary organizations. Later writers, especially since the 1930s, have made similar claims for good 'human relations'. It is claimed that if management shows concern for the welfare and satisfaction of the workforce this will lead to improved output and organizational performance. Better human relations are said to encourage initiative and generally motivate staff. Both these approaches throw some light on organizational success. Both, however, underestimate the importance of the environment, that is, of the world outside the organization.

Writers on organizations increasingly stress the importance of monitoring and adapting to external conditions. Empirical studies of organizations suggest that there are no rules of sound organization which apply universally. Different organizations, rather, and even different parts of the same organization, need to be managed differently. In particular, external conditions are crucial. Factors such as organizational structure and human relations are important, but each organization needs to adapt them to its own external environment.

Anything outside a business organization is part of its environment. Some parts of the environment, such as competitors or legal restrictions, are clearly of more immediate impact than others. Many of the most far-reaching changes affecting business organizations, however, stem from general changes in the domestic or international environment. For instance, changes in population structure, in technology or in the balance of international economic power may mean changing demand for the services of all sectors.

The environment provides businesses with resources and opportunities but it also imposes certain constraints on their activities, such as those imposed by market forces or by law. The way any business combines its resources, which include manpower, ideas, technology and finance, and organizes itself to identify and exploit opportunities is likely to be a major determinant of its success.

Resources, opportunities and constraints are not, however, easily separable. Businesses need adequate resources in order to exploit opportunities. It has been frequently claimed, for example, that financial institutions in Britain are unwilling to lend to inventors and innovators. In some industries outdated technology or shortages of skilled labour have been cited as reasons for British firms not taking advantage of opportunities available to them, and so losing customers to their foreign competitors. The constraints imposed on businesses may also prevent them from fully exploiting their opportunities. Government price controls and laws safeguarding the rights of consumers and employees are examples of constraints which may severely handicap business operations. The constraints of one organization may, however, create opportunities for others. Cuts in National Health Service spending, for instance, create opportunities for private health insurance schemes.

The importance of the environment in providing resources, opportunities and constraints is such that each business and voluntary organization needs to be alert to the features of its own environment. It must also monitor and adapt to changes in that environment. Success in these tasks ensures that the organization survives; failure can endanger its existence. For example, building societies both receive deposits and grant mortgages, and they need to keep these in rough balance. Uncompetitive interest rates and poor service will drive borrowers and investors to other financial institutions. In order to keep in balance the societies adjust their interest rates according to economic conditions and, less frequently, change their personnel, policies, technology and structures in order to improve services. By careful monitoring of environmental changes the societies are able to maintain themselves and grow.

The activities of business organizations cannot, however, be understood solely in terms of the need to adapt to the environment. Decisions taken by enterprises are a result of bargaining, negotiation and conflict between managers, workers and different sections or interests within the enterprise. Nevertheless, these groups and interests are not isolated from the environment. The experiences which people have outside work, in the family, at school and in the community are powerful influences on their attitudes and behaviour at work. The strong solidarity and class consciousness of miners, steelworkers or ship-builders, for example, is a reflection of the isolated and relatively closed communities in which they live, as well as their work experience.

1.4.1 The variety of environments

The environments in which business and voluntary organizations operate can vary greatly in complexity and uncertainty. Large diversified organizations frequently operate in extremely complex environments. A multinational corporation, such as ICI, has plants in many countries and has diversified into several industries. Similarly, a local authority provides a wide range of services to varied groups of clients. In each case the organization needs to adapt its outputs and methods to a variety of clients and conditions. This problem has become increasingly common due to the trend towards larger units in all business sectors.

Environments also vary according to their uncertainty and rate of change. Comparisons of different industries often highlight the different rates of change in their markets. For example, a study of the American plastics, food and container industries was based on evidence that they experienced respectively high, moderate and low rates of change in demand, products and technology. Moreover, the study showed that divisions in the same company may operate in different environments. In the plastics firms, for instance, research divisions faced the most uncertain environment. There were great changes in the state of knowledge about products and a long timespan before ideas could be tested on the market. In contrast, marketing divisions faced less uncertainty. There were limited changes in customer demand or the actions of competitors and also a fairly rapid feedback from customers on the acceptability of the product. The environment of the production divisions was the least uncertain. There were few changes in products or methods and these divisions had the most immediate tasks of providing a set quantity of output at a set quality. Failure in these tasks was obvious almost immediately. This study showed that the environment of a business may be very complex and that different parts of the same organization may operate in environments with very different levels of uncertainty.

1.4.2 Dependence on the environment

Although all organizations are influenced by the resources, opportunities and constraints provided in the environment, businesses vary in the degree to which they can control the environment. In highly competitive industries businesses are influenced by conditions which they cannot control. In the international currency markets, for instance, there are numerous brokers buying and selling currency in many countries. Competition is intense and no one is able to dominate the markets. Rather, brokers must respond quickly to changes in currency rates in order to survive.

Most organizations do not, however, operate in such a competitive situation, and most are able to influence their immediate environment to some degree. There has been a marked trend towards concentration in British industry. An increasing number of industries are dominated by just a few large firms which may serve to limit competition. Competition may be further reduced and markets manipulated by price-fixing or market-sharing agreements reached secretly between companies. For instance, the history of the oil industry for a century up to the 1970s shows that despite great uncertainty and successive gluts and shortages the major oil companies, frequently acting together, were able to regulate output and prices to stabilize markets and protect their profits.

In some cases the dominance of a business over its environment is so great that it is able to insulate itself from the outside pressures of shareholders, competitors, consumers and governments. This may be especially true where private or state monopolies exist. Even when organizations are able to dominate their immediate environment, however, they are still affected by the broader changes in the environment. For example, the major oil companies, which are among the richest and most powerful businesses, have been affected by the rise of the Organization of Petroleum Exporting Countries (OPEC) and the desire of an increasing number of oil-producing countries to control their prime national asset. Even the most powerful businesses cannot insulate themselves from society completely.

1.5 The plan of the book

In this chapter the broad scope of the business world has been emphasized together with the existence of several major business sectors.

The importance and variety of the environment of business have also been stressed together with the different degrees to which businesses are dependent on the environment. In Chapter 2 the difficulties of interpreting phenomena will be explained and two contrasting views of business in society outlined. One view focuses on consensus and harmony whilst the other stresses conflict and disorder. Chapter 3 will describe the development of British business over the last century together with the increasing government intervention in economic affairs. These three chapters comprise Part A of the book and will provide a background and conceptual framework for Parts B and C.

Part B, comprising Chapters 4–7, will examine the four major business sectors which have been identified. Voluntary organizations will also be examined in these chapters as well as in Part C. Part C, comprising Chapters 8–12, will explore the social, political, legal and international environment affecting organizations in all four business sectors. Possible future developments in business and society are explored in the final chapter.

Guide to further reading
General

Donaldson, Peter (1978). *Economics of the Real World*, 2nd edn, Penguin, London. A lively introduction to the workings of the economy.
Kempner, T., MacMillan, K. and Hawkins, K. (1976). *Business and Society*, Penguin, London. Chapters 1–4 deal with the changing environment of business.
Thomas, R. E. (1976). *Government of Business*, Philip Allen, Oxford. Chapters 1 and 2 describe the main types of business and the changing context in which they operate.

Subsections
1.3

Prest, A. R. and Coppock, D. J. (1978). *The U.K. Economy: A Manual of Applied Economics*, 7th edn, Weidenfeld and Nicolson, London. Chapter 4 provides data on industry and commerce.
Eldridge, J. E. T. and Crombie, A. D. (1974). *A Sociology of Organisations*, Allen and Unwin, London. Chapters 3 and 4 give a useful summary of various classifications of organizations and the significance of the environment.

1.4

Child, John (1977). *Organisation: A Guide to Problems and Practice*, Harper and Row, London. Chapter 7 discusses the factors affecting organizational performance including environmental factors.

Burns, T. and Stalker, G. M. (1961). *The Management of Innovation*, Tavistock, London. The classic British study of the importance of the environment for business.

Brown, R. G. S. and Steel, D. R. (1979). *The Administrative Process in Great Britain*, 2nd edn, Methuen, London. Chapter V stresses the distinctively political environment of the public sector organizations.

Exercises

Review questions

1. In what ways has the distinction between business and government become obscured?
2. Distinguish between the four main business sectors. Give examples of organizations to be found in each sector.
3. What is meant by the term 'environment'? Describe the three ways in which the environment affects business enterprises.
4. Explain why different organizations, or different parts of the same organization, may operate in different environmental conditions.

Investigation and application

Information on employment in different industries is available in the *Annual Abstract of Statistics* published by the Central Statistical Office. Use this source to estimate the current size of each of the four business sectors. Compare the current position with that 5 years ago. What are the major difficulties of making such comparisons?

Project

Select organizations in any two of the business sectors and compare and contrast the ways in which the environment provides them with resources and opportunities and imposes constraints. Where possible make use of Annual Reports or other information provided by the organizations.

Chapter 2

Interpreting business in society

2.1 Introduction

Facts do not speak for themselves. They are open to different interpretations. Frequently, facts are selected and interpreted according to preconceived ideas and beliefs. Certainly there are different beliefs about the role of business in society which affect the selection and interpretation of facts. Wherever debate and controversy take place, such as over trade unions or the European Economic Community (EEC), different overall viewpoints are brought to bear on the issues. These debates are not just about the facts but about how things should be viewed and about how evidence should be interpreted. In order to understand the role of business in society an awareness is needed of the major perspectives which can be employed and of the different values and beliefs which underpin them.

2.2 Perspectives on business in society

The views people hold about business are closely related to their political views on a range of social and economic issues. Throughout this book reference will be made to three political positions, those of the Left, the Centre and the Right. Each viewpoint has a number of distinctive features which result in rather different approaches to many of the issues that will be dealt with. The existence of these differences is hardly surprising given that an evaluation of business in society touches on many controversial issues of power, status and wealth. These differences reflect deep-seated beliefs on how the economy, the political system and society should operate.

The Centre and Right political views have one fundamental feature in common. Very broadly, they each accept the present organization of society and the role of business in it. Each also rests on the belief that there is widespread agreement that the existing organization of society is satisfactory. In the language of social science, they are both Consensus approaches since they assume an absence of fundamental conflict in society and in particular they believe that the interests of business and the rest of society are compatible. The Left political view broadly rejects the existing organization of society and the role of business in it. It holds that substantial disagreement exists about whether or not the existing order of society is satisfactory. This view is a form of Conflict theory. Throughout the book, there will be considerable emphasis on the different interpretations and explanations provided by those on the Left, employing Conflict theory, and those in the Centre and on the Right, employing Consensus theory.

2.2.1 The Consensus perspective

The basis of the Consensus approach is the belief in widespread agreement on the desirability of existing economic, political and social institutions. Those on the Right and those in the Centre share the view that the production of goods and services is best left, as far as possible, to the operation of the free market. They put considerable stress on the value of the profit motive, competition and private property as the basis for economic activity.

The profit motive is valued for the incentive it creates for businessmen to work efficiently, while competition is seen as a means whereby the efficient prosper at the expense of the inefficient. Private property gives citizens a stake in society and promotes responsible attitudes.

An economic system based on these principles will produce goods and services cheaply and efficiently. The market will ensure that the demands of consumers are met, and economic progress will result from the competition between firms to produce the goods consumers want, at prices they can afford. Within this perspective, however, those on the Right of the political spectrum emphasize the benefits of a free enterprise system with minimal government intervention. This is known as *laissez-faire*, and it was the dominant view in Britain from the mid-nineteenth century to the mid-twentieth century. Those on the Right wish to see a return to these values and policies. This right-wing variant of the Consensus view will be labelled the individualist perspective because of the importance it attaches to individual initiative and freedom of choice. This view is commonly found amongst those on the right wing of the Conservative Party.

The other version of the Consensus approach does not place so much emphasis on the virtues of the entirely unregulated free market. This view is typical of the Centre ground of British politics and is found in sections of the Conservative Party and of the Labour Party. It will be labelled centrist or moderate throughout the book. Moderates share the individualist's belief in the profit motive, private property and competition but support the use of the power of the state to remedy deficiencies in the free market. These deficiencies arise where consumers suffer because industries are monopolistic, where the economy fails to produce full employment and where an unacceptable level of poverty occurs. These deficiencies are remedied by state management of the level of economic activity using Keynesian techniques, by policies to regulate and control certain areas of business and by the setting up of a limited system of publicly owned enterprises and social services. While the private sector of business is to retain its dominant position in the economy as a whole, the ideal of the moderates is not the free enterprise economy of the individualists but a 'mixed economy' with a 'welfare state'. The moderates do not wish to abandon market forces, merely to guide their operation.

Whether they are in the Centre or on the Right those who adhere to a Consensus view usually support a 'pluralist' interpretation of the political system. They hold that if all citizens have the right to support the parties and pressure groups of their choice then governments will have to be responsive to the wishes of the population as a whole. Parliamentary democracy, therefore, gives everyone a say in political decision-making and prevents any one group from wielding a disproportionate influence. Government is seen as an impartial arbiter reconciling the various competing interests in society. The machinery of state, the Civil Service and the legal system, is seen as a neutral mechanism for regulating society in the interests of all.

Other institutions outside of the economic and political spheres are also seen to command widespread support in the Consensus approach. Society is viewed as offering its members a rich and varied existence. The opportunity to obtain the material rewards of life is open to all with the necessary talent. Family life and leisure offer everyone the chance of a full life and where social problems do arise the means exist to solve them.

The Consensus view, therefore, adopts a favourable evaluation of existing society. While those in the Centre and on the Right differ concerning the desirable level of state intervention, each maintains that the drastic changes proposed by those on the Left are not necessary, and indeed harmful. The implications for business are clear. The Consensus approach involves leaving things much as they are, or at least only making changes very gradually.

The Consensus approach rests on a set of assumptions about the nature of economic, political and social institutions. It can be summarized as involving the following ideas.

- Over a long period, economic, social and political inequalities have declined.
- No fundamental conflicts of interest exist in society.

- Economic and political power is widely dispersed.
- Economic, political and social institutions generally work to the benefit of all.
- There is genuine and widespread support for the existing order of society.

2.2.2 The Conflict perspective

The basis of the Conflict approach is the belief that existing economic, political and social institutions do not work in the interests of the majority of members of society. Those holding left-wing political views are most likely to adhere to a Conflict approach. In this book these people will be referred to as radicals. Radicals are to be found on the Left of the Labour Party, in parts of the trade union movement and in other smaller groups and organizations supporting left-wing views. Many radicals, both political activists and academics, draw their inspiration from the work of Marx. Marxism is the most common kind of Conflict theory, though by no means all Conflict theorists are Marxists.

The Conflict approach takes a critical view of the workings of the market system and the values on which it is based, the profit motive, private property and competition. The profit motive is seen as a demeaning reliance on greed as the basis of the economic system. Private property is seen as a means whereby those who own and control enterprises are able to exploit the labour of those who have to work for them to earn a living. Competition is seen as the means whereby whole industries come to be dominated by a few firms, exploiting workers and consumers alike. Those on the Left who support a Conflict approach are more likely to be in favour of the public ownership of productive assets and of cooperation and planning as the basis for the economic system.

The Conflict view sees the market as inefficient and unjust. Goods are produced for profit, not to meet people's needs. The division between the owners of enterprises and their employees results in endemic conflict and excessive outlay on the supervision and management of an uncooperative workforce.

State intervention in the economy is seen as a means whereby the resources of government are enlisted to aid the survival of the market or capitalist system. Economic and social policies are largely designed to reduce opposition to the system by ameliorating its worst effects without fundamentally altering it.

Radicals seek a fundamental change in the economic system. They wish to limit the rights of private enterprise, perhaps by taking industries into public ownership. They seek much greater state control of the economy in the form of planning. They are also likely to support increases in the rights of employees and a limitation of what are seen as the arbitrary powers of senior management. The overall purpose is to redistribute income and wealth, end economic exploitation and create a more equal society.

Radicals view the existing political system as a means by which those with wealth are able to exercise disproportionate power and influence. They suggest that the major parties are unlikely to challenge the position of the owners of wealth. Indeed, they see the Conservative Party as a defender of these interests, while the Labour Party leadership pursues policies which do not threaten their position. Radicals suggest that while many pressure groups exist, the decisive influence on government is normally those groups representing industrial, commercial and financial interests. Governments, therefore, normally act to support the interests of capital. The machinery of state is seen as a further means whereby upper class interests are furthered, in part because senior positions in the Civil Service and the Judiciary are held by people from upper class backgrounds.

The Conflict view has a distinctive approach to many other social arrangements. Opportunities are seen as highly restricted since children from upper class families obtain many of the top positions. Poverty and deprivation are viewed as ineradicable conditions without fundamental changes in the system. It is suggested that lack of resources and lack of power mean that most people are unable to develop their full potential.

The Conflict approach, therefore, involves a critical evaluation of existing society. In contrast to the Consensus views in the Centre and on the Right, it maintains that drastic change is necessary. There are considerable implications for business. To the extent that these views influence policy, or indeed, the general attitudes and behaviour that people hold, then business may find itself operating in a new kind of environment and subject to strong pressures for change.

The Conflict approach makes a number of assumptions about the nature of economic, political and social institutions. These can be summarized as follows.

- Economic, social and political inequalities have remained substantially unaltered.
- Fundamental conflicts of interest exist in society.
- Economic and political power are concentrated in the hands of an unrepresentative minority.
- Economic, political and social institutions do not work to the benefit of all.
- The basis for widespread opposition to the existing order of society exists and will appear under the right conditions.

Table 2.1 indicates the main terms used in the discussion of the two perspectives. These terms will be used throughout the book as different issues are discussed.

Table 2.1 Perspectives on business in society

	Conflict views	*Consensus views*	
Political position	Left	Centre	Right
Political label	Radical or leftist	Moderate or centrist	Individualist or rightist
Economic ideal	State-controlled economy	Mixed economy	Free market economy

2.3 Using the perspectives

The versions of the Consensus and Conflict perspective given above are not meant to be definitive; they are merely an attempt to put down two coherent but opposed viewpoints. While each, as presented, is an adequate representation, other authors would probably choose to organize the details of the account rather differently. There is then, no single Consensus or Conflict perspective which is correct. In fact, these perspectives are two ends of a spectrum and there are many intermediate positions which are neither wholeheartedly one nor the other. Most writing on business and social science occupies a position somewhere on this spectrum. The literature on business, however, is usually written from a Consensus perspective, though the authors frequently fail to state this. A novel feature of this book is the explicit use of both perspectives.

The issue of whether one of these views is right and the other wrong is often debated. Some authors believe that one or the other is correct, others believe that the two can be combined into some kind of compromise viewpoint, while others believe that either may be applicable depending on what is being explained. Ultimately, however, it is not possible to prove that one or the other view is right and it becomes a question of how each person is able, to his own satisfaction, to make sense of things.

What can be learnt about business in society from an understanding of these perspectives? First, a great deal of the information and debate in the mass media about matters relevant to business is biased towards one or other of these views. The same is true of much of the relevant academic literature. A recognition of this enables material to be more sensibly evaluated. Secondly, these viewpoints have a direct relevance to many occupational roles where it is often necessary to anticipate the motives and behaviour of others. These can often be seen more clearly through the use of these perspectives. Thirdly, people may be able to formulate their own views more clearly if they are aware that there is frequently an alternative way of looking at things. Fourthly, these perspectives are of importance in understanding the issues dealt with in this book. The ideas, theories and controversies discussed here will frequently be related to them. Last, as the concluding chapter will show, views on how business and society are likely to develop in the future will largely depend on which of these perspectives is adopted.

2.4 Social science and business in society

The perspectives discussed above demonstrate that it is possible to make sense of business in society from more than one point of view. These views occur in everyday life and are used to provide a frame of reference for understanding events. They are also used in the more academic discussions which take place within 'social science'.

The term 'social science' refers to a number of subjects, including economics, politics and sociology, which study various aspects of life in society. The word 'social' is used because these subjects do not focus on the individual as such but on aspects of his relationships with other people. Behaviour is 'social' because it takes account of, and is affected by, the behaviour of others. The businessman making decisions about his business, the elector deciding how to vote and the trade unionist formulating a pay claim are all acting in ways which are affected by how others have behaved in the past and by how they are expected to behave in the future. These subjects also examine the organizations within which behaviour takes place, such as firms, trade unions and families. At a wider level, they deal with the large-scale arrangements necessary for man to exist in society, such as the economy and the political system.

The word 'science' refers to the fact that these subjects claim that they provide 'scientific' knowledge about their subject matter. However, the 'social' sciences are generally newer, less well developed and less well established in the public mind than the 'natural' sciences such as physics or chemistry. They also deal with matters about which people have a great deal of direct knowledge and experience, such as work, politics and family life. Social science claims that it provides a more valid view of these matters than people's everyday understandings. This claim is based on the special way in which social scientists obtain their knowledge. An example is the cause of industrial disputes, an issue on which most people have a definite opinion, such as, 'they are caused by bad management', or perhaps, 'militant shop stewards are to blame'. A person holding one of these views would probably do so as a result of the kinds of attitudes he had been brought up with, the sorts of people he mixed with, the newspaper he read, his personal experience, or lack of it, of labour relations and so on. In other words he would come to his view on the causes of strikes simply in the course of everyday life. By contrast, a social scientist interested in industrial disputes might reach opinions of a similar kind but in a very different way. He might have carefully read the available literature on the topic and analysed existing data. He might have examined the various explanations offered by other authors and attempted to discover which was the best. He might even have done his own research into particular industrial disputes. In doing all this he would try to prevent his personal views and values from influencing his conclusions so that his results would not just be his own opinions, but would be objective and 'scientific'.

From this, it might seem that the social scientist possesses valid and objective knowledge whereas the layman's knowledge is simply a set of unproven opinions illustrated by highly selective 'facts' and based on value-judgements. In reality, the contrast is by no means as great. Although social scientists might want their work to be objective, value-free and 'scientific', in fact they are also members of societies and have their own values and viewpoints. The values a social scientist holds can affect:

- the topics which are chosen for study,
- the questions which research is designed to answer,
- the concepts he chooses to use in his explanations,
- the kind of explanation he chooses to give,
- the emphasis given to various possible conclusions.

As a result, if two different people study the same topic, there is no guarantee that they will produce the same explanations. It might seem from this that social science cannot provide better explanations than everyday opinions. However, it needs to be remembered that any science is a collective activity. Theories, arguments and conclusions are published, debated and criticized by specialists in the area. This debate helps to ensure that poor arguments, inadequate data and unjustified conclusions are exposed while soundly based knowledge is accepted. Thus, while individual social scientists may put forward mistaken or ill-founded explanations, or allow their work to be adversely affected by their own values, a check in the form of open academic debate exists. As a result the findings of social science have some claim to validity.

2.5 Conclusion—facts, theories and perspectives

This book utilizes a great deal of factual material about various aspects of business in society. Providing an accurate account through the use of facts is important in social science. These facts have been obtained in a variety of ways. Often they have been collected by others. Government departments, commercial and non-commercial organizations and international agencies all publish substantial amounts of relevant material. In addition, social scientists obtain their own data through questionnaire surveys, the examination of documents and through becoming members of the groups or organizations they wish to study.

Facts on their own, however, are of limited usefulness. They may form the basis of a simple description but they do not explain why things happen. This is the job of theories. Theories are usually statements about how things are caused. The assertion 'monopoly leads to increased prices' is a theory. The relevant facts can be examined to see if this is true. If it is, the theory is confirmed. There are many theories in social science, some well established, others very tentative. New theories are constantly being put forward. All theories need to be examined critically. The reasoning and the evidence on which they are based may be open to question. Finally, the selection, presentation and interpretation of the data in a theory is likely to be coloured by the perspective adopted by the author. The fact that people have a perspective, which is usually some variant of a Conflict or Consensus approach, does not invalidate their theories. It is, nevertheless, the case that theories can be more clearly understood and assessed when the perspectives of those who hold them can be identified.

Guide to further reading
General

George, Vic and Wilding, Paul (1976). *Ideology and Social Welfare*, Routledge and Kegan Paul, London. Contains an account of the main political approaches in Chapter 2 (Right), Chapters 3 and 4 (Centre) and Chapter 5 (Left).

Marx, Karl and Engels, Frederic (1967). *The Communist Manifesto*, Laurence and Wishart, London. Parts I and II contain an excellent summary of a major Conflict viewpoint.

Worsley, Peter (1970). *Introducing Sociology*, Penguin, London. Chapter 2 contains a discussion of theories in social science, and sources of data. There is also a very clear account of the Conflict and Consensus perspectives on pages 373–392.

Subsections

2.1 and 2.2

Budd, Alan (1978). *The Politics of Economic Planning*, Fontana/Collins, Glasgow. Chapter 2 provides a useful summary of different perspectives on state economic intervention.

Exercises

Review questions

1. How do moderate and individualist approaches view the role of the state?
2. What are the main differences between the Conflict and Consensus views?
3. Why do radicals criticize the workings of the market system?
4. What differences exist between common-sense knowledge and social science?
5. How do values influence the research carried out by social scientists?

Application and investigation

1. Identify the perspective adopted in another textbook in this area with which you are familiar. Describe how the perspective has coloured the account given by the author.
2. Outline your own perspective using the concepts introduced in this chapter. Give the reasons why you hold these views.

Project

Formulate a set of questions to discover the extent to which people hold Consensus or Conflict views on economic and political questions. Try it out on a suitable group of respondents and summarize your results in a research report.

Chapter 3

The changing economy and its management

3.1 Introduction

This chapter will examine Britain's economic system as a whole. The impact of the changing economy upon the nation's social, political and legal institutions will be analysed in later sections of the book.

Two central facts distinguish the economy of 1980 from that of 1900: first, the economy is vastly more productive today than 80 years ago; secondly, the involvement of the state in that economy is very much larger. This chapter will examine these features as well as the causes and results of economic development—the changing resources used by the economy and the way these resources have been deployed to create an economy which is not only richer but qualitatively different. Development means not only more goods, services and jobs, but different types of goods, services and jobs. Attention will then turn to the policies by which the government has sought to keep the economic machine running smoothly, ideally providing jobs for everyone without the general price level rising. The policies open to the state will be analysed in terms of the two approaches described in Chapter 2.

3.2 Economic growth

Some physical measures of this century's economic expansion are set out in *Figure 3.1*. Broadly speaking, the volume of goods and services produced has quintupled.

3.2.1 Labour resources

This prodigious rise in output has been caused in part by the larger number of people at work today. The number of those economically active has risen by almost a half, a much faster rise than the increase in

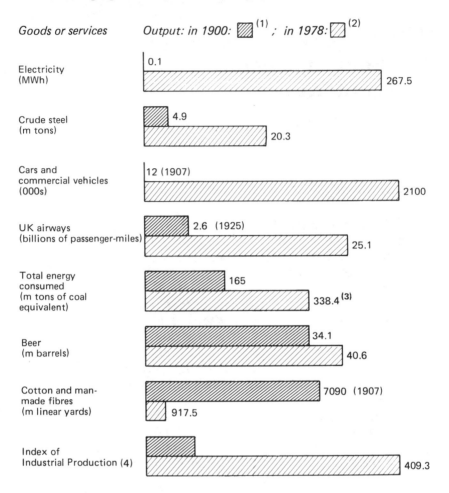

Figure 3.1 Production in the UK, 1900–1978

Sources: (1) *The British Economy, 1900–1972, Key Statistics*, London and Cambridge Economic Service; (2) *Annual Abstract of Statistics*; (3) *Digest of UK Energy Statistics*; (4) Feinstein, C. H. (1972), *Statistical Tables and National Income, Expenditure and Output for the UK 1855–1965*, Cambridge University Press (author's calculation from *Economic Trends* for 1965–1978)

the total population. The largest contribution to the expansion of the workforce has come from married women.

The number of hours worked has not risen by the same proportion. Employees nowadays work shorter weeks—normal hours for all manual workers in 1976 were 40.2 hours, compared to 46.7 hours in 1920. Forty-one per cent of women employees work part-time. There are also fewer working weeks in the year as paid holidays have become more widespread. Balancing the trend to shorter hours, labour has become

Table 3.1 The economically active population

Group	Number in millions		
	1901	1975	Change 1901–1975
Males	11.5	15.8	+ 4.3
Females	4.8	9.8	+ 5.0
(of whom: married)	(0.7)	(6.6)	(+ 5.9)
Total	16.3	25.6	+ 9.3

Sources: *British Labour Statistics, 1886–1968, Table 102; Social Trends 1980*, HMSO, 1979, *Table 5.1*

more productive. The educational qualifications of the labour force have risen as the education system has expanded. Industrial training has also grown, with various Industrial Training Boards and the Manpower Services Commission now supplementing the efforts of individual firms.

3.2.2 Capital and technology

The efforts of the workforce are enhanced by the stock of 'capital goods'; industrial machinery, such as lathes, blast furnaces, robots, transport and communication networks and buildings. The process of investment has trebled the British economy's stock of capital goods between 1900 and 1978.

The growth in output has, however, been faster than the increases in labour and capital alone would warrant. The explanation lies in the ideas that are now used in production—the technology which is employed. Today's capital stock is not only bigger than that of 1900. It is qualitatively different, for it embodies more advanced research. One of the most important aspects of the history of the twentieth century has been the introduction of the new technologies such as electricity and motor transport. These new technologies had mainly been developed during the latter part of the nineteenth century. Steel began to be produced in the 1860s; public electricity generation started in 1882; and Britain's first motor cars were constructed in 1896. The necessary consequences of the use of these new technologies have been the abandonment or decline of older products and processes. Coal-driven railways have yielded pride of place to the road system and, in the factories, production in batches has frequently given way to assembly-line methods, or, as in the case of chemicals, to continuous-flow systems. Old industries like textiles or agriculture have been transformed, and new ones like electronics or plastics have been created.

As a result of these changes in technology, all industries have achieved higher labour productivity, that is to say, a given volume of output can today be made with less labour. Some industries have expanded as demand for their output has advanced, such as chemicals, while others have lost ground in terms of both output and employment, such as coal. Some have been virtually eliminated, such as Cornish tin-mining. Thus the relative sizes of the primary sector of the economy (agriculture and mining), the secondary sector (manufacturing) and the tertiary sector (services) have altered fundamentally during the last 80 years. Future changes will be even more far-reaching and rapid. Technical developments have been made in the past decades which are currently in the process of adoption—nuclear energy, lasers, 'biological engineering', microprocessors and so on. Without doubt the transformation of the industrial scene will accelerate in the coming decades.

3.2.3 The organization of business

The twentieth century has seen the growth—in response to technological and other pressures—in the scale and form of business organization. Large firms are much more important today than in 1900. In 1909, the hundred largest firms accounted for 16% of Britain's manufacturing output; in 1970 the figure was 41%. Partly this change has come about as employment has become concentrated in the larger factories. More important, however, has been the tendency for firms to own more than one establishment: the biggest 100 firms each owned, on average, 72 plants in 1972, compared with 27 in 1958. In consequence, large firms are generally engaged in several lines of business simultaneously. Unilever's range of goods, for example, includes frozen food, margarine, soap and detergents and animal feed.

A more recent phenomenon has been the proliferation of multinational corporations (MNCs), owning production and distribution facilities in many parts of the world. Most are based in the USA, but Britain and the other Western European countries have produced several giant MNCs themselves.

Today's big companies are partly the results of natural growth, and partly they are the products of mergers. These have tended to come in waves: the 1890s, 1920s and the 1960s and 1970s. The first wave involved mainly the amalgamation of firms in the same industry, such as the formation of Imperial Tobacco out of 16 companies. Recently mergers have more often involved firms from different industries, such as Cadbury and Schweppes, in so-called 'conglomerate' mergers.

Big organizations may come into existence to employ 'economies of scale'. These occur when large-scale production is cheaper per unit than small-scale production. A single large plant may be more efficient than two smaller ones. Economies of scale also exist in distribution, marketing and finance. For example, a nationwide advertising campaign may cost twice as much as a regional one, but may reach 10 times as many consumers.

A result of the development of big firms has been the concentration of production in the hands of small numbers of sellers. In 1968, a survey looked at over 330 product groups. In one-quarter of the cases, nearly all the output was accounted for by five firms or fewer. Comparison with earlier years shows that the overall trend has been toward greater concentration since World War II.

Within the firm, increased size has meant a move away from 'family' firms, constituted as partnerships or private companies. Economic leadership has passed to the large, public joint-stock company. Despite the fact that the majority of enterprises remain private companies, they are a force in but a few areas of activity, such as construction, retailing or catering. As the large firms have come to the fore, so has professional management tended to replace the owner-manager, though in many cases managers own shares in the firms for whom they work.

The trend to gigantism has been evident in all business sectors in recent years: conglomerate mergers have created large corporations in banking and finance; the extension of public ownership has produced large organizations in the industries concerned; and public bodies such as local authorities have been reorganized into huge units. The biggest organizations, however, are to be found amongst the nationalized industries—the Post Office was the nation's largest employer, and the Central Electricity Generating Board is the biggest buyer of industrial capital goods.

For the employee, work has also altered fundamentally. In 1900, jobs were frequently done by gangs, with the foreman not only acting as supervisor but often as a subcontracting employer also. Employment, especially for labourers, was frequently casual, with no security of continued employment. Today both practices have been replaced in the central sectors of the economy by direct and more stable employment contracts. A further feature is trade union membership. Spreading from skilled workers to the unskilled in the late nineteenth century, membership is now well established also among female and white collar workers.

3.2.4 International links

The development of the British economy has not been shaped only by domestic forces. The UK has long had an 'open' economy, that is to say, economic links with the rest of the world have traditionally been more important for the UK than, say, for the USA, a relatively 'closed' economy. These economic links operate through trade in goods and services, through the export of capital and the migration of labour, through the ownership of assets and through Britain's role in international organizations. All these spheres have been transformed no less fundamentally than domestic industry during the course of this century.

In 1900, Britain imported mainly food and raw materials, which were largely paid for by the export of manufactured goods—indeed Britain then accounted for over 32% of world exports of manufactures—and by the provision of services like shipping and banking—so-called 'invisible exports'. Trade was largely with the Empire, which also received an enormous flow of investment from Britain. It is estimated that between 1907 and 1914 annual investment abroad exceeded net real investment at home. As a result, in 1914 Britain held a vast stock of assets overseas and was the centre of a huge empire. Many of the colonies had substantial numbers of emigrants from the UK.

During the twentieth century the direction of trade has shifted away from the Commonwealth and towards the industrial countries of Western Europe, with whom Britain is joined in the European Economic Community (EEC). At the same time the proportion of manufactured goods in Britain's import bill has grown prodigiously. Whereas Britain was virtually self-sufficient in finished manufactures at the start of the century, by 1979 these accounted for over one-third of all imports. Foreign goods now account for a quarter of home sales of manufactures, while a similar proportion of Britain's manufacturing output is sold abroad.

Although the flow of outward investment has continued on a relatively smaller scale, Britain's stock of overseas assets is much depleted, partly as a result of two world wars. Inward investment, particularly by American MNCs has grown, so that these companies now have a significant presence in such industries as vehicles, electronics and, of course, oil extraction.

3.2.5 Consumption

The development of technology, an expanding labour force and capital stock, and increasing traffic with other economies have placed immense possibilities at the disposal of the British economy. The ways in which these possibilities have been exploited will now be examined. One of the most significant features of the modern age is the sheer volume of goods consumed by the population at large. Compared with the poverty which was the lot of the labouring classes in mid-Victorian times, today's consumers live in opulence. Real consumer spending has risen by over

2.5 times this century; allowing for the growth of population, this amounts to a rise of over 80% in per capita terms between 1900 and 1979. The major beneficiaries of this expansion have been wage- and salary-earners, for income from employment has climbed as a proportion of Gross National Product (GNP) from 48% in 1900 to 69% in 1977.

The structure of consumption has altered with rising living standards. Food, which absorbed about half of the average working class family budget in 1900, now accounts for about one-quarter. Housing, fuel and clothing have also receded in importance. The extra purchasing power has been devoted rather to 'superior goods', that is those goods whose consumption rises as people become richer. Thus, durable household goods (furniture, domestic appliances), transport and vehicles, and entertainments have all expanded their share of the consumer's budget. Of today's 19 million households, over 10 million have cars, 17 million have washing machines, and nearly 9 million have telephones, whereas in 1900 these things did not exist or were the preserve of the rich. Consumers also benefit from increased public spending on the social services, such as education and health, which absorb a significant proportion of the nation's labour resources. This public provision is sometimes called the 'social wage'.

Associated with rising standards of living have been major changes in Britain's political, social and legal systems. These changing structures will be discussed in later chapters.

3.2.6 What sort of economy?

There is much controversy over the question of whether increasing state intervention has altered the nature of the economy. On the Right of the political spectrum, those who believe in the virtues of free competition decry the advance of state regulation and taxation. It has, they argue, reduced incentives and smothered free enterprise. This 'creeping socialism' constitutes a real threat to economic and political liberty.

In the centre-ground of politics, other Consensus theorists describe the system as a 'mixed economy'. They praise the partly-public, partly-private economy as a means of avoiding the worst excesses of total state ownership, as displayed in the USSR, and of uncontrolled capitalism, as seen in this country in the early nineteenth century. A mixed economy combines the benefits of innovative entrepreneurship with a degree of social responsibility.

From the Left of the political spectrum, radicals argue that the economy is basically run on capitalist lines. Describing the system as 'state monopoly capitalism' they argue that state intervention merely serves to support free enterprise, by providing cheap commodities from the nationalized industries and by securing the cooperation of labour through welfare spending.

3.3 National Income

Hitherto, this chapter has concentrated on physical quantities: tons of steel or millions of telephones. The following sections will, however, use monetary units—£s—in discussing economic theories about problems such as inflation. The monetary value placed upon a country's production is called its National Income (NI).

NI can be derived by two principal methods. The **expenditure method** aggregates spending by consumers, government and foreign buyers of UK exports with spending on capital goods during a particular year. Care is taken to allow for the distorting effects of indirect taxes, such as value added tax (VAT), and subsidies.

The **income method** seeks the same destination by another route. It involves totalling up all incomes derived from economic activity: income from employment and self-employment, trading profits and rents. 'Transfer incomes' such as unemployment benefits, which do not derive from economic activity, are not included. The income method, significantly, includes income received by UK residents from the ownership of assets which are located in other countries.

Economic activity has the effect of wearing out the country's capital stock, and this must be made good if production is to be maintained. 'Capital consumption' or depreciation is accordingly deducted, to arrive at Net National Product, or National Income.

The primary use of NI statistics is to quantify the rate of 'real' economic growth. The effect of rising prices must therefore be eliminated to permit comparison between different years. Attention must also be paid to population changes and to the distribution of the NI between the various income brackets. Between 1900 and 1978, NI rose by over 280%, an annual average rate of growth of some 2%.

The significance of the NI statistics is a matter of interpretation. Orthodox economic theory, popular toward the Right of the political spectrum, believes that a higher NI indicates, simply, more output and more well-being. Other Consensus theorists in the centre of politics accept that the NI figures are only a rough guide to welfare, for they contain an arbitrary element. They record only monetary transactions, yet welfare may be affected by other things. The NI statistics may show higher output, but worsening pollution, for example, may simultaneously reduce people's welfare.

Some Conflict theorists argue that economic growth brings the disruption of long-established communities as well as greater volumes of consumer goods. This disruption may engender unemployment, crime and other social problems. If police and welfare services expand as a result, National Income will record an even greater rise, but on balance people's lives may be actually impoverished.

3.4 Theories of the macroeconomy

The size of NI is a matter of much concern. Should the level of economic activity be too low, unemployment will occur and businesses selling consumer goods will face sluggish demand. A level of demand which exceeds the economy's capacity to supply will, on the other hand, lead to a large volume of imports and so to balance of payments problems. High demand also contributes to the process of rising prices: inflation. The British economy has experienced all these types of problem during the course of the twentieth century.

The policies which governments have used toward them have been shaped in part by theories of the behaviour of the whole economy: 'macroeconomic' theories. This section will examine three such theories—monetarism, Keynesianism and the so-called alternative economic strategy. These theories correspond respectively to the individualist, moderate and radical perspectives.

3.4.1 Monetarism

Monetarism is an economic doctrine with a long history. Out of favour in the 1950s and 1960s, it returned to prominence during the 1970s because it appeared to offer a solution to the problem of inflation. Modern monetarism is associated with the work of Professor Milton Friedman of Chicago, who is a firm advocate of *laissez-faire* policies. Monetarists believe that the market is the best medium for organizing economic affairs and that government intervention can only be harmful. Inflation, for example, can be traced to governments' printing money, rather than to high pay claims. This belief in the market stamps monetarism quite clearly as a Consensus theory.

The central tenet of monetarism is that *a rise in the quantity of money in the economy will produce a rise in the price level.* Inflation can be attributed to an expanding money supply and can be reduced by controlling the money supply. Money, in the modern economy, consists mainly of bank deposits. 'Sterling M3' ($\pounds$M3), as one measure of money supply is called, was composed of £9 billion in notes and coin and £47 billion in bank deposits in January, 1980. The control of inflation demands, therefore, the regulation of the banking system.

Banks create additional bank deposits by lending. A bank loan to a customer raises the amount of money in his account immediately. When he spends the money, his account falls, but that of the shopkeeper rises. The process is termed **credit creation**. Conversely, the repayment of bank loans leads to a fall in total bank deposits and thus to a contraction in the money supply.

Bank lending occurs when two circumstances hold: first, potential borrowers must be willing to pay the interest charges; secondly, the banks must have sufficient **reserve assets**. These are liquid assets, which can readily be turned into cash. They include bankers' balances at the Bank of England, Treasury bills and money-at-call which has been lent out on the money markets at short term. Reserve assets earn lower yields than other bank assets such as loans to customers.

The Bank of England has stipulated that banks must hold reserve assets equal to $12\frac{1}{2}\%$ (one-eighth) of their liabilities, that is, customers' deposits. The Bank of England is therefore able to influence the level of bank deposits by influencing the banks' holdings of reserve assets. Given a ratio of deposits to reserve assets of 8:1, the Bank of England knows that a £1 billion rise in reserve assets will lead eventually to a rise in bank lending, bank deposits and £M3 of £8 billion. This relationship is known as the 'banking multiplier'. In consequence, the regulation of £M3 depends upon the control of the banks' holdings of reserve assets.

Reserve assets consist largely of Treasury bills. These are sold by the Bank of England to the commercial banks and are redeemed 3 months later. They are a means whereby the government borrows at short term to make up the difference between public spending and taxation. For the commercial banks, Treasury bills are reserve assets and so are a basis for further lending. When the government borrows in this way, it is also helping the banks to lend, and the process is therefore called 'printing money'.

Inflation is caused, the monetarists believe, by governments' borrowing through the issue of too many Treasury bills and thus printing money. To control inflation, monetarists advise governments to resort to other forms of borrowing which do not present the banks with new reserve assets. The government should sell long-dated gilt-edged stock (gilts) to investors—a process known both as 'funding' and 'open market operations'. They should also try to attract funds through National Savings. Such methods would, however, involve raising interest rates. High rates of interest not only make investors willing to buy government stock but also tend to deter people from borrowing from the banks. The Bank of England can influence all interest rates by changing the Minimum Lending Rate (MLR), the interest rate it charges on emergency loans which are sometimes granted to the banks.

Monetarists would not generally approve of such large-scale government borrowing, on the grounds that it diverts funds away from productive use in the private sector. Monetarists, therefore, prefer the government to borrow less money in total. The government deficit, the Public Sector Borrowing Requirement (PSBR) should be reduced, by raising taxes and cutting spending. Policy may also involve instructions to banks to restrict their lending, but monetarists would generally disapprove of any policy measures which distort the market. They prefer to prescribe the nasty medicine of higher taxation, lower public spending and higher interest rates in order to restrict the growth of £M3 and so to control inflation.

3.4.2 Keynesianism

Keynesian economics does not share monetarism's faith in the market. Left to itself, the market can produce undesirable results, such as the prolonged mass unemployment of the 1930s. Keynesians believe the state should intervene to correct such imbalances. This policy recommendation is the opposite of monetarism's *laissez-faire* ideals. Keynesians believe, however, that state intervention can ensure an outcome which is satisfactory to all members of society; it is thus a Consensus theory which is popular in the centre of the political spectrum.

Writing in the 1930s, Lord Keynes looked at the economy as a whole, rather than at particular markets: his theory was at a macro-, rather than a microlevel. He began by identifying the **circular flow of income** from firms to householders (as wages, dividends and interest on exchange for the hire of labour and capital) and back to firms as expenditure on the outputs of the enterprise. The circular flow is clearly NI in another guise: a large flow will be recorded as a high NI, a small flow as a low one.

The flow can, however, be reduced by 'withdrawals', and augmented by 'injections'. Not all income is spent upon the products of firms— some is saved, some goes to the state in taxation and some is spent outside the economy on imports. Savings, taxation and imports are all, therefore, withdrawals from the circular flow. Conversely, expenditure can arise from outside the circular flow, thus constituting an injection into that flow. Under this heading are investment, public spending and exports.

Should withdrawals and injections be of the same size, the circular flow would remain a constant size. There is, however, no guarantee that

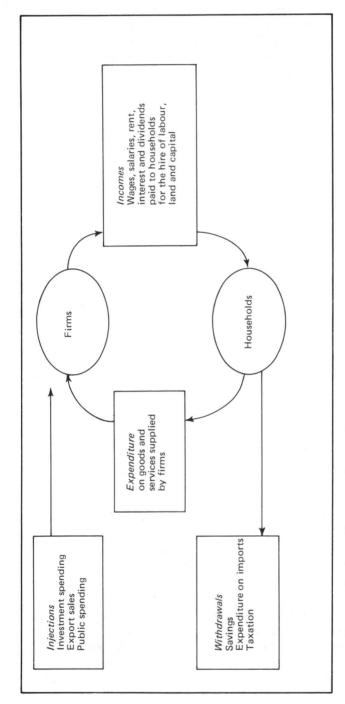

Figure 3.2 The circular flow of income and expenditure

withdrawals and injections will be equal. Suppose that businessmen's plans for expansion are shelved for some reason. Withdrawals, all else being equal, will now exceed injections. There will be a leak in the circular flow, and the flow will accordingly contract—a slump will develop. The process of contraction will end only when savers' plans are revised downwards. The probability is that this will indeed happen, for as more people are thrown out of work with the deepening slump, they will, most probably, stop trying to save. In time, planned savings will again be equal to planned investment. Both will be at lower levels than before, for investment and savings plans will have been revised downward during the course of the slump. The contraction of the circular flow has ended; NI has stabilized. The stabilization of NI at the low point of the slump means, however, that unemployment will stay high until something happens to make injections exceed withdrawals, say, a spontaneous surge of investment. The 1930s seemed to be a period in which the world had become stuck at the slump phase of the business cycle.

Keynes' analysis appeared to explain the persistence of mass unemployment. It also suggested a means of solving that problem. Injections should be raised, or withdrawals decreased, so that the former exceeded the latter. The circular flow would expand, NI would rise and workers would find jobs. Expansion would end when rising incomes had pushed up savings and other withdrawals so that injections and withdrawals balanced once again. Furthermore, Keynes argued, it lay within the power of the government to produce this state of affairs, by raising its own spending (an injection into the circular flow) or cutting taxes. He advocated a programme of public works without a corresponding rise in taxation. The Budget would not now be balanced—indeed there would be a deficit, the opposite of the policies pursued in the 1920s and early 1930s—to be covered by borrowing.

Conversely, to temper the problems of a boom, such as inflation or excessive imports, the government should raise taxation or reduce expenditure, thus creating a Budget surplus. The manipulation of spending and taxation was ideally to be operated 'countercyclically', with the state promoting expansion during slumps and helping to deflate NI in the boom periods. This policy is known as 'demand management'.

The amount of government spending necessary to reduce a given level of unemployment would depend upon the size of the 'multiplier'. An injection into the circular flow induces a rise in NI of a somewhat greater magnitude, and the ratio between the two items is the multiplier. The initial spending by the state on, say, a power station will raise NI by the amount of the spending as the contracts are fulfilled. The incomes of the construction workers, their employers, the suppliers of the turbines and so on will go up—and so will their spending on goods and services. This spending in turn will raise the incomes of brewery workers, landlords, garages and of anyone else who sells things to the power station construction men. In their turn, the brewery workers, landlords and garage mechanics will spend their extra money on various items and so raise the incomes of, say, farmers, cinema owners, publishers, home decorators and so on. The initial expenditure by the state spreads through the economy in a widening ripple.

As it proceeds, its effect becomes weaker. Not all the extra income is spent, for some is saved. Of the spending, some leaks away in taxation and some into imports and cannot be respent in the domestic economy. The strength of the multiplier will depend upon consumers' marginal propensity to consume domestically produced goods. If consumers spend a high proportion of any extra money on locally made items, the money remains in the economy to be respent, and the value of the multiplier will be high. If, however, consumers save their money or spend it on foreign goods, the multiplier will be low and the government's attempts to raise NI will be less effective. A recent estimate suggests that the multiplier may have a value of 1.45.

Keynesians believe the problems of inflation, unemployment and foreign trade deficits can be overcome by demand management by the government. Public deficits can reduce unemployment, while inflation can be controlled by reducing demand. With their predilection for state intervention, Keynesians also favour deliberate government policies on prices and pay settlements. Monetarists believe, of course, that public deficits are the cause of inflation and that incomes policies are powerless to control it. Both economic doctrines, however, believe that satisfactory solutions can be found within the existing economic system, for both are Consensus theories.

3.4.3 Radical theories

There are various economic doctrines which may be classified as Conflict theories. One coherent example is the 'alternative economic strategy', which draws its support from the Left of the political spectrum. It rejects both the monetarists' faith in the market and the Keynesian policy of guiding the market by public intervention, for it is mainly concerned with the distribution of power within the economy. The free enterprise or capitalist system, according to this view, is dominated by the giant firms. These corporations wield enormous power by virtue of their access to technology, their control of prices, industrial location and investment, and their ability to manipulate consumers and to exploit their employees. These firms are a law unto themselves, being able to evade public control by virtue of their power, expertise and international connections. They are able to avoid the effects of restrictive credit policies and corporation taxes by their power to move funds between subsidiaries.

Competition between these business empires in the pursuit of profit is seen as fierce and anarchic. The market is no longer the delicate mechanism for allocating resources seen by the monetarists, but a tumultuous battlefield. 'Monopoly capitalism', as the modern age is dubbed, is inherently unstable, and even Keynesian tinkering and guidance will not save it from generating problems. Problems like inflation, unemployment, low growth, regional imbalance, poverty and the squandering of resources are the results of uncontrolled—and uncontrollable—capitalism. In the UK specifically, the large firms are held to be 'failing the nation' by directing their investment overseas.

From this interpretation of the economic history of the twentieth century, the alternative economic strategy itself arises. If the uncontrolled power of the big companies is the problem, then these institutions must be brought to heel. The alternative strategy accordingly demands that the big companies be controlled by the government. Many of them have received vast sums of public money in the past. The defence industries have clearly been dependent on public contracts, and have also received the benefits of government-funded research and development (R & D) work. The same is true of the electrical engineering industry with regard to its involvement in nuclear power construction. Many large manufacturing firms have received development grants to set up factories in the depressed regions and all firms benefit from government spending on roads, industrial training and so on. Hence, the protagonists of the alternative strategy argue, these firms should be made accountable to the state and their activities controlled.

The mechanisms of control could include outright nationalization and planning agreements (whereby firms would submit their plans for their activities to the government for approval and possibly financial support). The establishment of works councils through which employees' representatives could influence the policies of a firm (industrial democracy) would also weaken the power of the capitalist groups controlling the big firms. Publicly owned companies in the major industries would use public funds to undertake greater investment and expansion. This competitive threat to the remaining companies would force them to invest also, thus reviving the performance of the whole economy. There would need to be strict control of imports if the anarchy of competition on the international plane were not to disrupt the British economy. Central planning would be carried as far as practicable, again to limit the instabilities of the system and to reduce the power of the owners of capital. Such large-scale state intervention is viewed with distaste by moderates and is, of course, anathema to individualists.

3.5 Economic policy

Elements of all three economic theories can be found in the policies of successive British governments from 1900 to the present. At the beginning of the century, the orthodox belief was a form of monetarism. Britain's trading and financial position demanded a stable currency, for sterling was the most widely held international currency. Stability would be best attained, it was thought, by avoiding excessive public borrowing.

In the 1920s and 1930s, unemployment in the UK rose to high levels, and tax receipts fell as economic activity slowed. Governments' response was to cut public spending, in line with falling taxation, in 1922 (the 'Geddes Axe') and in 1931 (following the May Report). Indeed, the Labour government's distaste for these cuts lead to its resignation in 1931.

Unemployment continued to stand at over one million throughout the Depression of the 1930s and government policy was widely criticized. One of the critics was Keynes, who argued that cutting public spending made the situation worse rather than better. Keynes worked at the Treasury during World War II and assisted Beveridge with his proposals for major reforms in health and social security. Many of these plans came to fruition shortly after the war with the creation of the 'welfare state'. Among the new policies was a commitment to full employment, based on Keynes' theories.

Keynesian policies of demand management were used consistently during the 'long boom' of the 1950s and 1960s. Government deficits were increased ('reflation') in order to reduce unemployment; and aggregate demand was reduced ('deflation') to correct the problems of high demand, such as inflation and excessive imports. Persistent deficits in foreign trade emerged as the main problem of the period, and successive governments resorted to increasingly severe rounds of deflation in attempts to achieve a balance of payments equilibrium. Indeed, a political cycle could be seen, as governments attended to the alternating problems of trade deficits and unemployment. In the early years of their term of office, governments frequently deflated to deal with a trade imbalance. As the next election drew nearer, they tended to cut taxes to reduce unemployment and boost their popularity.

Keynesian policies successfully eliminated unemployment, but seemed ill-equipped to deal with the major problem which developed in the 1960s: inflation. Following the Keynesian tradition of active state policies, governments sought to contain inflation by intervening in the setting of prices and wages. For most of the time between 1966 and the close of the 1970s, Britain had an incomes policy of some form. Policies ranged from statutory policies with fixed limits to voluntary policies using suggested 'norms' for pay rises.

In the mid 1970s, the Labour government went to great lengths to secure the cooperation of the trade unions as part of the 'social contract'. In return for the limitation of pay increases, the government enacted various reforms in employment law, cut taxes and subsidized food, housing and the nationalized industries. Some of their policies such as the creation of the National Enterprise Board, whose original brief was to use public funds to make British industry more competitive, derived from the thinking behind the radical alternative economic strategy. Though some progress was made in curbing inflation, prices continued their upward spiral.

The large PSBR which the social contract entailed began to worry investors in the foreign exchange market and the gilt-edged market. In 1976, a crisis developed, as sterling slumped badly against the dollar and as investors refused to buy newly issued gilt-edged. The government felt it had no alternative but to apply to the International Monetary Fund (IMF) for assistance. The IMF, an international agency which grants loans to countries in financial difficulties, employs monetarist economic theories. Accordingly, it imposed monetarist conditions upon the loans to the UK: higher taxes, lower public spending and increased interest rates.

The Conservative government elected in 1979 firmly believed in pursuing these policies with even greater vigour. Their success remains to be judged. The previous sections of this chapter have shown that success will depend not only on economic theories but upon political factors as well. Economic policy depends upon an underlying economic philosophy, which is related to a more general perspective on business and society. Economic management is also subject to powerful political pressures, domestic and external, as the troubled story of the 1970s shows.

Guide to further reading
Subsections
3.2

Pollard, Sidney (1969). *The Development of the British Economy 1914–1967*, Edward Arnold, London. Provides an informative and readable account of Britain's economic history in the twentieth century.

Hobsbawm, E. J. (1968). *Industry and Empire*, Weidenfeld and Nicolson, London. Another informative history, with Chapters 9–15 being the most relevant.

Hannah, Leslie (1976). *The Rise of the Corporate Economy*, Methuen, London. Gives a readable account of the development of large firms.

3.3 and 3.4

Stanlake, G. F. (1979). *Macro Economics: an Introduction*, Longman, London. Gives a description of the methods of computing NI in Chapter 2, and describes Keynesian macro-economic theory in Chapters 3–10 and 20.

Lipsey, Richard, G. (1975). *An Introduction to Positive Economics*, 5th edn, Weidenfeld & Nicolson, London. Part 8 discusses the nature and importance of money and the creation of credit.

Goodhart, C. A. E. and Crockett, A. D. (1970). 'The importance of money', in the *Bank of England Quarterly Bulletin* Vol. 10 (June), pp. 159–189. Discusses the differences between the monetarist and Keynesian approaches to the role of money in the economy.

Gould, Bryan *et al.* (1979). *The Politics of Monetarism*, Fabian Society Tract, London. Shows the relation between the economic theories of monetarism and the underlying political philosophy.

Lord Robbins (1977). *Liberty and Equality*, Institute of Economic Affairs, London. Sets out briefly the individualist view of the relationship between political freedom and economic affairs.

Galbraith, J. K. (1974). *Economics and the Public Purpose*, Deutsch, London. Discusses the power of large firms in the capitalist economy in Part III, especially Chapters 14 and 16.

Holland, Stuart (1975). *The Socialist Challenge*, Quartet Books, London. Sets out a radical analysis of the economic and political system in Chapters 2, 3 and 4, and outlines a radical political strategy in Chapters 7 and 8.

Campbell, M. P. (1981). *Capitalism in the UK*, Croom Helm, London. Provides a readable analysis of the British economy from a Marxist viewpoint.

Exercises

Review questions

1. Why has production in the UK risen during the last 80 years?
2. What are economies of scale?
3. What is the National Income, and what is the usefulness of this figure?
4. Gross income from employment
   Net income from employment
   Consumer expenditure
   Exports

   Imports
   Capital formation
   Company trading profits

What items would be used for computing NI by (*a*) the income method and (*b*) the expenditure method? (*see* 'Blue Book': *National Income and Expenditure*)

5. What other items would be needed to compute NI by (*a*) the income method and (*b*) the expenditure method?
6. What is money, and how is it created?
7. What are 'withdrawals', and 'injections', and how do they affect the economy?
8. What are the results of industrial competition according to radicals?
9. What theories are current government policies based upon?

Application and investigation

1. (*a*) What are the major differences between the monetarist and Keynesian approaches to the workings of the economic system and government economic policy?
   (*b*) Why do radicals believe the state should intervene more widely in the economy?
2. What are the economic consequences of a government deficit, according to (*a*) Keynesians and (*b*) monetarists?
3. What have been the levels or rates, over the last 5 years, of unemployment, inflation, economic growth, interest rates, growth of £M3, the exchange rate of sterling?
4. Explain how the banking multiplier works.

Project

Examine the macroeconomic strategy of the current government in terms of its underlying philosophy, objectives and methods. Assess its success to date and outline what you believe to be the most likely developments in this area in the next few years.

Chapter 4

The industrial and commercial sector

4.1 Introduction

This chapter will examine the industrial and commercial sector using the framework outlined in Part A. After defining and describing the sector and its evolution, it will discuss its significance for the rest of the economy. Frequently, this sector is described as the 'wealth-producing' sector. Certainly the industrial and commercial sector exerts a dominating influence on the whole of modern society, which is revealingly described as an 'industrial society' or an 'advanced industrialized economy'. Not only does this sector determine the material conditions of life and the tempo of change, but the ideas and values of the sector—such as the profit motive, private property and 'efficiency'—are the dominant ideas of society as a whole.

Because of its importance, governments have sought to assist the sector's growth and development. The means of attaining this have ranged from detailed intervention to non-interference. Bitter controversy has raged from time to time on the extent, and form, of public intervention. Many different policies, each with its particular implications for business, have been pursued over the years. The goal of faster economic growth has nevertheless proved to be rather elusive.

4.2 Scope and development

This chapter will be concerned with private commercial organizations other than financial institutions. They are to be found in agriculture (SIC Order I), manufacturing (III–XIX), construction (XX), transport (XXII), distribution (XXIII) and miscellaneous services (XXVI). They grow, mine, make or process things, selling them through the distributive network, and they employ the services of the transport and marketing trades in so doing. Others, such as firms in the entertainment business, perform services rather than dealing in merchandise. Consumer and capital goods are produced for private and public sector customers and for export.

Organizational forms range from self-employment, through partnerships and private companies, to public companies. The overwhelming majority of firms in this sector—perhaps 93%—are small, unincorporated businesses. Their 4 million employees constitute 30% of employment in the sector, and they account for some one-fifth of its output. Small firms may also be an important source of innovation, though their importance in the economy has declined through much of the present century.

Among the largest organizations in retailing and wholesaling is the cooperative movement. Cooperative societies were established in the nineteenth century to sell food and other goods to working class families. The intention was to bypass the ordinary shops owned by private capital. The societies were run democratically by the membership, and thus had a different pattern of ownership and control from the rest of industry and commerce. In recent years, competitive pressure from the private chain stores has forced the cooperatives to modernize, joining into

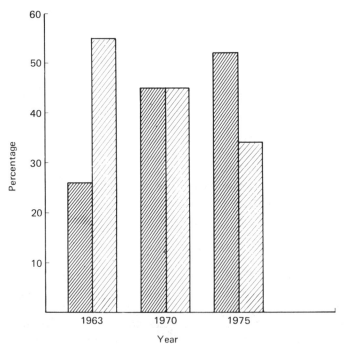

Figure 4.1 The changing pattern of share ownership. Percentage of UK quoted ordinary shares held by: individuals ▨ ; institutions ▨

Source: Committee to Review the Functioning of Financial Institutions. *Evidence on the Financing of Industry and Trade*, Vol. 3: *The Stock Exchange*, p. 194

larger, more concentrated societies and adopting more aggressive business attitudes. A new wave of smaller cooperatives in retailing and handicraft production has also been in evidence of late.

In terms of the volume of output, employment and assets, the private sector is dominated by the large multiproduct, multiplant, multidivisional enterprise. The 100 largest public companies held 64% of the net assets owned by all public companies in 1973. In manufacturing industry, the largest 100 firms employed over 3 million people in 1972, accounting for one-third of total jobs. The share of the large chains and supermarkets had also been increasing in the distributive trades.

One effect of the growth of large concerns has been the appearance of the professional manager. Legally, control rests with the owners of a firm, that is, the shareholders. In practice, they frequently have little power. Without access to technical information, shareholders have severe difficulty in over-ruling the professional managers. Indeed, the twentieth century has seen the decline of the private shareholder : shares in quoted companies are to an increasing extent owned by the financial institutions, notably the pension funds and insurance companies.

4.2.1 Competition and concentration

Private organizations in general relate as buyer and seller, customer and supplier. 'Vertical' links like these can take many forms : subcontracting from a main contractor, forming consortia of firms to undertake joint projects, hiring (leasing) rather than buying equipment, or hiring ideas through franchises and licensing agreements.

The normal form of 'horizontal' relationship is that of competition between firms, whereby buyers are offered a choice between the products of different firms. Firms may offer identical goods at different prices, in which case the consumer is at liberty to buy the cheaper product. Alternatively, firms may offer goods which are similar at prices which differ to some degree. The customer must then weigh the relative advantages of extra cost against quality differences, and so decide on the best value for money.

Consensus theories stress the incentives which this system gives to firms to seek the most efficient methods of manufacture and to improve the quality of their goods. The beneficiary of this process is, they argue, the consumer, who is thereby presented with a growing range of consumer goods. This is the doctrine of **consumer sovereignty**. It argues that output should be determined by consumer choice. The goods and services which people truly value are shown by people's purchases in the market place. At one time economists argued that only agricultural goods were truly valuable, and that the other parts of the economy produced mere luxuries. Modern economic theory has turned away from this notion of value and has replaced it with the proposition that value is in the mind of the consumer. If customers are willing to pay for something, regardless of whether it is an agricultural crop, such as tomatoes, a manufactured article like a pan, or a service, such as watching a football match, then it has value. An economy dominated by service industry is no less useful, by this logic, than one which is given over to industry or agriculture.

The theory of consumer sovereignty implies that anything which interferes with consumer choice is wrong. It follows that governments should adopt a *laissez-faire* policy and stay out of economic affairs. Governments should, however, prevent the emergence of monopolistic firms who could thwart consumers' wishes, for consumer sovereignty requires competition between producers.

Conflict theorists question the extent of competition, believing industry to be largely monopolized. They frequently argue that, where it exists, competition induces firms to skimp on safety arrangements and safety testing, to reduce the quality of products and to over-exploit natural resources. It is also argued that firms can create the demand for their products by persuasive advertising, which thus undermines free consumer choice.

The working of the market may lead to a reduction in competition as firms grow bigger and become fewer in number. Large firms may arise simply because of the success of a business products or services in the market place. An organization may market a new product which may become an established consumer good. Large firms are also able to exploit economies of scale in production, administration, finance, distribution or research and development (R & D). Typically, big firms are diversified, selling many commodities made in several different factories. Diversification frequently proceeds by way of 'conglomerate' mergers, whereby a firm takes over another company involved in a different activity.

In the nineteenth century, competition was seen as the source of industrial efficiency and ultimately of human progress. In the 1880s and 1890s, however, there was a distinct trend away from the competitive ideal, as firms in the same industry merged together to form powerful monopolistic units. During the interwar Depression, the restriction of competition became more widespread. Firms frequently colluded to share business out amongst themselves, often with government approval. Since World War II, British industry has continued to become more concentrated, as an increasing proportion of output is accounted for by the large firms. In 1968, there were 156 instances of a single firm's accounting for over half the output of a particular commodity. One-third of all sales of manufactured goods was into markets where five firms accounted for 90% of domestic output. Almost half of all sales was into markets where the top five firms controlled 70% or more of output. Examples included food, chemicals, electrical engineering, beer, wines and spirits, and cigarettes and tobacco.

4.2.2 Competition and industrial change

Critics of highly concentrated markets argue that the smaller the number of sellers, the easier it is for firms to collude—to refrain from competing by making agreements on pricing, or market shares, by setting up exclusive dealerships or by other methods. Rising concentration levels do not, however, mean an end to competition. Most industries face stiff competition from imported goods, which have advanced as a proportion of home sales of manufactured goods from 3% in 1950 to 26% in 1979. Competition from this source is likely to become even fiercer in future as countries from the Third World become industrialized.

Mere statistics on concentration do not, furthermore, convey the full story. The typical 'market structure', as the number and sizes of competing firms is known, is not monopoly, a single seller, but oligopoly, a few sellers. Competition among the few can be as fierce as competition among the many. Oligopoly may, furthermore, be conducive to innovation. Only large firms, it is argued, have the resources for R & D work. Large firms are better able to bear the risk of trying out new products. Their fortunes will not be solely dependent on any one product, and they will have had experience of marketing new goods in the past. The prospect of being—temporarily—the sole supplier of a new product may also be a spur to innovation.

Even when competition within an industry appears to be limited, competitive challenges may come from outside. Competition also exists between industries: glass competes with plastic; coal with oil and gas. All firms face the possibility of threats from successful innovations in other industries as well as from their direct competitors. The process of competition demands that firms constantly change their activities: products must be redesigned, lower cost production techniques adopted, new marketing approaches used. This leads to changes in firms' product ranges, the size and composition of their labour forces, their plant and their prices.

Industrial change involves the decline and closure of industries facing contracting markets. It also means the creation of new firms. The process of industrial change is **metabolic**: new firms appearing and old ones closing. Even if firms survive, their component units, the factories and offices, will be changing as new locations replace old.

As a result of such changes, the location of economic activity in Britain has altered fundamentally since 1900. At that time the coalfields of Wales, Scotland and the North of England were the industrial centres of Britain. These are, however, the areas where job losses through closures and contraction have been heaviest. The staple industries of coalmining, textiles, shipbuilding and steel have reduced their labour forces dramatically. These regions have therefore been characterized by relatively high unemployment rates. Expansion in the 1930s and since the war has been heavily weighted towards the South East and West Midlands: Birmingham and Coventry have grown rapidly in the twentieth century with the booming motor and electrical engineering industries.

The change in the numbers of people at work has been accompanied by a change in the nature of work done in the various regions. Management functions tend to be heavily concentrated in London and the South East—indeed, 65% of the headquarters of the top 500 firms were to be found in London in the early 1970s. Mergers accentuate this concentration, for, by this process, firms based in the South East frequently take control of provincial enterprises. At the same time, the 'peripheral' regions have tended to become the locations of branch plants of multinational companies. Although these factories provide jobs, the work tends to be routine, while the strategic decisions are made at head office. A spatial division of labour has thus been emerging, with the regions playing different roles, ranging from managerial functions to the performance of allotted tasks.

Parallel to the alteration in national industrial location has been a change in location at urban level. Land is cheaper in the suburbs, and the growth of road transport has freed factories from the ties of rail and train networks. The suburbs have accordingly attracted new industrial development and industry near the city centre has dwindled as old plant is not replaced.

4.3 The role of the industrial and commercial sector

The industrial and commercial sector, sometimes called the 'wealth-creating sector', employs 12.6 million people (58% of the labour force), generates 63% of the Gross Domestic Product (GDP) and accounts for 61% of investment. It is the source of 84% of the manufactured goods sold in this country, which constitute the basis of our material standard of living. Its exports make up over 80% of Britain's foreign earnings, which go to pay for the imported remainder of our consumption of manufactured goods as well as other foreign expenditure, such as tourism and government services (Armed Forces, Diplomatic Services, aid). It also constitutes the taxable base. Nearly all public spending is financed by taxes levied on the income and expenditure generated by the private sector—although the private sector in turn depends upon state provision of law and order, social services, communications and so on.

The significance of the private sector is not indicated by the size of its contribution to GDP, exports or employment. It is a force of overwhelming significance in determining the structure of the whole economy and society. Industrial and commercial wealth is one of the principal sources of power and status. Ownership and control over the processes of production and distribution are thus major determinants of the allocation of power between individuals and groups.

The sector also sets the tempo of society. Most economic and social change ultimately originates in the activities of the industrial and commercial sector. The development of motor transport, for instance, has not only meant the growth of new industries, but it has also helped to alter the layout of cities and has indirectly contributed to changes in community relationships and family life.

For the state, industrial change presents new challenges. New industries with higher skill requirements will demand more educational services; the need for faster transport will demand a motorway network; a higher standard of consumption will demand a more extensive refuse disposal service; industrial change will produce derelict factory sites and slag heaps to be reclaimed; and improving health and dietary standards will result in more surviving old-age pensioners to be looked after. Of great importance, too, is the overall strength of a nation's industry and commerce in determining the international standing of the state. Britain rose to be a world power as a result not only of successful diplomacy and victorious military campaigns, but also as a result of her economic success. This success was indicated by her huge share of world trade (over 30% in 1900) and the record of her businessmen in pioneering new products and processes. On both these counts Britain's economic power, and, in consequence, her political influence, are now waning.

4.4 The performance of British industry and commerce

Britain's economic performance has attracted much concern and comment. Some measures of Britain's recent industrial performance are set out in *Figure 4.2*. As an economic power, Britain has been in relative decline. She has been losing her position in world markets—a

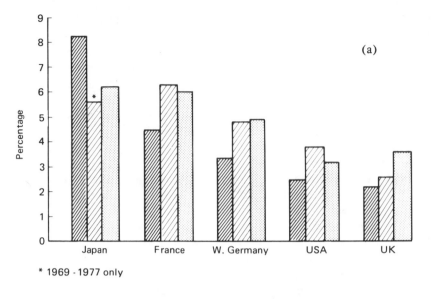

* 1969 - 1977 only

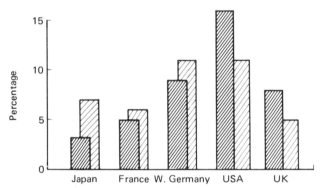

Figure 4.2 International economic performance, 1960–1975. (a) Selected indicators. Average annual rates of change in: GDP per head ▨ ; manufacturing output ▨ ; manufacturing output per employee ▢ . (b) Shares of world exports (%) in: 1960 ▨ ; 1975 ▨

Sources: *UN Yearbook of National Accounts Statistics, 1978,* Vol. II, *Table 64; OECD Main Economic Indicators, Historical Statistics, 1960–1975; UN Yearbook of International Trade Statistics, 1977*

trend which has been in evidence throughout most of the century. In absolute terms, sales have risen, but not as fast as those of other countries. Besides the figures on market shares is the record of British entrepreneurs. During the late eighteenth century and most of the nineteenth, major industrial innovations were made in Britain, particularly in textiles, steam, iron and steel and engineering. In the twentieth century, however, British industry has more often been following the initiatives of foreign competitors. The chemical, automotive, electrical and aerospace industries were born and developed in Germany and the USA. Today several industries in the UK are dominated by the local subsidiaries of American, Japanese or other overseas-based multinational corporations (MNCs).

A further symptom of Britain's industrial weakening, according to many, is the falling share of manufacturing in GDP, total employment and investment. This decline can be dated from the mid-1960s. Since then, industrial production has failed to advance, and rising productivity has meant that fewer workers have been required and that plants have been shut down. Profits also pursued a downward course during the 1960s and 1970s. These developments have been termed 'de-industrialization'. In the context of increasing international competition and uncertain supplies of fuel and raw materials, industrial decline has been identified as a symptom of economic weakness.

Attacks have been levelled at most aspects of British industry. For example, design, quality and aftersales service have been criticized as inferior to those of rival producers. Delivery dates are frequently not honoured, as production is held up—often by industrial disputes. The financial system is believed by some to have directed insufficient funds into industry. Other commentators, acknowledging the inefficiency of management in particular, blame the lack of incentives which management is offered as a result of high rates of taxation and a narrowing of differentials during successive incomes policies. None of these has been established as the ultimate cause of Britain's economic retardation. More comprehensive analyses of the relative decline of British industry have also been put forward, each with its implications for government policy. These analyses will now be discussed.

4.4.1 Overburdening the wealth-creators

An important interpretation of the failings of the British private sector has been put forward in recent years by Bacon and Eltis (1978). Their fundamental thesis is that the problem with the industrial and commercial sector is that the state has starved it of resources.

They divide the economy into a 'market sector' and a 'non-market sector'. Their market sector corresponds to the industrial and commercial sector discussed in this chapter, with the addition of the financial institutions, the nationalized industries and parts of the public services which charge for their output, such as council housing. They stress the

56

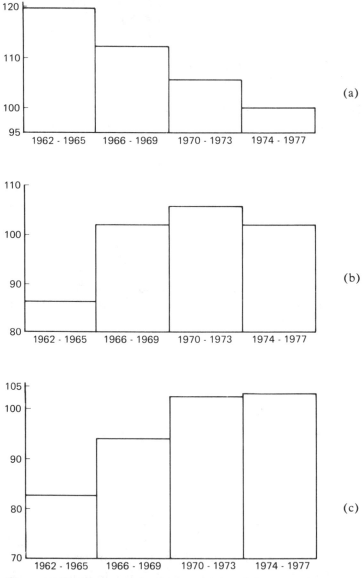

Figure 4.3 Trends in employment, output and investment,
1962–1977 (1975 = 100). (a) Employment in production
industries. (b) Investment in manufacturing industry. (c)
Index of industrial production

Source: *Economic Trends*, Annual Supplement

role of the market sector as the ultimate provider of private consumption, exports and investment.

In examining the record of the market sector from 1955 to 1974, they found that productivity in Britain grew more slowly than in West Germany, France or Italy. The difference was, however, not very large. The gap was also found to be closing during the later years, as productivity in Britain grew rather more rapidly. The performance of the British economy as a whole, however, deteriorated badly. Inflation accelerated, output stagnated, unemployment rose, the exchange rate of sterling fell and industrial disputes became more frequent. Although outside influences such as the world recession have not helped, Bacon and Eltis argued that Britain was less able to withstand these shocks than other countries. The responsibility for this lay squarely with the state.

The 1960s and early 1970s saw a prodigious rise in the public services. Between 1964 and 1973, the health and education services and public administration grew by about one million workers, while the total labour force remained virtually static. This growth demanded a shift in resources away from the market sector, and this shift was measured by Bacon and Eltis. In 1961 the market sector was able to use three-fifths of its output for the consumption of its workers and for investment, while the non-market sector took two-fifths of that output through taxation. Thirteen years later, the burden of taxation was far greater. In 1974, the non-market sector was claiming three-fifths of the output of the market sector, which was left with just two-fifths for its own use. This resource shift was imposed through higher tax burdens upon the market sector and through a reduced supply of labour. Workers reacted to the higher tax payments by seeking wage increases to defend take-home pay. Companies were, however, hindered in their ability to pass on higher labour costs in increased prices by international competition and, later, by price controls. Profits fell and, with them, investment. Industrial capacity ceased to expand. British industry was unable to meet peaks in demand, and in boom periods imports flooded into the home market. The lack of expansion in output meant that rising productivity led to labour shedding, and the manufacturing labour force shrank.

The strategy which Bacon and Eltis favour in order to remedy this malaise is a right-wing 'pro-market sector solution'. Deliberate steps should, they argue, be taken to expand the market sector and to reduce the non-market sector's claims upon its output. This would involve cuts in government spending and a reduction in public service employment, so as to release resources. At the same time investment incentives would help the market sector to expand capacity. A further useful measure would be to charge the users of public services wherever possible, rather

Business sectors and society

Part A gave a framework for analysing business in society, and examined the macroeconomy and its management. Of equal importance for business is an understanding of the pattern of events at a more detailed level. For this, a microlevel analysis is needed. Part B will accordingly focus upon the four major business sectors which have been identified: industry and commerce, finance, public enterprise and social services. Each sector will receive a similar treatment, covering the following areas.

- The growth and development of the sector.
- Its contribution to the economic system.
- The sector's performance.
- The pattern of control both within the sector and in relation to the rest of society.
- An evaluation of the sector, using the alternative perspectives set out in Chapter 2.

than giving access to the services free of charge. One objective here would be to reduce taxation. A second would be to establish directly the value which consumers place upon health, education and housing. Consumers would be able to take responsibility for their own service requirements, rather than receiving these services freely from the state as the so-called 'social wage'. Elements of this solution appear, indeed, as part of the intended economic strategy of the Conservative government elected in 1979.

Among the recent policy developments which reflect 'pro-market sector' thinking are those which stress the importance of small firms. These have come to be regarded as a reservoir of entrepreneurial talent and innovation. The continued existence of the small firm sector is believed to be essential for the regeneration of British industry. To help it to survive, the Employment Act of 1980 reduced the obligations which previous legislation had laid upon it with regard to maternity leave and dismissal procedures.

It is no coincidence that the analysis of Bacon and Eltis should find favour with a Conservative administration. This brief outline of their theories has drawn out several themes encountered before. First, there is the general presumption that the private sector is able to perform satisfactorily, if left alone. The recommendation that the government should minimize its role by cutting taxes and public spending is quite in keeping with the *laissez-faire* tradition. The other prong of policy, charging users of public services, again betrays an individualistic ethic, which holds that people should take responsibility for their own education, health and housing. Quite clearly Bacon and Eltis are Consensus theorists with an individualist approach.

Conflict theorists criticize Bacon and Eltis' analysis, arguing that wealth creation does not only depend upon the private sector. Public services such as education and health are needed by an industrial workforce. Rejecting *laissez-faire* policies, Conflict theorists question the ability of the market sector to achieve a satisfactory rate of growth without state support.

4.4.2 Overmanning

Another analysis which is accepted on the Right is the view that labour bears the blame for Britain's poor economic performance. The starting point is the fact that production in the UK generally requires more labour than in other industrialized countries. Typically, workers in other countries benefit from using more and better equipment. The argument that British labour itself is less productive rested mainly on subjective assessments, for statistical studies were rare. During the

1970s, studies were undertaken which included comparisons between identical production lines in the UK and in Europe. It was found that car assembly in the UK, using identical equipment to European lines, required twice as many man-hours, while engine and transmission units needed 50–60% more labour. The explanation for this differential was thought to lie with the slower pace of work on British lines, a higher incidence of faulty products and poor maintenance. While some commentators have blamed management for these results, the main line of argument has been to blame them upon the poor motivation and attitudes of the workers themselves.

Trade unionists, it has been argued, obstruct the efficient use of labour by maintaining various 'restrictive practices'. These include apprenticeship regulations, which restrict the supply of labour to time-served men and women; the pre-entry closed shop, where recruitment has to be from among union members; and insistence upon craft distinctions so that a worker can only undertake a specific range of tasks. More broadly, unions have been accused of general opposition to technical change. Instances can easily be found: the dock workers have successfully resisted the introduction of barge and catamaran container systems which would facilitate international container traffic, and, on the railways, the footplatemen retained the 'second man' in the cab long after his job, stoking, had been eliminated by the switch to diesel. The cause of this behaviour by unions is said to be a desire to preserve jobs for union members. Rising productivity and new technology typically involve labour-shedding. British unions, with unemployment rates of up to 22% in the 1930s in their memories, attempt to ensure that jobs are retained. Restrictive practices may also slow production, thus forcing management to pay overtime rates for the extra hours needed to fulfil orders.

Overmanning and poor industrial relations are not easy problems to solve. Individual restrictive practices may be 'bought out' with high pay rises: so-called 'productivity agreements'. Skillful manpower planning can avoid the need for redundancies, say, by cutting recruitment and allowing natural wastage to reduce the labour force. Given entrenched attitudes, however, new restrictive practices will tend to arise continually. Changes in the legal powers of trade unions in relation to closed shops have been put forward repeatedly in recent years and have invariably produced heated political controversy.

Poor industrial relations have also been put forward to explain Britain's relative decline. Strikes disrupt production, causing companies to fail to meet delivery dates and so to lose customers. Frequently British trade unions are accused of being too ready to strike. While management have also been subjected to the counter-accusation of failing to recognize fully the role of unions, and thereby bear the responsibility for disputes, right-wing commentators have also alleged that labour is less easy to direct and is less motivated in the UK.

Critics of unions from the Consensus viewpoint delight in pointing out that these attitudes are self-defeating. Resistance to new technology, for example, fails to preserve jobs, for the firm becomes uncompetitive. It loses its markets to rivals who have brought in new methods of production, goes bankrupt, and the jobs disappear. Job preservation is best attained, they argue, through cooperation between unions and management.

Conflict theorists see unions in a rather different light. They are an inevitable aspect of class society. Workers are seen as having no control, as individuals, over their pay and the conditions of their work. The only way to protect their interests is to organize into trade unions. Strikes and poor industrial relations are blamed upon the nature of the system which demands the exploitation of labour by capital.

4.4.3 Under-investment

Radical analyses of Britain's economic record draw attention to industry's poor capital stock. British workers are relatively unproductive, the argument runs, because they work with outdated machinery. Slow growth reflects a consistent record of low investment by management, who thus bear the responsibility for the UK's industrial decline.

Various explanations of this low level of industrial investment have been put forward by radicals. Some commentators have argued that British managers have become decadent and do not share the pioneering

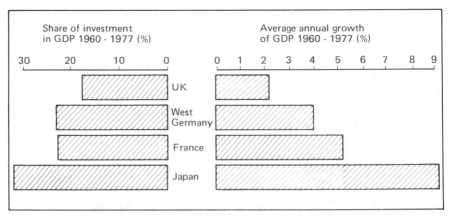

Figure 4.4 Investment and growth

Source: *UN Yearbook of National Accounts Statistics, 1977, Vol. II, Tables 2A, 6A*

spirits of their forefathers; they are content to distribute their profits as dividends rather than ploughing them back into investment. A more sophisticated version of this argument draws attention to the 'amateur' nature of British managers. They have, typically, fewer technical qualifications than their counterparts in other countries, and are less at home with the more advanced technologies of the twentieth century. A consequence of this is Britain's lagging position in the new industries of chemicals and electronics, and one aspect of this position is a low rate of investment.

Other commentators attribute the low level of investment to British investors' relatively easy access to overseas opportunities. Britain's foreign links are strong, and Britain has a tradition of lending capital abroad. In their private pursuit of the highest profit, investors are seen as neglecting the productive capacity of home industries. Radicals also stress the importance of MNCs in this context. MNCs operate on a global level and are able to move funds from one subsidiary to another through accounting procedures such as 'transfer prices'. If, for example, a motor firm has an engine factory in Spain and an assembly unit in Britain, the Spanish subsidiary will 'sell' engines to the British subsidiary at a 'transfer price' which is simply an accounting device. The British subsidiary will sell the cars to distributor firms at a real market price. Profits made in Spain can be moved to Britain simply by lowering the transfer price for engines, while profits made in Britain can be moved to the Spanish subsidiary by setting a high transfer price. Radicals accuse MNCs of moving profits out of the UK to finance investment overseas.

Some have defended British management on the grounds that profits in UK industry are low, and any investment would yield low returns. The rebuttal is that low profits reflect high costs. These in turn come from using outdated methods as a direct result of failing to invest in new machinery. Other causes of low profits have existed, however: corporation tax reduces companies' net incomes, and price controls have intermittently trimmed profit margins.

In summary, radicals argue that privately-owned industry has been 'failing the nation' by not investing in the UK on a sufficient scale. The solution, they argue, is to boost industrial investment using state funds. The state should take over many large firms and make them invest in new plant and machinery. Other firms could be given subsidised loans. They would be made accountable to the state and the public over the use of these funds by making 'planning agreements' with the government, covering their forecasts for sales, output, investment and so on. This large-scale public intervention in industry is part of the radicals' economic strategy. It is put forward not only as an economic programme for raising the rate of growth, but also as a means of restricting the power of the owners of capital. Elements of it were found in the industrial policies of the Labour government between 1974 and 1976.

Critics of this approach from the Consensus viewpoint argue that a programme of state investment in industry is unlikely to yield much benefit to the nation. First, civil servants and politicians do not always have business ability. Secondly, public investment projects are frequently characterized by over-spending, delay and waste. Evidence also suggests that British industry's existing capital stock is used inefficiently by international standards. In any case, the critics argue, it may be futile to try to keep heavy manufacturing industry alive, when market forces indicate that it should decline. If manufacturers in other countries are more efficient, they should undertake production. Britain should abandon such industries and redeploy its resources into new, high-technology industries. Capital should, moreover, be allowed to flow abroad from the UK where returns are low to other economies where returns are higher. This will aid the process of industrializing the poorer countries. The outflow of funds should also depress the value of sterling on the foreign exchange market and so make British firms more competitive.

These criticisms amount to a restatement of confidence in the market mechanism. Radicals, in contrast, prefer state regulation. The radical analysis and the criticisms of it can be seen to reflect the underlying values and philosophies of Conflict and Consensus. While the discussion of the causes of Britain's economic record has generated many useful insights into industrial conduct, no single theory as to the ultimate cause of low growth has been proved to the satisfaction of all. There is disagreement not only over the facts but also over the interpretation to be given to those facts.

4.5 The government and the industrial and commercial sector

The state is involved in the private sector, regardless of the fact that politicians may be committed to *laissez-faire* ideals. The electorate are deeply interested in their own prosperity and security, which can only be safeguarded in a competitive world by continued economic advance in the private sector. The international standing of the state is also affected by the country's economic success. The state has, moreover, responsibilities in the fields of unemployment and general social welfare. The process of economic change, entailing the abandonment of old industries, organizations and locations, creates many of these social problems such as prolonged unemployment. Economic growth nevertheless provides the resources to meet these problems, and governments of all persuasions seek to promote it. The specific policies which they adopt are, of course, of great importance to business. A main influence on policy is the political and economic beliefs of policy-makers.

The *laissez-faire* school of economics holds that the state should refrain from interference in the economy. The government should restrict itself to providing the framework for business operations: defence, law and order, a stable currency and a road network. It must also establish the rules under which goods and services, including labour, are bought and sold. The 1960s and 1970s saw significant changes in these areas through legislation on health and safety, employees' rights, racial and sexual discrimination and consumer protection.

Laissez-faire theory also enjoins governments to ensure that competition is not obstructed by monopolies or collusion between firms. A dominant firm in an industry may suppress competition by, for instance, refusing to supply to retailers who stock rival goods. Again, a powerful supplier may compel retailers to buy additional ranges of goods from him. If there are only a few suppliers, they may form a cartel to fix prices and to share the market between them. They may operate discriminatory pricing systems whereby different prices are charged to different classes of customer.

These restrictive practices allow firms to exploit consumers, and are frowned upon by *laissez-faire* theorists. The last hundred years have seen, however, many instances of these practices. Mergers began to appear at the end of the nineteenth century and in the Depression of the 1930s, many cartels were formed.

Steps were taken to restore competition after World War II. Restrictive agreements were made illegal and 2800 such agreements were subsequently abandoned. The Monopolies and Mergers Commission was also established. It may investigate any firm which accounts for over 25% of sales of a particular product, or mergers involving firms with assets of over £5 million. The presumption of the Commission is that monopolies and mergers will generally be beneficial to the economy, by attaining economies of scale or increasing the market share of a well-managed firm. Exports and employment may therefore be increased. The official view is also that, even in markets with few sellers, conditions are usually competitive and conducive to economic progress. As a result, only 3% of the 1500 mergers qualifying for investigation since 1965 have been examined, and only 2% have been abandoned. Market processes in this area have not suffered from much state interference.

After World War II, interventionist Keynesian policies came into favour at the level of macroeconomic policy. Governments also adopted a more interventionist stance at microlevel. For example, firms have been offered tax incentives to stimulate investment. In the Assisted

Areas, where unemployment is higher, investment incentives are even greater.

The increasing complexity of life has also demanded closer contacts between firms and the state. Businesses and trade associations are constantly putting their views to government on trade policy, tax regulations, safety codes and so on. The Department of Industry 'sponsors' industries, monitoring their performance and representing them in international trade negotiations. The government is also in constant contact with the trade unions. Consultation between government, industry and the unions has been given institutional form in the National Economic Development Council (NEDC). Set up in 1962, the NEDC provides a forum for discussion of economic performance and policy. Perhaps the most significant document to emerge from this process of consultation was the National Plan of 1965, which sought to create conditions for faster growth. It was abandoned in 1966 as Britain's external payments position deteriorated.

Below the NEDC proper are the Economic Development Councils (EDCs), each concerned with a particular industry. These EDCs are also composed of trades union and employers' representatives and Civil Servants, and their aim is to examine ways of raising industrial performance.

Government involvement in industry has at times been even more direct, bordering at times on policies favoured by radicals. The first significant step in this direction came with the establishment, in 1966, by the Labour government, of the Industrial Reorganization Corporation (IRC). Its brief was to promote the formation of large firms, better able to compete in world markets, through the merger of existing firms. The IRC assisted in some 70 mergers before its abolition in 1970 by the Conservatives.

In 1974 the Labour Party took office and announced an 'industrial policy'. They were, first, to seek to reach planning agreements with major companies. Secondly, they created the National Enterprise Board (NEB), which was to channel investment funds into promising firms, in return for which it would take a shareholding. State ownership would thus be moved away from the traditional nationalized industries into the more dynamic sectors of the economy, and the private sector would be made accessible to state control. The NEB made little progress towards discharging its responsibilities. It acquired Fairey engineering, and other, smaller firms, and helped to establish Inmos, a microprocessor firm, in order that this technology be available to Britain. Technological development had long been a major theme of industrial policy, which has also seen substantial aid for computing, nuclear engineering and aerospace. There was, however, intense political pressure to use NEB funds to prop up ailing firms, in the same way that the declining shipbuilding industry had been subsidised for some time. In the space of a few years in the mid-1970s, Rolls Royce, Alfred Herbert (Britain's biggest machine tools maker), British Leyland and Chrysler all went to the brink of bankruptcy, and were given state subsidies to keep them in existence. In the case of Rolls Royce, Alfred Herbert and British Leyland, the funds came from the NEB, at the behest of the government. The Board was thus diverted by political pressure from its intended goal—promoting high-technology, growth industries into subsidising outdated, uncompetitive 'lame ducks'. The policy of making planning agreements likewise foundered, as firms refused to cooperate.

The Conservative government elected in 1979 was committed to *laissez-faire* policies. Labour's industrial policy was reversed: planning agreements were dropped and the NEB's activities severely curtailed. The government also proposed the establishment of 'enterprise zones'—specific areas where state interference would be at an absolute minimum. As in macroeconomic policy, the wheel has turned full circle as policies based on individualist thinking have superceded interventionist approaches.

Guide to further reading
General

Allen, G. C. (1966). *The Structure of Industry in Britain*, Longman, London. Chapters 1–5 provide a useful if dated survey of industrial organization.

Dunning, J. H. and Thomas, C. J. (1963). *British Industry*, Hutchinson, London. Is similar in content to the above in Chapters 1 and 2 but is likewise dated.

Prest, A. R. and Coppock, D. J. (1978). *The UK Economy: A Manual of Applied Economics*, 7th edn, Weidenfeld & Nicolson, London. Provides a brief but more up-to-date survey of industrial trends in Chapter 4, especially Parts I–III, VI and VII. Part V is also useful on subsections 4.2 and 4.5.

Subsections
4.2 and 4.3

Schumpeter, J. A. (1976). *Capitalism, Socialism and Democracy*, Allen & Unwin, London. Chapters V–VIII provide a sympathetic account of the process of industrial change from a Consensus point of view.

Community Development Project (CDP) (1977). *The Costs of Industrial Change*, CDP/Home Office. Chapter 1 gives a radical analysis of the process of industrial change.

4.4

Bacon, Robert and Eltis, Walter (1978). *Britain's Economic Problem: Too Few Producers*, MacMillan, London. Sets out the individualist analysis of Britain's poor growth rate in Chapters 1, 2 and especially 4, together with their suggested solution in Chapter 5.

Central Policy Review Staff (1975). *The Future of the British Car Industry*, HMSO, London. Chapter III compares British and European car assembly lines, showing the different rates of output.

Trades Union Congress (1975). *Economic Review*, London. Argues that underinvestment is a major cause of low growth rates, and sets out radical measures to overcome them in Sections I, II and III.

4.5

Budd, Alan (1978). *The Politics of Economic Planning*, Fontana/Collins, Glasgow. Sets out the different ideological perspectives on economic planning in Chapter 2, and gives a brief history of planning in the UK in Chapters 3–7.

Budd, Alan (1978). *A Review of Monopolies and Mergers Policy*, HMSO, London. Discusses the extent of concentration and competition in the UK and concisely reviews policy in Chapters 3–5.

Beckerman, Wilfrid (1972). *The Labour Government's Economic Record 1964–1970*, Duckworth, London. Has useful chapters on planning (4) and industrial policy (5).

Exercises

Review Questions

1. How has the organization of industry and commerce changed during the twentieth century?
2. What is the doctrine of 'consumer sovereignty'?
3. What is meant by 'market concentration' and why do Consensus theorists disapprove of it?
4. Why is the industrial and commercial sector important for the rest of the economy and for society as a whole?
5. What is meant by 'de-industrialization'?
6. What do Bacon and Eltis see as the cause of Britain's poor economic performance?
7. How do they believe the situation can be changed?
8. What role have the trade unions and management been accused of playing in Britain's economic performance?
9. What economic theories lie behind the policies of the current government? How can you tell?

Application and investigation

1. Take a sample of local firms and see how many are independent, how many are subsidiaries of larger groups and how many have subsidiaries of their own. How have their profits, employment, sales and investment changed in recent years? Take a nationally known firm and see how many subsidiaries it owns and how many products it sells. (Sources will include company reports and Extel cards, which should be available in a local reference library. *Who Owns Whom* will also provide information on ownership).
2. (*a*) What trends have there been in the volume of industrial production in the last decade? Which industries have been growing and which have been contracting?
   (*b*) Are the markets for the following products competitive or oligopolistic? Think of reasons why their market structures are different.
   (*i*) Motor vehicles
   (*ii*) Brewing
   (*iii*) Fresh vegetables
3. Both central and local government adopt policies toward private industry. Compare the kinds of policies which, first, individualists, secondly, moderates and, last, radicals would recommend to them.
4. Trace the effects which the following technical innovations have had upon economic and social relations, and the effects which they may have in the future.
   (*a*) Television
   (*b*) Computers

Project

What instances of industrial change have occurred in an area with which you are familiar in the past few years? What have been the effects upon first, the local economy; secondly, the local community; and last, the local authorities?

Chapter 5

The financial sector

5.1 Introduction

This chapter will be concerned with the activities of the banks, the insurance companies, the Stock Exchange, the building societies and the other institutions which make up the financial sector (SIC Order XXIV). Businesses and individuals use these institutions when they wish to borrow or lend, whether for long or short periods. All businesses, in fact, engage in borrowing and lending, and all are in consequence affected by what is going on in the financial sector. The aim of this chapter is to examine the operations of this sector and its role in the economy, showing its importance for the rest of the business and for society. It will explore commentaries upon the sector's performance, again showing how these commentaries reflect the two interpretations of social life outlined in Chapter 2. In the Consensus view, financial markets simply allocate funds between borrowers. In the Conflict perspective, by contrast, the financial sector is not merely a neutral mechanism but is also a centre of power, able to impose its will on the economy and on economic policy.

5.2 Finance for business

Running a business involves day-to-day expenditure on suppliers and employees. This spending is known as current expenditure, running costs, revenue spending or prime costs. Funds to meet them derive from trading receipts such as sales revenue or rents, from payments for franchises or leases, or from taxes and grants. While private companies rely almost exclusively on trading income, public authorities rely primarily upon grants and taxes.

Capital spending—the purchase of more capital stock such as equipment or buildings—is, by contrast, financed not out of current receipts, but out of savings. The savings may be those made by the organization itself, in the form of retained profits or, in the public sector, 'revenue contribution to capital outlay'. More commonly, the savings are made by other parties, and are made available to the capital spenders by the activities of the financial sector. This is sometimes referred to as the 'City' because the head offices of the financial institutions are mainly located in the square mile of the City of London.

5.2.1 The flow of funds and the means of borrowing

Industrial and commercial companies, taken as a whole, are net borrowers, for their investment spending is higher than their own savings. The same is true of government, whose receipts from taxation are almost invariably less than expenditure. The personal sector, by contrast, is generally a net lender. The 'savings ratio', which is the ratio of savings to personal incomes, in fact rose from 6% in the 1950s to about 16% in the 1970s. Investment in this sector, which includes small unincorporated firms and voluntary organizations as well as households, is usually far less than savings. As a result, its 'financial assets' (bank and building society deposits, pension rights, holdings of insurance policies) are constantly mounting. These savings are lent to the deficit sectors, companies and the government, and the movement of savings into the hands of borrowers is known as the 'flow of funds' (*Figure 5.1*). The

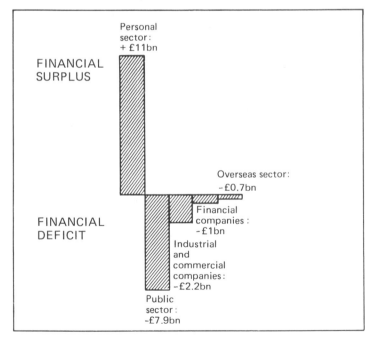

Figure 5.1 The flow of funds, 1978
Source: *Financial Statistics*

overseas sector is also involved in this flow. Saving by this sector indicates that the rest of the world is increasing its financial assets in this country, with Britain going deeper into debt.

The deficit sectors borrow funds in many different ways. Companies borrow from each other through trade credit. Credit also comes from banks, typically in the form of 6-month, but often renewable, overdrafts. Longer-term funds are raised through issuing bonds bearing a fixed interest coupon or through the sale of shares on which dividends are paid. Public authorities borrow by issuing financial instruments in return for cash. Unlike shares, these public sector instruments are redeemed—bought back by the issuer, that is, the government—at a predetermined date. The state borrows directly from the public through the issue of 'non-marketable debt', such as National Savings Certificates and Premium Bonds. The term 'non-marketable' reflects the fact that once bought these cannot be resold to another citizen. On a far grander scale is public borrowing through the issue of Treasury bills and gilt-edged stock (gilts). The former are redeemable in 3 months, and are bought mainly by the banking system, for they constitute part of the banks' liquid or reserve assets. Gilt-edged stock, however, is the principal source of public borrowing. In this case the government sells certificates, bearing a fixed interest return, to be redeemed at some date in the future. The sale of gilts is known as 'funding', and the main purchasers are pension funds and insurance companies. Local authorities also borrow short and long term, from the banks and from individuals. During 1979, the government sold £10.1 billion worth of gilts.

Treasury bills, company shares, and gilts may be resold by the original buyer. There are in consequence, second-hand or secondary markets for these securities, and prices fluctuate according to economic conditions. Events which are seen as threats to sales, output and profitability, such as disruption to energy supplies, industrial disputes, the imposition of tariffs in export markets or rising interest rates, could induce falls in security prices. Changes in prices are recorded in the Financial Times Share Index and the Government Securities Index, both of which attract press coverage. Private individuals rarely have recourse to these methods of obtaining credit. Bank loans, building society mortgages, hire purchase and credit cards account for most of their borrowings, while bank and building society deposits, pension fund contributions and insurance premiums make up the bulk of their savings.

5.2.2 Capital markets

Borrowers and lenders meet in the capital markets. The Stock Exchange is the principal such market, where new company shares and gilts are issued, and where second-hand shares and gilts change hands. Treasury bills and similar short-term securities are bought and sold on the 'money market', and other markets are formed around the purchase and sale of different assets such as local authority debt. In the new issues of gilts and shares, savings are used to buy financial assets. Each asset has its own return, expressed as a rate of interest, which is a proportion of the initial sum that the lender receives each year from the borrower. In 1979, local authority bonds yielded a return of about 15%, while gilts yielded about 13%.

Rates reflect the type of lending undertaken. Long-term lenders demand higher rates of interest than short-term. The riskier the project or the lower the 'credit-rating' of the borrower, the higher is the interest rate that will be charged. Lenders will also evaluate the prospect of the price of the financial instrument changing when assessing rates of return, for this will mean a capital gain or loss. An expectation among investors of low returns by a private firm will reduce its share price, making it easier for another firm to take the company over.

Investors in government stocks also evaluate the returns offered. They may take the view that the interest on gilts is insufficient to compensate them for the decline in the real value of their funds caused by inflation. In consequence, there may be a widespread refusal to buy newly issued gilts, and the government would then be unable to borrow money by this means. Financial pressure may also be exerted by the foreign exchange market. If foreign investors feel that the economic situation is deteriorating, with inflation accelerating, they may sell sterling. The exchange rate of the pound will fall. In either case, the government would suffer financial embarrassment.

5.3 Financial institutions

The main kinds of institutions making up the financial sector are shown in *Figure 5.2*.

The banks are the core of the system. The banking mechanism is highly complex, with subdivisions including the foreign banks (which are now larger than the British banks), the discount houses, merchant banks and finance houses, as well as the more familiar clearing banks.

The largest institutions after the banks are the building societies. They take deposits from the public, and lend most of this money back to the public for house purchase, in accordance with various rules for risk assessment such as the borrower's income and the value of the property. In recent years the societies have grown rapidly, partly because their competitive net-of-tax rates have attracted the greater

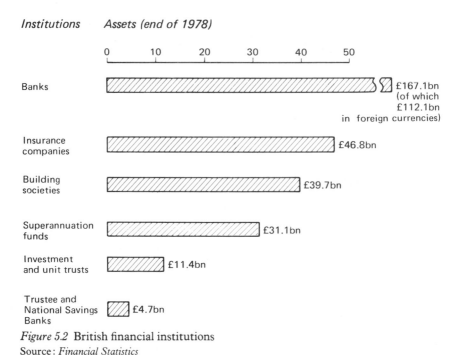

Figure 5.2 British financial institutions
Source: *Financial Statistics*

part of the rise in savings since the war. Indeed, in 1977 they had become as large as the clearing banks in terms of sterling assets.

Like the building societies, the savings banks (National Savings Bank and Trustee Savings Banks) began in the nineteenth century as savings institutions for the working classes. They take deposits from the public, but all their lending is to the government. Like industry and commerce, the savings banks movement and the building society movement are relatively concentrated, with a few large organizations accounting for most of the assets.

Unit trusts and investment trusts display the principles of **financial intermediation,** which occurs when funds are channelled from saver to investor through an intermediary like a bank or building society. Investment trusts and unit trusts are institutions which buy shares in the UK and abroad on behalf of their contributors and who are thus able to pool the risks of many different shareholdings. Insurance is another familiar form of risk-pooling. Of much greater financial importance, however, are life assurance and pension funds. Life assurance offices collect premiums which they invest in shares, gilts and other assets in order to be able to meet claims and to pay out on maturing endowment policies in the future. Pension funds receive contributions from workers and employers, with which they buy assets. The intention is to receive a sufficient yield to provide pensions for employees on retirement. Both are subject to favourable tax treatment, and both have expanded very rapidly in recent decades. Occupational pension schemes are now mandatory, and life assurance has become increasingly linked to transactions such as house purchase or the payment of school fees. As a result, the pension funds and life assurance offices are continually searching for new investment outlets and are major forces on the Stock Exchange. They are among the principal buyers of new issues of shares and of gilt-edged securities. Indeed, over 50% by value of the shares in British companies is held by such funds, compared with 26% in 1963. Private individuals, who once owned the bulk of shareholdings, have, by contrast, been consistent sellers in aggregate and now hold only some 30% of all shares. In consequence, share ownership is becoming indirectly more diffused, in that shares are being transferred from the relatively small group of private shareholders to the institutions, who hold them on behalf of a much larger number of people. At the same time, control over investment funds is becoming more centralized in the hands of the institutions.

5.3.1 The commercial banking system

The banking system is the lynch-pin of the financial system. Its several divisions are shown in *Figure 5.3*. Common to all of them is the basic procedure of banking, taking deposits from firms and individuals and lending the funds out on different terms. These principles are applied in quite different ways by the different kinds of banks.

Domestic banking is dominated by the six London clearing banks, the 'clearers', so called because they participate in the London Clearing House to settle cheques drawn upon each other. Other deposit banks include the Scottish and Northern Ireland banks, which are in some cases subsidiaries of the clearers, and the state-run National Giro. Their funds come from the current or deposit accounts of their customers. Some of these funds are kept as 'liquid assets' or reserve assets, that is, as cash, or assets which are readily turned into cash such as Treasury bills or money-at-call. For the most part, however, funds are lent out in the form of advances or overdrafts to customers or, as investments in gilts, to the government. Because deposits are short term, assets are also short: overdrafts are frequently for 6 months, and gilts may be readily sold on the gilts market. Profits arise from the difference between the lending rates and borrowing rates, with about one-third of the funds coming free to the banks as current accounts. The banks administer the payment systems of the economy through the clearing of cheques, and hence maintain an extensive branch network. There were over 14 000 clearing bank branches in the mid-1960s, but the merging of several banks since then has permitted some rationalization. This kind of banking is known as retail banking, and entails the holding of a stock of liquid assets to meet customers' demands for cash.

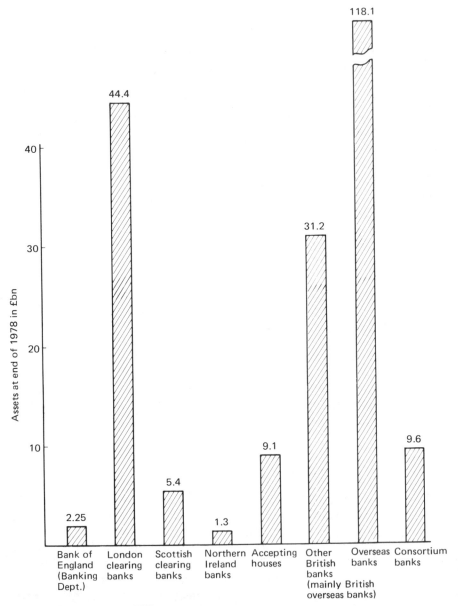

Figure 5.3 Banks in the UK
Source: *Financial Statistics*

Like industry and commerce, banking has undergone major structural changes during this century. The main developments have been the influx of foreign banks and the rise of the highly competitive 'parallel markets'. During the Depression, banking, like many other industries, became cartelized, and competition was restricted. The deposit banks all agreed to link their rates for depositors and borrowers to Bank Rate, so that all charged the same. It was not, moreover, the practice for banks to borrow from each other. The deposit banks have traditionally lent money to the discount houses. This 'call money'—so named because it can be recalled at a moment's notice, and is thus a highly liquid asset—is used by the discount houses to buy newly issued Treasury bills from the Bank of England. In the 1930s, this market too was cartelized: the houses all agreed to offer the same price for Treasury bills. The Bank of England concurred in this, with the condition that the discount houses would buy all the bills on offer.

The discount market, as the institutions which engage in the buying and selling of Treasury bills and other short-term securities are known, is more than a means by which the Bank of England borrows money from the banks via the discount houses. It is also the source of funds used for settling claims between banks. One bank, say National Westminster, may find its customers are spending money in shops owned by customers of another bank, say Lloyds. National Westminster will find itself running out of cash and will recall its short-term loans to the discount houses, to turn these into cash. Lloyds, by contrast, will have too much cash, and this surplus they will lend to the discount houses. The houses remain unaffected on balance, but the clearers have been able to adjust their assets in line with the changing patterns of deposits.

A more complex situation arises when all the clearers experience a simultaneous loss of cash, as may be caused, for example, by their customers paying more taxes. All the clearers will recall their call-money loans, and the discount houses will be short of cash. They may sell parts of their portfolio of Treasury bills, but if cash is generally short they may not find buyers easily. Under these circumstances they will be forced to borrow from the 'lender of last resort', the Bank of England. The rate at which the Bank makes funds available in these times of stringency is the Minimum Lending Rate (MLR), formerly Bank Rate.

These markets and institutions—deposit banks, discount houses, MLR—have been referred to as the 'classical markets' for financial assets. Their central features have endured through the twentieth century. There have been changes, of course, perhaps the most significant being the fall in the number of clearing banks from 26 in 1924 to six in 1980. This may be compared to the 14 000 banks in the USA, where the legal framework is rather different.

The cartel and the poor rates offered by the banks, however, gave scope for other companies to move into the credit business, particularly consumer credit. The 1950s and 1960s saw a rapid expansion of hire purchase (HP) business, in which consumers borrowed money from the finance houses to buy durable goods. The finance houses obtained their funds from the public as deposits and from the banks through the wholesale money market, where banks and financial institutions borrow and lend funds. Not to be excluded from this flourishing area, the clearers quickly bought controlling interests in the finance houses. Competition between banks was therefore resumed, albeit indirectly. The acquisition of subsidiaries in new credit fields has continued. The clearers now have a presence also in unit trust management, factoring (collecting payments on behalf of another industrial or commercial firm), leasing (purchasing equipment for hire to an industrial firm), computing, credit cards and insurance.

The clearers have also moved into merchant banking, traditionally the preserve of highly specialized institutions. The merchant banks are concerned with the management of investment and unit trusts and with corporate finance, advising on mergers and acquisitions.

Merchant banks are a subdivision of the secondary banking sector, which also embraces the British overseas banks, foreign banks and the 'new' secondary banks, whose principles differ from traditional retail banking. In retail banking, banks borrow a large number of small short-term deposits, and hold a cash reserve for customers' withdrawals. Secondary banks, however, operate on the principle of 'matching'. They take a small number of large deposits for fixed terms and lend the funds out for the same fixed terms at marginally higher rates of interest. Deposits and loans may be in any currency, as long as they match. The secondary banks take deposits mainly from industrial companies and from the clearers, pension funds and other institutions through the money market and seek borrowers in industry, commerce and local government in the UK and abroad. They lend money amongst themselves, something the clearers have never done.

Secondary banking has been more aggressively competitive than traditional banking. The secondary banks bid high for funds and offer low rates to borrowers. This style of banking has been most successful: the secondary banks have grown much faster than the banks in the 'classical markets'. They have introduced many new financial instruments such as the Certificate of Deposit, and have set up new markets—the 'parallel markets'—through which they are traded. Banks and financial institutions trade deposits on these markets, where banks who have unsatisfied borrowers may obtain funds from institutions who have more than they can, directly, find borrowers for. This is contrary to the convention in the classic markets of banks not lending to one another. There is, of course, no lender of last resort in the parallel markets. These new markets developed partly through the changing practice of old institutions, such as the merchant banks and British overseas banks, partly through the establishment of new secondary banks and partly through the influx of foreign banks, particularly from America.

The American banks began to arrive in the early 1960s, following the establishment in Europe of manufacturing subsidiaries by American industrial firms. Tight regulations on banking in the USA also prompted American banks to seek business abroad. Their dealings in dollar deposits outside the United States, known as Eurodollars, created the largest parallel market, the Eurodollar market. Similar markets in other Eurocurrencies grew up in the 1960s and 1970s. Here funds are borrowed and lent to conduct business operations on a multinational scale. Because of the variety of its institutions and the flexibility of its markets, London became the centre for Eurocurrency dealing, and there are indeed more foreign currency assets than sterling assets held in banks in London today.

The size and flexibility of the foreign currency markets in London and other centres has meant that techniques of regulation, such as foreign exchange control, have been rendered inadequate. Central banks have now largely surrendered the determination of exchange rates to the markets.

5.4 The role of the financial sector

There has been considerable debate over the influence which the City has had over events in Britain. Controversy has centred upon the power which the City possesses to shape economic policy, and upon the contribution which banking should make to Britain's industrial performance.

5.4.1 Economic policy

Like all business interests, the banking community has its views on the way economic policy should be conducted. With its long history of worldwide business, the City has traditionally held *laissez-faire* and monetarist doctrines, favouring free trade and the free movement of funds. Until the early 1970s, it also set great store by the maintenance of the exchange rate. A stable pound was felt to be essential for world trade in general, and Britain's trade in particular. Stability of the currency was also thought absolutely essential if foreign businessmen were to continue to deal with British banks. The City accordingly disapproved of changes in the foreign exchange rate of the pound, and strongly opposed domestic policy which could have stimulated inflation, such as large government deficits. While the City no longer deals exclusively in sterling and no longer, therefore, feels its fortunes to be completely bound up with the currency's exchange rate, domestic monetary stability still remains among its prime concerns. In contrast with many other business interests, however, the City appears to have enjoyed fairly consistent success in seeing its desires with regard to policy come to fulfilment. In 1925, for example, the pound was 'returned to the Gold Standard', meaning that the external value of the pound was raised by 10%, back to its 1913 level, in terms of gold and other currencies. This was in response to the explicit demands of the City. The decision, however, created new difficulties for industry, for costs and prices had risen during World War I. British goods were now over-priced in foreign markets, and were accordingly more difficult to sell. During the 1950s and 1960s again, it has been argued, governments paid more heed to the City than to industry. Faced with repeated balance of payments problems, successive administrations had to choose between, on the one hand, devaluing sterling, and so restoring the competitiveness of industry, and on the other, deflating the economy in order to maintain the exchange rate, which was the policy favoured by the City. The second option was selected time and again; devaluation was only adopted with the utmost reluctance in 1967. The role of the City—the gilts market and the foreign exchange market—was likewise crucial in prompting the government to adopt a monetarist approach to the control of inflation in 1976.

The success of the City in forcing governments to pay attention to its ideas and demands illustrates the power of the banking community. Commentators have drawn attention to the close contact which bankers have traditionally had with government and the Civil Service through the Bank of England, whose officials are found on committees throughout Whitehall, and through the shared family and social connections of senior bankers, politicians and Civil Servants. These contacts have been far closer than those between industry and government. The financial sector also has, as the historical record shows, an ability to precipitate crises in the sale of gilts and on the foreign exchanges.

Commentators have frequently drawn attention to the relatively greater weight which the banking system carries in the UK as compared with other industrial countries. Left-wing critics of the City argue that this power has been used to promote the interests of finance to the detriment both of industry and of radical social policies. The banks, they argue, prevented Britain from adopting tariffs in the 1920s despite the fact that every other country had imposed them, and so contributed to unemployment. Similarly, foreign exchange rate crises constrained the Labour governments of 1964–1970 and 1974–1979.

Defenders of the City, who normally adopt a Consensus view, argue that foreign exchange crises result not from conspiracies by bankers but from ordinary business decisions. Governments who 'print money' and permit inflation must expect investors to take their funds elsewhere. The responsibility for financial crises rests, they believe, with governments and their overspending, not with the financial sector.

5.4.2 The provision of industrial finance

The British financial tradition is one of market relationships between borrowers and lenders; they do not become any more involved in one another's affairs beyond the lender's assessing the credit-worthiness or the dividend potential of the borrower. Traditionally banks have supplied funds to industrial borrowers through 6-monthly overdrafts, though these are frequently renewed upon expiry. Between 1970 and 1977, just over half of industry's funds for investment came from this source.

Industry may also raise funds through the issue of shares to investors on the Stock Exchange, which deals in securities issued by public authorities and companies from many countries. Indeed one of the City's main functions before 1914 was to channel savings overseas to acquire foreign assets, and the British economy still records a relatively high level of overseas investment. The Stock Exchange's readiness to deal in foreign securities has been criticized by left-wingers for providing investors with easy access to overseas investment opportunities which draw funds away from domestic industry.

The links between industry and finance are rather different in other countries. In Germany, banks supply funds to firms by buying shares, and, in consequence, become involved in their strategic management. In France, *banques d'affaires* specialize in investing in particular industries, while in Japan, banks and industrial firms frequently operate as different branches of a single financial and manufacturing conglomerate. In all these cases, banks tend to commit funds to industry for longer periods, adjudging their clients' prospects over the long run.

British banks have been often criticized, by moderates as well as radicals, for taking a very short-term view of the prospects of industrial companies. These criticisms were made with renewed force following the bankruptcy of Rolls Royce Ltd in the mid-1970s. The banks, it was alleged, had precipitated the collapse by shortsightedly refusing to renew overdraft facilities during the costly development phase of Rolls Royce's RB–211 engine. The banks were said to be generally failing to meet industry's need for medium-term loans of 5–10 years, and also to be ignoring the financial needs of small firms. Reporting in 1980, the Wilson Committee on the financial system was divided on the issue. A minority of the Committee felt that the institutions—pension funds and life assurance offices—were committing too few funds to industry, and recommended the direction of 10% of their annual inflow of cash to industry through a new agency to be run by employers, government and unions.

Defenders of the banks and financial institutions, normally arguing from an individualist point of view, insist that they could only lend to profitable, credit-worthy borrowers. They are constantly looking for outlets for their funds. If industry has failed to invest, it cannot be due to a shortage of finance. Partly as a result of the debate, however, the banks have made medium-term finance available. At the behest of the Bank of England, the early 1970s also saw the creation of Equity Capital for Industry, an institution which it was hoped would provide long-term finance.

The controversy over industrial finance reflects the perspectives which have run through this book. On the one hand is the *laissez-faire* tradition, whose supporters believe the marketplace to be the best mechanism for allocating resources for the benefit of all. On the other hand are those who hold that funds are allocated by a small but powerful group of financiers. The financial market must therefore be controlled in the interests of the majority.

5.5 The Bank of England and the regulation of the financial system

The responsibility for the general supervision of the City rests with the Bank of England, which was a privately owned bank until its nationalization in 1945. It administers the various regulations relating to banking, such as those pertaining to reserve asset ratios, operating traditionally through personal contact and advice. It is not the Bank's practice to rely on the legalistic enforcement of written regulations. The financial sector is strongly characterized by self-regulation rather than external supervision. Standards of prudence and reliability are maintained by associations and committees drawn from the City itself, like the Foreign Exchange and Currency Deposit Brokers Association. The Bank of England's role is to guide this system. It also acts as the spokesman for the City, representing its views and interests to government.

The Bank is better known, of course, for issuing bank notes and coin; and the state's bank accounts, such as those of the Exchequer and the

Paymaster General, are held at the Bank. The Bank also, in conjunction with the Treasury, borrows cash for the state through the sale of Treasury bills and gilt-edged securities. It is the 'lender of last resort' to the discount houses (and so, indirectly, to the commercial banks), making funds available at MLR when cash is short. For the classic markets, MLR (formerly Bank Rate) was thought of as the 'cost of funds', in that it was the rate which the banks would have to pay for any extra cash should they be faced with a high demand for cash from the public. It was the practice, accordingly, to base their own lending rates to customers upon the 'cost of funds' to them, that is, upon Bank Rate. In the context of the banking cartel, with the clearers all charging the same rates, the Bank of England was able to raise or lower overdraft and deposit rates, and thus all other interest rates in the economy, by changing Bank Rate.

Through their sales of Treasury bills and gilts, the authorities (the Treasury and the Bank of England) are also able to influence the volume of reserve assets held by the commercial banks. Thus they influence the banks' ability to lend and so they can affect the supply of money in the economy. The control of the money supply and of interest rates is the core of monetary policy. The type of monetary policy pursued at different times has altered, depending in part upon the economic philosophy of the government of the day.

5.5.1 Keynesian policies toward money and banking

During the 1950s and 1960s, economic management centred upon fiscal policy—the manipulation of public spending and taxation. Money supply and interest rates played a decidedly minor role in the management of aggregate demand. The primary economic problem of this period was Britain's persistent balance of payments weakness, and governments periodically deflated the economy in order to cut the demand for imports. In these circumstances, monetary policy was used to support fiscal deflation.

The form of monetary policy reflected the interventionist tendencies of Keynesian economic policy. Bank Rate could be raised deliberately to deter bank lending, and thus depress investment. It would also attract foreign funds to London, to the direct benefit of the balance of payments. Hire purchase (HP) restrictions could be imposed, making credit harder to obtain and thus depressing demand.

With regard to the banks, Keynesian policies would attempt to restrict their ability to lend money. First, banks could be called upon to place a proportion of their reserve assets as 'special deposits' with the Bank of England. These special deposits would no longer be counted as reserve assets, and a call for special deposits would amount to a cut in banks' holdings of reserve assets. Since the banks' ability to lend depended on their reserve assets, a reduction here meant a decrease in bank lending. Another Keynesian technique for limiting bank lending was to issue directives to the banks. Known as quantitative and qualitative controls, these directives laid down a recommended ceiling on bank lending and suggested that certain borrowers, such as exporters, be given priority.

Problems arose with the implementation of these interventionist policies. Industries selling durable goods saw demand fluctuate violently as HP regulations were changed. Directives on bank lending proved ineffective as the banking system devised new methods of granting credit. Controls also bore most heavily upon those in closest contact with the Bank of England, the clearers. The newer secondary banks, operating in the parallel markets, were subject to few hindrances. These problems led to the temporary abandonment of interventionist methods of regulating the banks. In 1971, a new system, known as Competition and Credit Control (CCC) was introduced, based upon *laissez-faire* ideas. Direct controls on bank lending were ended, and emphasis was placed upon market forces.

5.5.2 Monetarist policies toward money and banking

Monetarist thinking places supreme importance upon the money supply. Monetarists believe that the growth of the money supply governs the rate of inflation. They also have great faith in the free market, and view with disfavour any state intervention, which inevitably distorts the market. Most of the tools of Keynesian policy toward money and banking are accordingly rejected by monetarists.

The policy techniques favoured by monetarists are as follows. The money supply and bank lending should be controlled through the level of reserve assets (mainly Treasury bills) issued by the Bank of England. Changes in HP regulations, which discriminate against certain industries, and directives to banks, which discriminate against certain kinds of bank, should be abandoned. Bank Rate should not determine other interest rates in the market for credit; rather, market forces should determine Bank Rate. Interest rate cartels, like that of the clearers, should be discontinued. The intention of Competition and Credit Control was to bring these ideas into operation, and promote free competition in the market for credit. Bank Rate was renamed Minimum Lending Rate, and made to vary according to the level of interest rates in the money markets.

As with Keynesian policies, the new scheme also had its problems. First, money supply grew extremely rapidly at this time. Secondly, many secondary banks exploited the more liberal system of controls and extended their operations dramatically. Many of their ventures were, however, unsound, involving speculation in the property market. When property prices fell in 1974, many were driven into bankruptcy. In most cases, depositors were protected by the Bank of England's 'Lifeboat Committee' which was drawn from the City's leading institutions. They lent money to the ailing secondary banks and paid off their creditors, before taking over their assets. Radical critics of the City saw the 'Lifeboat' as a measure taken by the banks to forestall any outside investigation of the practices of the financial sector. Defenders saw it as an instance of the usefulness of the City's informal, rapid and personal system of self-regulation.

5.5.3 Radical policies toward money and banking

Radicals focus their attention upon the power which they believe the City uses irresponsibly. They are accordingly not over-concerned with the details of interest rate policy or reserve asset ratios. Their wish is to curb the power of the financial sector, and they see nationalization and the regulation of credit as the principal methods. After taking the main banks and savings banks into public ownership, radicals would direct credit into their priority areas—lending to the government to finance public spending, and lending to industry for investment. Lending abroad, lending for speculative purposes and lending to consumer luxury industries would be strictly limited.

These ideas are rejected by individualists. They argue that such measures would destroy London as an international financial centre, and so lose foreign earnings and jobs. They also believe that controls would prove impossible to administer, because the financial markets are so complex and flexible.

5.5.4 Recent developments

Monetary policy displaced fiscal policy as the main technique of economic management in the late 1970s. Governments' attention has been fixed upon the money supply since 1976, when a dramatic financial crisis occurred. Money supply was expanding rapidly, inflation was high and public borrowing was on a massive scale. Investors in both the gilts market and the foreign exchange market began to lose confidence and stopped buying. Unable to sell gilts, the government resorted to borrowing through the issue of Treasury bills. This had the effect of raising the commercial banks' stock of reserve assets, enabling them to undertake more lending and in this way creating more money. The government, in short, was resorting to 'printing money', and thus the outlook for inflation deteriorated even further. The exchange rate of sterling fell from over $2 to almost $1.50 and the government felt obliged to apply to the International Monetary Fund (IMF) for a loan. The IMF insisted that the government take steps to restrict monetary growth and that it publish annual targets for the permitted expansion in the money stock.

In the struggle to contain the money supply, important elements of Competition and Credit Control were abandoned. MLR was no longer allowed to respond to market pressures but was to be fixed by administrative decision as Bank Rate had been. Controls on bank lending also reappeared, under the name of the Supplementary Special Deposits Scheme (also known as the 'corset'). Thus there was once again detailed public intervention in the financial system.

5.6. Conclusion

Competition in the markets for credit has once again been restricted, despite the fact that many financial markets are among the most competitive markets in the whole economy. Funds can be allocated to whoever can pay the going rate and so are put to the optimum use. The capital markets thus illustrate the operation of the market mechanism as an impersonal instrument for allocating resources in the best way.

The City can also be viewed as one of the most powerful pressure groups in the country. As the crisis of 1976 showed, the concentrated power of the financial sector can be a decisive force in shaping both government policy and the general pattern of business life. Some argue from a Conflict point of view that this power, wielded by a small minority of wealthy people, is used to protect the interests of the rich. Others, from a Consensus standpoint, advance the view that the financial institutions act simply as other businesses and thus, through the market mechanism, help to allocate resources in the best and most productive ways for the benefit of the whole economy and society. The responsibility for financial crises lies with governments who follow lax monetary and fiscal policies. These interpretations clearly reflect the two perspectives on business life developed in this book.

Guide to further reading
General

Carter, H. and Partington, I. (1979). *Applied Economics in Banking and Finance*, Oxford University Press, Oxford. Provides a general survey of money and banking, especially in Chapters 4, 5, 6 and 7.
Prest, A. R. and Coppock, D. J. (1978). *The UK Economy: A Manual of Applied Economics*, 7th edn, Weidenfeld & Nicolson, London. Chapter 2, Parts II and III, provides a readable and brief introduction.
Revell, J. (1973). *The British Financial System*, Macmillan, London. Another readable description of the financial sector, especially Part B.
Channon, Derek F. (1977). *British Banking Strategy and the International Challenge*, Macmillan, London. Chapters 1–3 and 5–8 give an excellent short description of the organization of the financial system and an outline of recent changes.

Subsections
5.4 and 5.5

Keegan, W. and Pennant-Rea, R. (1979). *Who Runs the Economy?*, Maurice Temple Smith, London. Chapters 4 and 5 discuss, in somewhat journalistic fashion, the power of the City over economic affairs.
Crouch, Colin (Ed.) (1979). *State and Economy in Contemporary Capitalism*, Croom Helm, London. Chapter 5 by Frank Longstreth contains an interesting, if more analytic, discussion of the same topic from a moderate perspective.
Wilson, Sir Harold (Chairman) (1980). *Report of Committee to Review the Functioning of Financial Institutions*, HMSO, London. Outlines the radical view of industrial finance in a Minority Report.
Gowland, David (1978). *Monetary Policy and Credit Control*, Croom Helm, London. Chapters 1–4 discuss the theoretical basis of Competition and Credit Control, and describe the history of that system in the early 1970s, including the secondary banking crisis.

Exercises
Review Questions

1. What is meant by 'funding'?
2. What is the 'flow of funds'?
3. Name four types of financial institution, and define financial intermediation.
4. What are (*a*) reserve assets and (*b*) special deposits?
5. What are MLR, discount houses, and money at call?

6. How do parallel markets differ from classic markets?
7. What criticisms of the City do Conflict theorists make?
8. What are the functions of the Bank of England?
9. What is meant by the 'corset'?
10. What innovations did CCC introduce?

Application and investigation

1. (a) What is the government's current policy on money and banking?
   (b) What are current rates of interest on:
      (i) building society deposits
      (ii) local authority bonds (of your local local authority),
      (iii) Minimum Lending Rate,
      (iv) bank accounts (deposit accounts and current accounts),
      (v) National Savings Certificates,
      (vi) credit card facilities.
   (c) Why are these rates broadly similar for the most part, and why are some different?
2. Compare and contrast the Keynesian and monetarist approaches to the regulation of banking. How do they both differ from the radical view of the financial sector?
3. What have been the major developments in the past 2 years in interest rates, money supply, public borrowing and banking regulation? What economic and political forces have been operating to produce these results? (The section in *Economic Trends* entitled 'Recent economic developments' may be of some assistance.)

Projects

1. Obtain the balance sheet of a major clearing bank. Explain how its profits arise. Explain how the bank would be affected by:
   (a) higher government spending,
   (b) the payment of taxation,
   (c) funding,
   (d) the issue of Treasury bills,
   (e) an increase in interest rates.
2. What is meant by investors 'losing confidence'? Under what circumstances would they lose confidence, and what would be the consequences of such an event? How would Conflict and Consensus theorists interpret this?

Chapter 6

The public enterprise sector

6.1 Introduction

Chapters 4 and 5 examined the role and performance of the privately owned organizations in industry, commerce and finance. It is time to turn to public enterprise. State involvement in the economy is not limited to regulation and manipulation, but extends to the public ownership of commercial organizations providing goods and services. The largest industrial and commercial concerns, in fact, are those owned by the state.

Prominent among the trading organizations of the public sector are the nationalized industries, which cover important parts of the energy, communications and transport industries, and which are controlled by Boards of Directors appointed by the government. Local government trading services such as housing and local transport services constitute a second category of public enterprise. A third is composed of 'mixed enterprises': those businesses such as British Petroleum (BP) in which the state has a minority holding. In the case of BP, the shares are held directly by the state, while in others state ownership is indirect, with the shares being held by a public agency such as the National Enterprise Board (NEB). This chapter will concentrate upon the nationalized industries, for they are the most important, but the roles of municipal and mixed enterprise will not be overlooked.

6.2 Forms and development of public enterprise

State ownership of trading organizations ran counter to the dominant *laissez-faire* ideas of early nineteenth-century Britain. Government involvement in commerce was extremely limited. The Post Office, set up in 1840, was the most important instance. At local government level, however, more initiatives were taken, both by Labour councils, in the name of 'municipal socialism' and by Conservative councils, in the name of local 'self-help'. By the end of the nineteenth century, local authorities were running many commercial operations including housing, electricity, gas, road transport, recreation facilities and laundries. In many cases these have now been taken over by the nationalized industries and utilities, as with gas, electricity and water. The remaining trading services fall into two categories. First are those common throughout local government, such as housing, transport and leisure services. Many of these never make profits and are permanently subsidized, like housing. Secondly, various local authorities retain their own particular ventures: Hull's telephones, Birmingham's bank and Bradford's Wool Conditioning House are all owned by their respective local authorities.

6.2.1 Nationalized industries

The predominant form of public enterprise in the twentieth century has been the nationalization of whole industries, such as rail or electricity. Nationalization was frequently the last stage of a process of increasing state involvement in private companies in that industry. Control of the railway system, for example, was taken from the hands of the 130 private companies and assumed by the state during World War I. After the War, in 1921, the government forced the companies to amalgamate into four large units. After being taken over once again for the duration of World War II, the railways were finally nationalized in 1947.

The nationalized industries are wholly owned by the state. Managerial powers are vested in Boards of Directors appointed by the government. Prior to World War II there were only a few nationalized industries: the BBC had been set up in 1923 and the Central Electricity Board in 1926. The principal period of nationalization was the postwar Labour government's term of office from 1945 to 1951. The late 1940s saw the nationalization of coal, electricity, rail, gas, and iron and steel, then termed the 'commanding heights' of the economy, as well as parts of the air and road transport industries and the Bank of England. In the 1950s, the Conservatives returned road transport and parts of the steel industry to private hands. The overall structure of the public enterprise sector was, however, little changed. The 1960s and 1970s have seen the addition of some manufacturing industries such as steel, shipbuilding and aerospace to the public enterprise sector.

Such is the extent of public ownership that modern Britain is said to have a 'mixed economy', with both public and private sectors. The nationalized industries account for 11% of the Gross Domestic Product (GDP), 8% of all employment, and 19% of gross domestic investment in the production industries (SIC Orders II–XXIII). The nationalized industries also occupy a strategic place in the economic system, dominating energy supply and transport and communications.

Table 6.1 The Nationalized Industries

Organizations	Total assets (£m, 1978)	Employees ($\times 10^3$, 1978, worldwide)
Major nationalized industries		
British National Oil Corporation	751	1
British Steel Corporation	2235	210
British Aerospace	322	70
British Gas Corporation	2078	100
British Airports Authority	509	6
Post Office	6881	401
British Rail	1593	178
National Coal Board	1333	239
Electricity Council	6511	159
Bank of England (Banking Department)	2483	7
Private firms (for comparison)		
ICI	3977	151
Grand Metropolitan	1147	107
Unilever	3525	385

Sources: Annual Reports and Accounts

6.2.2 Mixed enterprise

When an industry is nationalized, private ownership is replaced by state ownership. Shareholders in the former companies surrender their shares and are given gilt-edged government stock in compensation. There are now, however, an increasing number of mixed enterprises, which are jointly owned by private shareholders and the state. Their growth reflects, to some extent, a disillusionment with the performance of the nationalized industries and a desire for a more flexible structure for the management of state assets. Mixed enterprise has been seen as a means of influencing the policies of private firms more effectively than exhortations and incentives while avoiding outright nationalization.

There is nothing new about state shareholdings in private firms: BP has had a large government shareholding since before World War I. In recent years there has been increasing interest in applying the 'BP solution' to more government acquisitions. State holding companies such as the NEB and its Scottish and Welsh counterparts were established in 1975 to acquire holdings in private companies. The

Conservative government elected in 1979 views the NEB and public ownership with disfavour. Their policy is to allow partial private ownership of sections of some nationalized industries. This is sometimes referred to as 'privatization'.

6.3 The debate over public ownership

Nationalization is identified with the Labour Party's commitment to socialism. Clause four of the party's constitution sets as an objective 'the common ownership of the means of production, distribution and exchange'. Public ownership is seen as a means of redistributing power and wealth, as control over major industries is removed from the hands of capitalists. Political justifications for this include the assertion that the power of business, and especially of monopolies, is excessive and should be limited. Running industries in order to secure private gain is criticized as immoral and as a source of injustice in that the poor may be deprived of basic goods. Public ownership, it is argued, would permit industries to pursue social objectives, providing goods and services for the public, and employees would benefit from improved working conditions. Private enterprise is also accused of duplicating facilities and wasting resources. Public ownership would allow industry to be planned efficiently to meet social needs.

Political opponents of nationalization on the Right argue that public ownership of industry can be a first step towards an all-powerful, undemocratic state. Political liberty is rarely found in societies where individuals do not have the economic liberty to own property. The progressive abolition of private property will, in the long term, undermine citizens' political freedom.

Opponents of nationalization also argue, on a more concrete level, that public ownership makes industries respond to the dictates of planners rather than to the requirements of their customers. There will be, accordingly, no incentive for firms to be efficient and resources will be squandered.

Even on the Left, there has been no agreement on the desirable extent of nationalization. The dominant view among the Labour Party leadership and Labour governments has been that the UK should have a 'mixed economy' in which public ownership is limited. Their political objectives could, they felt, be achieved through a range of alternative methods, including taxation and regulation as well as public ownership. The left wing of the Labour movement, by contrast, has seen increased public ownership as the key to achieving their social and political objectives. Only public ownership will, they argue, permit industry to be controlled by the state in the interests of society; only the elimination of private property will allow society to move towards socialism.

There has also been disagreement over the form of public ownership. Some socialists, called syndicalists, have argued for workers' control: that state-owned industries should be run by the employees. The dominant view, however, has been that the authority to manage should reside with the government-appointed Boards.

Labour governments have been responsible for most public takeovers, and Labour-controlled local authorities have been keenest to develop municipal enterprise. The expansion of public ownership, however, owes more to a pragmatic response to circumstances than to ideological commitments. Governments of all parties have created nationalized industries. Despite international differences in political systems and traditions, most West European countries have similar public enterprise sectors embracing energy (gas, electricity, coal) and transport and communication (rail, national airlines, post and telecommunications).

The debate over nationalization has not been conducted purely in political terms, for economic and social arguments for public ownership have also been advanced. First, public ownership may permit **economies of scale** to be realized. These exist when large-scale production is cheaper per unit than small-scale production. A single large steel mill may be more efficient than two small ones for technical and organizational reasons. Large organizations may therefore be necessary to undertake the big investments appropriate to modern technology and to close the older, smaller units. This is known as 'rationalization'. Secondly, large-scale firms in private hands may become monopolies which are able to exploit the public, and it is argued that public ownership would prevent such abuse. Thirdly, it has been suggested that public enterprises are also better able to undertake a controlled reduction in capacity in a declining industry. Only a large organization, operating on an industry-wide basis, can plan redundancies and closures in an orderly way, as well as investing in modern capacity for the future.

Declining output and reductions in capacity, such as commonly occur in the nationalized industries, are frequently found in the later stages of the **'life-cycle'** of a product or service. All products, according to the theory of the product life-cycle, go through a series of stages. In the experimental stage, designs change rapidly as the product is improved. Design then becomes standardized in the growth stage when demand is buoyant, and profits are good. In the mature stage, the design is almost static and attention is placed upon finding more efficient ways of producing the product. As efficiency rises and sales stagnate, the industry's labour force shrinks. Profits tend to fall in the later stages, and the industry becomes unattractive to private capital. Many nationalized industries, viewed from this perspective, may be seen to be broadly concerned with products in their late stages of life. They are not concerned with developing new products, but with the performance of a well-defined job, at the lowest cost. Their work, in a word, is routine. While the nationalized industries are certainly engaged in technical change of the highest order, such as nuclear power or high-speed trains, the changes are in the production techniques, not in the products. Their labour forces are, mainly, shrinking under the impact of static outputs and rising productivity.

Public ownership may be supported by a further group of reasons, namely that the industry has some special importance to the community. Thus, bankrupt firms and unprofitable parts of the rail system are maintained for the sake of the communities that depend upon them. State participation in North Sea oil and gas production has been justified on the basis of their strategic importance, while military reasons have been put forward to support state ownership of parts of the defence industries.

None of these arguments—economies of scale, supervision of decline, and so on—is universally accepted. Many on the Right argue that the same objectives could equally well be attained without the state taking firms over. If large-scale production is truly cheaper, private firms will merge of their own accord. Monopolies can be regulated rather than owned—and strategic industries can be retained by subsidies. Indeed, the Conservative government elected in 1979 sought to sell off part-ownership of sections of some nationalized industries to the private sector. Their intention was first to reduce the extent of public borrowing, and secondly, to give greater freedom to market forces. The management of those industries accordingly would be accountable to the shareholders for the efficient use of their resources, rather than to ministers, parliament and the electorate. These moves reflect, of course, an Individualist approach to economic policy.

Table 6.2 Arguments over nationalization

	For	*Against*
Political	1. To run industry as part of an economic plan, rather than for private profit 2. To secure strategic or social objectives 3. To reduce power of business interests	To safeguard economic and hence political liberty
Economic	1. To attain economies of scale 2. To regulate monopolies 3. To facilitate large-scale investment or technological development 4. To smooth the problems of decline	To maintain the disciplines of the market place and ensure efficient use of resources

6.4 The obligations and objectives of public enterprise

The objectives of private firms are set by their directors and owners, who seek to make profits. Nationalized industries' objectives are determined by Parliament and the government. The statutes that took the industries into public ownership, such as the Coal Industry Nationalization Act, set down certain obligations, generally including the requirement that the Boards should consider the 'public interest'. The statutory obligations were extremely vague, and in practice governments have imposed many conflicting obligations upon the nationalized industries in the name of public interest. The Boards have generally been unable to resist this pressure.

The obligations of the nationalized industries include commercial obligations to earn a certain rate of profit on their assets. The particular rates demanded vary between industries and have been revised from time to time. Secondly, the nationalized industries have been used as instruments in the pursuit of economic objectives. The nationalized industries were thus forced into massive deficits in the mid-1970s as their prices were frozen to help to control inflation, while their costs rose. Nationalized industries have also been used to support British industry by buying UK-made equipment. Thirdly, nationalized industries are obliged to pursue certain social objectives. They have, for example, been used to assist the poorer regions and isolated communities by maintaining uneconomic operations.

The blurred and conflicting objectives imposed upon the nationalized industries are a cause of frequent problems. There is little incentive for management to pursue efficiency and cost reductions if it is known that the industry will receive a subsidy at the end of the year for any losses. The same comments apply also in principle to local authority trading operations. The different obligations—commercial, economic and social—frequently come into conflict. While restraining prices or keeping uneconomic rail lines open meets some objectives, they may produce inefficiency and will depress profits. The changing emphasis placed upon the different obligations at different times reflects the changing pressures that have borne upon governments, as well as their policies and beliefs.

6.4.1 Managing the nationalized industries

The dominant view in the UK has been that, to operate as successful commercial enterprises, the management of the nationalized industries need considerable freedom from ministerial, Civil Service and Parliamentary control. Managers must have the freedom and flexibility to manage. Yet the industries are state owned and should therefore be accountable to the government and Parliament which represent the public. The difficulty of reconciling these requirements is at the root of many of the problems of the nationalized industries, and is inherent in their objectives and obligations.

The conventional British solution to this difficulty is to establish each industry as a separate public corporation. A public corporation is a state agency which is not part of central or local government. It has been thought since the 1930s to be an appropriate way to manage nationalized industries as, in theory, it provides a balance between independence and accountability.

Some features of the public corporation are intended to insulate managers from political interference and guarantee them more freedom than their Civil Service or local authority counterparts. Such features include:

- establishing the industries as legal entities separate from government departments,
- vesting management powers in a Board of Directors rather than in ministers,
- financing the industries through borrowing and their commercial activities, rather than through taxation,
- allowing management to recruit, pay and deploy staff as thought appropriate rather than according to Civil Service practice,
- exempting the industries from the normal Parliamentary scrutiny applicable to ministries.

Other features, intended to safeguard the public interest and make the public corporations accountable, include the statutory imposition of non-commercial obligations, the publication of Reports and Accounts, having a government department with a certain degree of responsibility for each corporation, and establishing consultative councils. These constraints on the freedom of the industries are broad but are not intended to take away the prerogatives of management. In theory, ministers, Civil Servants and Parliament are supposed to exercise self-restraint and remain at 'arm's length' from the running of the industry.

6.4.2 The public corporation in practice

The balance sought between freedom and accountability has not been achieved. The national importance of the industries invites government intervention. Their supervisory and sponsorship responsibilities give ministers a direct interest in the commercial performance of the industries. Likewise, the national influence of the industries' decisions on wages, prices, investment and so on encourage detailed government intervention, often for short-term economic or political reasons. Similarly, Boards are conscious of their obligations to serve the public interest. Consequently, they are open to arguments and pressure from ministers who claim the right to interpret the public interest.

Ministers also justify intervention as a means of keeping Boards on their toes and improving management performance. The scale and form of the interventions has however been criticized for undermining the freedom of managers. Accountability, furthermore, is blurred as neither the public nor Parliament know on what basis, and by whom, decisions are made, and it is therefore impossible to assess the performance of the industries.

In the 1950s and 1960s, ministers intervened in quite detailed decisions to promote non-commercial obligations. The nationalized steel companies were, for example, induced to build works in areas of high unemployment, and the publicly owned airlines were forced to buy British rather than American planes. A White Paper on the nationalized industries' objectives, published in 1967, argued that governments could be expected to compensate Boards for such actions. Nevertheless, in the 1970s, interference occurred on a massive scale as governments sought to reduce inflation by holding down the prices charged by the nationalized industries. This situation led to a National Economic Development Office (NEDO) report in 1976 which reviewed the relationship between ministers and Boards. It identified four major weaknesses.

- A lack of trust and mutual understanding between Boards and government.
- Confusion about the respective roles of Boards, government and Parliament with a consequent blurring of accountability.
- The absence of systematic methods of reaching agreement on long-term policy and no assurance of continuity when decisions were reached.
- The absence of methods of assessing the performance of the industries and their management.

Such criticisms reflect the disillusionment with the public corporation as providing neither adequate public accountability nor adequate management freedom.

Although there is widespread agreement on what is wrong with the management of the nationalized industries, there is no such agreement on how it should be put right. Almost all the remedies proposed by MPs, academics and independent inquiries involve distinguishing the responsibilities of ministers and Boards more firmly, in order that accountability may be clearly established and performance evaluated. The intention of these proposals is to ensure that ministers can safeguard the public interest and approve the broad lines of policy, while leaving the Boards with sufficient commercial discretion to achieve their targets. Experience shows, however, that ministers have extreme difficulty in resisting the temptation to intervene. A decision such as a plant closure may seem like a managerial matter to a Board, but may appear as an issue of great social and political importance to ministers. It may be questioned, therefore, whether institutional changes of themselves will make any contribution to the problems of running the nationalized industries.

6.5   The performance of the nationalized industries

Having discussed the objectives of the nationalized industries and the problems of directing them, this section will go on to examine their performance. After looking at the main conventional measure of performance, namely profitability, attention will turn to the nationalized industries' pricing policies, their record on productivity and their management of change and decline.

6.5.1   Profitability

Comparison between the profitability of the nationalized sector and private industry can only be made with care. The burden of interest payments is far greater for the public corporations than private firms. The latter derive most of their funds from the issue of shares and from retained profits, and only pay interest on that part of their capital which is borrowed from the banks. The public corporations, by contrast, have to pay interest on the whole of their capital, whether borrowed from government or from private investors.

At the same time, profits cannot be taken as a straightforward indicator of performance. Efficient nationalized industries may record lower profits if they are obliged to pursue non-commercial objectives. Keeping uneconomic units in operation will raise costs and depress profits. Also, many nationalized industries are in a monopoly position and can gain high profits not through being efficient but simply by raising their charges.

Profitability has nevertheless been a focus of attention. After allowance has been made for the burden of interest payments and other factors, the returns of the nationalized industries have been low compared to private industry. An analysis of the public corporations' performance in the 1960s concluded that, with rates of return of about 6%, they were about half as profitable as private industry at that time. While the gas and electricity industries, National Bus and National Freight have managed to meet their interest charges, other industries have received subsidies and had their debts to the government cancelled ('capital write-offs'). British Rail and the National Coal Board (NCB) between them received over £3.4 billion in support between 1963 and 1974.

The lower rate of return in the public enterprise sector is a measure of the loss to the economy which public enterprise brings, say the critics. There has been an **opportunity cost** in allowing the nationalized industries to invest funds. Opportunity cost is the benefit which is foregone when resources are taken from one use and put to another. The opportunity cost to the economy of investing resources in the nationalized industries for one rate of return is the higher returns which would have been attained in the private sector.

The profitability and investment of the nationalized industries have long been among the concerns of governments. The Nationalization Acts had only stipulated that the corporations should break even, taking one year with another. That is, they were to earn sufficient trading profit to meet their interest charges. In 1961, a White Paper was published, which set target rates of profit for each industry, in an attempt to simulate market pressures. It was intended that investment would be restricted to projects which could earn the required returns. It was also hoped that attainable targets would give the industries a sense of purpose. The Boards were to seek to reach the targets by the best means they could. It was open to them, therefore, simply to exploit their monopoly position, if any, by charging higher prices. In the event, the electricity, gas and air corporations virtually attained their targets. The declining industries, coal and rail, however, sank into deficit.

During the 1960s, the social implications of commercial policies became evident. Closures of pits and branch lines entailed high social costs in terms of the disruption of small communities. In a second White Paper on the obligations of the nationalized industries, published in 1967, the government undertook to compensate the Boards for uneconomic operations undertaken at its behest.

The notion of a specific subsidy in order to attain a social objective was not new, but had been refined during the 1960s by the theory of **cost benefit analysis** (CBA). CBA, first developed in the USA, is an attempt to quantify all the effects of a public sector investment in money terms. The building of the Victoria Line for the London Underground, for example, was subjected to a cost benefit appraisal. The costs to society—the land, materials and labour used and the inconvenience of construction—were given monetary value, as were the benefits to society—shorter travel times, greater comfort and a reduction in road congestion as travellers switched modes of transport. Despite the fact that London Transport forecast a loss on the project, it was approved because the total social benefits outweighed the total social costs. Of critical importance in conducting a CBA, of course is the procedure for setting a monetary value on things like time-saving, noise or the loss of countryside. Although no CBA has convinced its critics, the procedure gave credence to the idea that social benefits may, in principle, be quantified. It is rarely, of course, used by private industry, nor is it applied systematically to all government decisions.

6.5.2 Pricing

In free, competitive markets, price is driven down to equal costs plus a normal profit mark-up. Price under competition also tends to equal **marginal cost**, that is, the cost of producing one more unit of the commodity. As the nationalized industries do not usually face direct competition, prices are not determined immediately by market forces, and pricing policy has been a matter of some public discussion.

Economists argue that prices should reflect the cost of resources used in production. Prices that are lower than costs will encourage consumers to buy more of the good in question, thus requiring large quantities of resources to be diverted from other uses. Artificially low energy prices, for example, stimulate demand and necessitate investment in new power stations, mines and oil installations. High prices, conversely, will restrict output to less than the volume that consumers desire.

In some cases, the marginal cost of supplying a good or service may be almost zero. Electricity produced at night is an example. The generating system is installed to meet peak demand during the day, and electricity sold then brings in enough money to pay for the fixed investment. In many cases, power stations are kept running all night, for this is cheaper than closing them down and starting them up again. Under these circumstances, the additional costs imposed upon the system by actually producing electricity at night are minimal. 'White meter' tariffs, which apply to night-time electricity, are below ordinary tariffs, reflecting the lower marginal costs. The same logic lies behind lower charges for off-peak telephone calls, cheap off-peak rail travel and cheap summer coal.

Economists have criticized the nationalized industries for setting prices at average cost rather than marginal costs, thus preventing the attainment of true economic efficiency. The 1967 White Paper accepted this criticism and enjoined the public corporations to base prices on marginal costs where possible. At the same time, the argument has not been fully accepted by the government or the public corporations. Charging prices equal to marginal costs could mean low prices, for if an industry had excess capacity, the cost of accommodating one extra consumer could be very small. Prices in that case could be too low to cover costs, and the industry would record a deficit. In requiring Boards to break even or to earn a target rate of return, the government implied that prices should be based to a large extent upon **average costs**. By their stress upon rates of return, governments have shown themselves unwilling to pursue economic efficiency at the expense of losses in the nationalized industries.

6.5.3 Productivity and industrial change

Poor financial results may be taken as an indication that resources are being used inefficiently. At the same time, virtually all the nationalized industries have been under competitive pressure both from other nationalized industries and from private operators. Some industries, facing expanding demand as their products went through their growth stage, were in a position to pioneer new services. British Airways and Post Office Telecommunications thus developed supersonic flight and data storage. Industries facing declining demand have been forced to reduce costs by raising productivity.

Technical change has been a prime concern throughout the sector. Labour-saving techniques have been adopted on a massive scale and old capacity has been scrapped. Mining, for example, has seen the widespread introduction of automatic cutting and loading equipment, as well as the wholesale closure of uneconomic pits.

An analysis of the period 1948–1958 concluded that productivity, both of labour alone and of labour and capital taken together, grew at least as rapidly in the public corporations as in manufacturing industry. Indeed, two publicly owned industries, electricity generation and aviation, were among the leaders of the productivity growth league. Comparing the nationalized industries' performance with that of equivalent industries abroad, whether privately or publicly owned, the study concluded that their record was not unreasonable.

Those findings were not universally accepted. They related, moreover, to public corporations like the Post Office, British Rail and the Central Electricity Generating Board (CEGB) which did not face direct competition. More recent additions to the public enterprise sector—the shipbuilding and steel industries and British Leyland—are, however, engaged in competitive struggle with overseas producers in the market place. Evidence from their performances suggests that productivity in the UK is frequently low by international standards.

All the nationalized industries have raised productivity by changing their production processes and organization. All industrial change involves the scrapping and closure of old plant and the commissioning of new. Most nationalized industries, as *Figure 6.1* shows, have shed labour in the process of modernization, and in this they are similar to many private manufacturing industries. The problems that face public corporations, while not unique, are made complex because the scale of their operation is frequently large, and because in some cases they are using very new and sophisticated technology. Indeed, a key aspect of the nationalized industries has been their management of industrial change and decline. There are two aspects to this process: the technical problems associated with new equipment, and the social and political consequences of technical innovation.

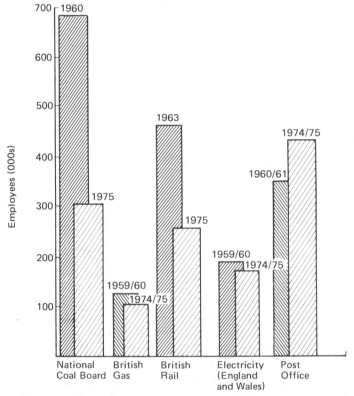

Figure 6.1 Employment in the nationalized industries

Source: *National Economic Development Office: Study of the UK Nationalized Industries, 1977,* Background Paper No. 4

Technological changes of the most advanced nature have been undertaken by some of the nationalized industries. Frequently the sole operators in their fields in the UK, the public corporations are generally the biggest buyers, by a long way, of their type of capital equipment. No one else in the UK buys power stations except the electricity corporations; equipment manufacturers thus sometimes become dependent on the public corporations. Problems have therefore arisen when orders are placed irregularly, or when the public corporations insist upon the development of their favoured design. The electricity industry, for example, was dogged for a time by the poor performance of the big generating sets which it demanded from the manufacturers. Similarly, its nuclear power programme has been little short of a catalogue of disappointment. Dungeness 'B', for example, was begun in 1965 but construction was subject to such delay that work was still going on in 1980.

The **political and social consequences** of technical change in the public enterprise sector have been varied. In areas of high technology, the state has favoured the creation of agencies with greater autonomy and, frequently, with a lower degree of public accountability. Examples are the NEB and the Atomic Energy Authority. Their creation has been criticized from the Right as more 'creeping socialism' and from the Left as the growth of an increasingly repressive capitalist state.

The closure of old capacity has had serious social consequences in some industries. Employment in mining, for example, fell from 700 000 in 1959 to 250 000 in 1975, with the bulk of the losses occurring in the depressed areas of Wales, Scotland and the north of England. This added greatly to the problem of high unemployment in these areas, and the government was prompted to try and retard the decline by taxing fuel oil and subsidising coal. The steel and shipbuilding boards also face the prospect of shedding labour in localities of high unemployment.

This illustrates the general theme of the problems of economic change. While new technology produces higher living standards, there are invariably groups who suffer losses. Communities in the coal, steel and shipbuilding areas lose employment opportunities, as the economy moves over to other fuels and patterns of production. The nationalized industries have sought to cushion the blows to the losers by subsidies. Uneconomic operations have been maintained, attempts have been made to attract new firms to employ displaced labour and large redundancy payments have been offered. The problems imposed by change and closure are unlikely to recede in the coming years, for the public corporations are as deeply affected by industrial decline as the private sector. How these problems are met will depend in part upon governments' views about the proper role and objectives of the nationalized industries.

6.6 The nationalized industries: evaluation and interpretation

The public corporations have not had an easy passage. Their progress has been dogged by poor financial results, the problems of modernization and closures, and accusations of inefficiency. Analyses of the causes of their problems, and of the remedies to be taken, vary widely. In broad terms they may be found to reflect underlying political or philosophical standpoints, Consensus and Conflict, and can be grouped accordingly.

The principle of nationalization is naturally anathema to the *laissez-faire* tradition. For the individualist school of thought, private enterprise and the free operation of market forces are the best ways to attain economic efficiency and growth. The institution of private property also means that power is distributed throughout the society and so forms the basis of democracy. The eclipse of private property in certain industries is interpreted, therefore, as a step toward the extinction of private property altogether. Not only does nationalization lead to subsidies for uncompetitive organizations, but it is also a move toward totalitarian dictatorship. The ideal solution is to sell the nationalized industries back to the private sector, and at all costs to avoid further state acquisitions. Indeed, the Conservative government elected in 1979 embarked upon a programme of selling shares in British Airways, British Aerospace and other nationalized industries to the public.

Moderates would accept a measure of state intervention, if the benefits can be shown to outweigh the costs. Looked at from this perspective, a measure of nationalization is good because a mixed economy balances the social structure and can improve the economic performance of the free enterprise system. This approach to nationalization favours the setting of guidelines for public corporations who should then be allowed commercial discretion to pursue them. Targets for prices and rates of return on investment should be both clearly stated and subsidised at a specific rate. Ministers, while maintaining a watching brief over the industry, should generally remain at arm's length. Extensions to public ownership are not to be accepted or rejected out of hand, but are to be judged on the contribution that nationalization would make to the nation's economic performance.

According to radicals, nationalization has merely relieved the private sector of the burden of running certain problematic industries. Consistent losses, large-scale investment needs and expensive research programmes can clearly make certain sectors unattractive to private capital, and the industries in question were transferred to the state. Investors were free to place their funds in new, profitable industries, while the public corporations provided cheap, subsidised inputs for the private sector. The public corporations, furthermore, retained the former management structures and, often, the previous managers. The nationalized industries also continued to compete against each other, rarely coordinating their activities. The only way in which nationalization can be made into a socialist measure is to carry it out in every industry, to pay no compensation and to place the industries under workers' control.

In the light of these approaches to nationalization, it is far from surprising that proposals to extend or to reverse public ownership arouse hot dispute. For like all features of the social environment of business, it is open to interpretation from contrasting standpoints.

Guide to further reading
General

National Economic Development Office (1976). *A Study of the UK Nationalised Industries: Their Role in the Economy and Control in the Future*, NEDO, London. A useful survey of modern problems.
Thornhill, W. (1968). *The Nationalised Industries: An Introduction*, Nelson, London. Describes the causes and development of nationalization in Chapter 1 and outlines the organizational forms used in Chapters 2 and 8.
Reid, G. L., Allen, K. and Harris, D. J. (1973). *The Nationalised Fuel Industries*, Heinemann, London. Gives quite a detailed description of the workings of public corporations in their sector, concentrating on their economic aspects.

Subsections
6.4

Coombes, D. (1971). *State Enterprise: Business or Politics?*, Allen & Unwin, London. Chapters 1–4 discuss the varying obligations imposed on the nationalized industries.

6.5 and 6.6

Webb, Michael G. (1976). *Pricing Policies for Public Enterprises*, Macmillan, London. Chapters 1–3 set out the logic of marginal cost pricing.
Pryke, Richard (1971). *Public Enterprise in Practice*, MacGibbon and Kee, London. Undertakes a sympathetic analysis of the nationalized industries between 1948 and 1968 from a moderate perspective.
Papps, Ivy (1975). *Government and Enterprise*, Hobart Papers 61, Institute of Economic Affairs, London. Analyses nationalization from an individualist standpoint.
Westergaard, John and Resler, Henrietta (1975). *Class in a Capitalist Society*, Heinemann, London. Part 3, Chapter 4 sets out a radical view of public enterprise.

Exercises

Review questions

1. What is meant by (*a*) the mixed economy, (*b*) mixed enterprise and (*c*) privatization?
2. Name the public corporations involved in energy, transport and communications and, manufacturing, and name their privately owned competitors.
3. What reasons have been put forward to support nationalization and on what grounds is nationalization opposed?
4. Why do radicals favour an extension of public ownership?
5. What problems arise in running the nationalized industries, and what solutions have been proposed?
6. Why should the reported profits of the nationalized industries not be taken as a straightforward indication of their performance?
7. What is meant by cost benefit analysis?
8. What is meant by marginal cost and average cost?
9. What technical changes have the nationalized industries been involved with?
10. What are the distinctive features of a public corporation as compared with first, a government department and, secondly, a private firm?

Application and investigation

1. Explain the principles of marginal cost pricing. Give examples other than those in the text.
2. Describe current government policy toward nationalization and the nationalized industries, giving examples from expanding and declining industries.
3. Compare and contrast the policies toward the idea of public ownership and the running of the nationalized industries favoured by individualists, moderates and radicals.

Projects

1. Examine a recent technological change such as the introduction of nuclear power in one of the nationalized industries. What caused it to be introduced? What problems, if any, have attended its

introduction? What consequences have there been or will there be in the future for the national economy and for your local area?

2. Select a nationalized industry and look at its accounts for the last few years. How would you assess its performance over that period? What could be done if anything to improve it?

Chapter 7

The social services sector

7.1 Introduction

The previous three chapters have been concerned with the commercial provision of goods and services by the private and public sector. This chapter will deal with the social services. The social services are those publicly financed and controlled forms of provision which distribute benefits in cash or kind to those in need. The major areas of provision are education, health, housing, the welfare or personal social services, and cash benefits. From the consumer's point of view the main feature of the benefits is that they are allocated on the basis of need rather than ability to pay. These services have a major impact on living standards through providing individuals in need with access to resources they might not otherwise have obtained. The system of personal taxation, in so far as it is adjusted to the needs of individuals, can be viewed as a form of 'fiscal welfare', which supplements the social services.

The social services sector also has very important economic implications. On the one hand it requires considerable amounts of taxation and makes heavy demands on the available supplies of resources, while on the other, it helps to improve the quality of the workforce through making education, health care and a guaranteed income widely available. During the twentieth century the social services have become established as a major element in the British economy. For many people indeed, the existence of widespread social services is the foundation of a distinctive type of society which they term the 'welfare state'.

The social services exist as a result of political decisions. They are surrounded by political controversy. Throughout the chapter, reference will be made to Left, Centre and Right political viewpoints. These differ in their interpretation of the origins and nature of the social services. These political views are usually closely related to the Conflict and Consensus approaches.

7.2 Development

Social policy expenditure, in common with other forms of state expenditure is much higher now than it was 60 years ago, as *Table 7.1*. shows.

Table 7.1 Growth of social service expenditure

| | Percentage of GNP at factor cost | | | |
	1921	1951	1975	1978
Education	2.2	3.2	7.6	6.1
Health and welfare services	1.1	4.5	7.1	6.3
Housing	2.1	3.1	4.6	3.4
Social security	4.7	5.3	9.5	10.8
Total	10.1	16.1	28.8	26.6

Sources: Gough, I. (1979). *Political Economy of the Welfare State*, p. 77, London, MacMillan; *Social Trends 1980*, HMSO, 1979, *Table 7.13*

The proportion of the National Income spent on each of the social services has increased in the period 1921–1975 although the rate of the increase has varied between the different services. The present social services also differ considerably in their scope, with a large private sector remaining in some areas, such as housing, and a small but significant private sector in others, such as health and education.

The social services have developed in response to changes in the overall economic, social and political organization of society. There is, however, considerable disagreement about precisely how these factors have influenced their development. The different viewpoints can be conveniently distinguished in terms of Consensus and Conflict approaches. Those who hold the Consensus view often see the development of the social services as a steady process of reform designed to meet the needs and problems arising from the growth of a modern industrial society. The Conflict view, however, sees social services as developing as a result of successful pressure from the working class for improvements in their living conditions. They may also be seen as a result of concessions granted by the dominant class as a means of maintaining their economic and political position.

Economic change has been a major factor in the development of social policy. The industrial revolution involved the growth of large-scale factory production, replacing the domestic system where goods were produced in the household. As a result of industrialization many new problems emerged. The industrial economy was subject to considerable fluctuations in the level of employment. When a downturn in the trade-cycle occurred, thousands would face destitution. The old and the handicapped, who had been able to make some contribution under the domestic system, could find few opportunities for work. Serious problems concerning health and safety at work developed. Changes in the patterns of family and community life also occurred. The skills necessary for work could no longer be learned in the household and as the requirement grew for a more literate workforce, the state took over major educational functions from the family and the local community.

The rapid growth of industrial towns and the considerable geographical mobility this involved often separated people from the network of support provided by friends and relatives. At the same time most of the rapidly expanding population of the industrial towns lived in slum conditions. These, together with poverty, poor working conditions and long hours of work, resulted in widespread disease and early death.

The first phase of development of the social services occurred during the nineteenth century. The Poor Law (Amendment) Act 1834 kept cash payments to the poor to a minimum and set up a system of workhouses to provide relief for the destitute. Conditions in these residential institutions were made as unpleasant as possible to deter their use and to keep down public expenditure. The state played little part in the provision of housing although there were some attempts to promote slum clearance. Apart from sick wards in workhouses there was little state provision of health care, although environmental health was tackled fairly vigorously through the Public Health Acts of 1848 and 1875. The other major development was in education, which was provided for all up to the age of 10 by the Education Act 1870.

In this century the two periods of most dramatic change in social policy were the years of the 1906–1914 Liberal government, and the period 1940–1950, when there was a three-party wartime coalition followed in 1945 by a Labour government.

The Liberal government of 1906–1914 made considerable reforms in the area of social security through providing pensions for the poor over 70 years of age and through setting up a scheme of National Insurance. This provided family doctor care for poor workers, and unemployment benefits for workers in industries subject to heavy seasonal unemployment. This scheme was funded by compulsory contributions from workers and their employers, with additional funds from central government revenue.

There is no doubt that this was a period when the attitudes of those in authority were changing. Research on poverty in York by Rowntree had demonstrated that almost a third of the working population lived at a standard insufficient to maintain their working efficiency. Rowntree's work was extremely influential. His attempt at an exact measurement of poverty through calculating a minimum necessary income formed the basis for subsequent discussions of poverty and the poverty line. Rowntree also showed how poverty most often occurred at particular phases of the life cycle, such as when there were small children in the family, or in old age.

Consensus interpretations of this period of reform tend to emphasize the influence of increased public awareness of poverty which resulted in part from contemporary research on the subject. They also point to the growing acceptance of the idea that labour efficiency would rise if working class living standards were improved. Those adopting a Conflict view point both to the impact of the growing industrial unrest in this period, as well as the fear of the Liberal leadership that the newly formed Labour Party would pick up much of their working class support unless concessions were made that assisted working people. This argument sees reforms as being reluctantly conceded in a bid by the propertied classes to hang onto power and to prevent the rise of a left-wing movement.

The next major phase in development came in the period 1940–1950. This saw the development of the modern welfare state through reforms providing comprehensive and free services for all in the areas of education, health and social security.

While the reforms were mainly brought in by a Labour government, the war itself played a major part in creating the conditions for them. This was because of the extension of the role of the state which occurred during the war and the changes in attitude and values that the war brought about. Much of the hospital system was brought under central control; and in the field of nutrition, rationing, a school meals scheme and a system of state-regulated canteens were set up. The state also took on responsibility for rehousing bomb victims, and providing day nurseries for the children of working women, rehabilitation facilities for the disabled, pensions for those widowed and family allowances for members of the armed forces.

A number of features of wartime life encouraged the mood of reform. The common experience of the hardships and dangers of total war, the massive extension of state economic regulation, the disruption of family life caused by the evacuation of children, and the conscription of military and civilian man- and woman-power all played a part. In turn the government realized the importance of maintaining civilian morale and early in the war began planning for postwar reconstruction. This culminated in a number of reports and White Papers which formed the basis for postwar changes, such as the Beveridge Report of 1942 on social security, and the White Papers of 1944 on a National Health Service and Employment Policy.

The Labour government elected in 1945, with a large majority, strengthened the system of social services largely in accordance with the wartime plans. These plans, together with the adoption of Keynesian economic policies embodied a widespread agreement on the need for reform which developed under the pressure of war and which was broadly supported, for a variety of reasons, across the political spectrum.

Since 1950 the two major political parties have in practice adopted similar policies towards the social services. Both have supported the growth of means-tested and earnings-related benefits which have been the two major innovations in the 1960s and 1970s. Except in the area of housing, where the Conservatives have generally put far less emphasis on council housing, and education, where Labour have been more in favour of comprehensive schooling, the policies pursued have been remarkably similar. A notable feature of the social services in most of the postwar period has been the very rapid growth of expenditure. There are a number of reasons for this.

- The quality of some services has been improved. In education, classes are smaller and in health increasingly sophisticated and expensive forms of diagnosis and treatment are being used.
- The extent of provision has increased. There are more old people's homes and more places in higher education.
- The number of people eligible for various services has increased.

The increasing number of old people has implications for expenditure on pensions, health, the welfare services and special housing for the old. The younger age at marriage increases the demand for housing because people desire an independent household earlier than in the past. Reductions in family size may lead to problems of over-capacity in education and other services provided for children. The increasing frequency of marriage breakdowns leads to more one-parent families and family poverty. A particular difficulty for the social services arises from the fact that birth rates, unlike death rates, are subject to substantial and rapid fluctuations. One obvious result is considerable year-by-year variation in the numbers starting school, and later, in the demand for further and higher education; but all the social services are ultimately affected. In recent years, in both major parties, there has been some decline in support for expenditure on social services as a result of the deepening economic crisis. The cuts in social services initiated by Labour in 1976 were continued by the Conservative government elected in 1979.

The explanation of the development of the social services in Britain is a matter of considerable controversy. A case can be made both for a Conflict and a Consensus interpretation. The view one takes is partly determined by the kinds of evidence that are appealed to. The Consensus view tends to emphasize the role of research and enquiry in improving the knowledge of social conditions and the role of humanitarian concern in creating the impetus for social reform. This view seems to be confirmed by the fact that most reforms are accompanied by relevant research and enquiry and by avowedly humanitarian motives on the part of reformers. Those who hold the Conflict viewpoint, however, suggest that research and humanitarianism are seldom decisive in themselves. They see the real influences as either the desire of those in power to improve labour discipline and efficiency, or fear of the political consequences of failing to make reforms.

7.3 Organizational structure

The social services differ considerably in their organizational structures. The two arms of the social security system, National Insurance and Supplementary Benefits are subject to a high degree of central control. All payments to claimants are made according to detailed rules by the local offices of the Department of Health and Social Security (DHSS). This highly bureaucratic structure is intended to ensure the uniform treatment of clients. Democratic control is exercised only through Parliament and local authorities have no influence over the working of the system.

In contrast, education, housing and the welfare services are administered by elected local authorities. Local authorities have Education, Housing and Social Service Committees and a separate director for each service. Within limits laid down by central government they are free to make their own decisions about the services to be provided. Central government control is exercised by the appropriate department—Education and Science in the case of education, Environment in the case of housing, and Health and Social Security in the case of the personal social services. Central control is exercised through statutory duties imposed on local authorities, through conditions attached to financial support, through advice or instructions from ministerial circulars sent to all local authorities and through informal consultations between central departments and local authorities. Central control is tighter in the area of education, where schooling has to be provided for all, than it is for housing and the personal services where local authorities have considerable choice concerning the standard and extent of provision. While this may mean that services are related to local needs and responsive to local political pressures, it also leads to variations in the standard of provision from one area to another.

The health services are organized in a hierarchy of control from the responsible minister in the DHSS, through the Regional Health Authorities down to the Area Health Authorities. Members of Health Authorities are appointed from among various interested parties, not elected. Democratic control therefore is only exercised at the centre. In theory, the DHSS lays down financial constraints and policy guidelines which are adapted to local and regional needs by the Health Authorities. There is supposed to be the maximum possible delegation. Considerable differences exist in the quality of service available in different areas although some attempts are being made to reduce these.

The services differ considerably in the extent to which central government is able or willing to control the service received by the clients. The bureaucratic framework of the social security system makes it possible for the government to determine with some precision the details of benefits available to clients. However, in the case of education and health this is not possible. Doctors and, to a lesser extent, teachers are generally free, within their sphere of professional expertise, to decide what service to provide for their clients and they strenuously resist outside attempts to regulate this freedom. In addition, both occupational groups are heavily involved in the administration of the services since schools and Local Authority Education Departments are run by teachers or ex-teachers and representatives of doctors have considerable powers of veto over decision-making in the health service. To a lesser extent this also applies to qualified social workers in Social Service Departments. As a result it is difficult to institute changes in these services where these are seen by the professional staff to impinge unfavourably on their roles.

In recent years there has been some concern about the efficiency of the administration of social services. Administrative changes have been made in an attempt to improve the coordination, control and planning of services. At central government level, the DHSS was created through a merger of the separate Health and Social Security Departments in 1968. In 1970 the local authority social services were reorganized and in 1974 the health services were given a new structure. In each case a number of functions which had previously been carried out by separate bodies were brought under unified control.

It has been argued that these changes have failed to achieve the desired goals of greater day-to-day efficiency, better long-term planning, greater responsiveness to social needs and more public involvement. In fact, many critics view the outcome as involving unnecessary increases in administration and a long period of disorganization and uncertainty resulting from the dislocation caused by reorganization.

Another aspect of organizational change in recent years has been the attempt to involve the public in decision-making in the social services through greater participation. This has been of particular importance in local authority planning since the 1968 Planning Act although some participation has also been encouraged in the National Health Service (NHS) through Community Health Councils. Proposals to increase participation of parents in education and of tenants in housing have also been made. Evidence from the area of housing suggests that attempts at organizing participation create hostility amongst many affected local authority staff and fail to involve a representative cross-section of the public, since it is mainly middle class people and interests who make their voices heard.

So far as administrative structures are concerned, the Consensus viewpoint suggests that it is possible to design organizational frameworks and procedures that will improve the general quality of decision-making through the application of sound principles of management. The reorganizations mentioned above were influenced by new management methods developed in business. In the case of the NHS the new structure was largely designed by McKinsey & Co. the management consultants. The Conflict view tends to be that blueprints for efficient management ignore the realities of widespread dissension within organizations which generally prevents the smooth operation of these schemes. In this view participation itself is seen as a device by which those in authority may attempt to manipulate people into supporting decisions which might work against their own interests rather than as a genuine attempt to involve the public in decision-making.

7.4 Role and performance

In this section the role and performance of the social services will be examined. The role of each service will be described by outlining its objectives and examining what it produces. Performance will be discussed in terms of the extent to which objectives are achieved. This is not an easy task as there is no universally applicable yardstick, such as profit, available for evaluating performance. In addition, objectives are often vague or conflicting and the evidence about the extent to which they are achieved is not clear-cut. Because the social services are very much a subject of political debate, discussion of their performance is often politically slanted. In looking at various views on the performance of the services their political implications will be brought out.

7.4.1 Education

The general objective is to provide an equal opportunity for every child to obtain an education that meets his or her needs. The content of this education is not defined by statute except for the requirement to provide religious education laid down in the Education Act 1944. The scale of the education system may be illustrated in terms of numbers (*Table 7.2*). Further information on output is provided by the overall level of educational achievements. In 1974, 12% of those in the 20–24 age group had qualifications above 'A' level. However, well over half the present working population have no educational qualifications at all, reflecting

Table 7.2 Numbers in education (1978)

Sectors	Pupils/students
All schools	11 221 000
Further education: Full-time	324 000
Part-time	1 379 000
Higher education: Full-time	464 000
Part-time	246 000
Total	13 634 000

Source: *Social Trends 1980*, HMSO, 1979, *Tables 4.1, 4.10 and 4.11*

the lower levels of educational provision in the past. In addition, the quality of provision varies in different parts of the country.

It is difficult to evaluate overall performance in eduation. From a right-wing political viewpoint there is criticism of 'progressive' teaching methods, lack of discipline in schools and low educational standards. The move to comprehensive schooling is often seen as diminishing the educational opportunities of the brightest children who are said to have fared better in the grammar schools. Those on the Right tend to stress the importance of providing for the 'high fliers'.

On the Left more emphasis is put on meeting the needs of children from poor homes. It is suggested that there is considerable waste of talent, with many people not being educated up to their full capacity. There tends to be more support for introducing new subjects and new teaching methods. Comprehensive schooling is supported on the grounds that a system of selective secondary schools is socially divisive.

7.4.2 Health

The objective of the health services is to provide a comprehensive system of health care, which makes available the best possible service to all who need it. Some indication of the scale of the hospital services is given by the figures in *Table 7.3*.

Table 7.3 Medical care (1978)

No. of beds occupied daily	380 000
Total inpatients per year	6 686 000
Total outpatient treatments per year	55 714 000

Source: *Social Trends 1980*, HMSO, 1979, *Table 8.30*

In addition, every member of the population visits a General Practitioner (GP) on average over three times every year. The standard of care provided is uneven. Some groups, such as unskilled workers, use the services rather less than their state of health would merit. Some types of patients, such as those in long-stay psychiatric hospitals, receive a very low standard of care relative to others. In addition, there are regional differences in the standard of care and treatment available.

There is some argument about how resources should be distributed between prevention, cure and care. Many argue that a great deal of illness results from preventable causes such as drinking, smoking and lack of exercise. They suggest that health levels could be improved by spending more on prevention and less on the more expensive and complex forms of cure. Critics have also pointed to the fact that many widely used drugs and surgical techniques are ineffective and often dangerous to patients, and that doctors frequently provide treatment with drugs, such as antidepressants and sleeping tablets, when patients really require reassurance or counselling. A major problem in evaluating the effectiveness of health care is that the services may often increase the numbers of unhealthy people by keeping alive people who otherwise might have died. Thus, successful treatment may increase the numbers of unhealthy people.

The debate about the effectiveness of health care does not easily fall into a political division between Left and Right. The main area of political controversy in health centres around the single issue of private provision of health care. This tends to be supported by those on the Right and opposed by those on the Left.

7.4.3 Housing

Postwar governments have sought to improve housing conditions, but there is no commitment to a minimum standard of housing as a right. The major form of provision is through council housing. By 1978, there were 6.79 million council dwellings accounting for 32% of the total. The chance of obtaining council housing varies from place to place. For example, in the South West it accounts for only 22% of dwellings, whereas the figure for the North is 41% and for Scotland 54%.

The government lays down standards for new council housing and there are norms for overcrowding and for judging the level of amenities. Considerable variations exist in the quality of housing. As *Table 7.4* shows, however, the lack of basic amenities is widespread in private rented accommodation where household incomes are lowest.

There has also been criticism of the effectiveness of housing policies, especially the massive schemes of slum clearance which were popular

Table 7.4 Housing standards 1978

Type of tenure	Percentage of households		
	Lacking sole use of bath or shower	Lacking inside WC	Lacking central heating
Owner occupied	3	3	36
Local authority	2	2	57
Private rented (unfurnished)	19	18	72
Private rented (furnished)	52	51	73

Source: *Social Trends 1980*, HMSO, 1979, *Table 9.11*

with local authorities in the 1960s and early 1970s. It is argued that many of these houses could have been cheaply renovated and that the process of clearance broke up the local communities with their long-established networks of mutual support. The new housing provided was frequently more expensive, of low quality and sometimes situated in inaccessible peripheral council estates. High-rise housing schemes were particularly subject to criticism. There is also debate about whether local authorities should emphasize improvement of dwellings rather than new building. In recent years there certainly has been more emphasis put on improvement, partly because it is cheaper than demolition and rebuilding.

Despite the improvement in housing standards which has taken place, it can be argued that the overall pattern of state expenditure on housing does not contribute effectively to achieving the objective of good housing for all. The money spent on housing is unevenly divided between the three tenure types. The cost of private renting is kept down by an incalculable amount, at no cost to the state, as a result of rent controls, while provision of new dwellings and a subsidy on rents exists in the local authority sector. Mortgagees receive tax relief on the interest payments on their mortgages. It is a matter of debate whether this should be considered a subsidy or not; the total value, however, is about the same as the figure for subsidies to local authority tenants. Some economists would argue that house owners are also subsidised by not having to pay capital gains tax when the value of their house increases.

There is no doubt that the costs to the state are lowest in the private rented sector, making up about 15% of all dwellings, which is where the worst housing conditions and the poorest and most overcrowded households are to be found. Rent controls have probably accelerated the decline in quality of private rented housing. It is by no means obvious that the main form of state intervention, the provision of houses for rent, is what people really want. There is also doubt about whether the 'points systems' used by local authorities to allocate houses actually ensure that they go to the most needy people. Clearly, in the field of housing, the policy objectives, vague though they are, are far from being achieved.

The main political controversy concerns the role of market forces in the provision of housing. Individualists prefer to encourage owner occupation, the reduction of council rent subsidies, private renting and the sale of council houses. Those on the Left are much more in favour of state intervention through rent controls and council housing. As a consequence, the level of council housebuilding fluctuates according to which party forms the government and varies from one local authority to another according to which party is in control locally.

7.4.4 The welfare services

Local authority Social Services Departments make a wide range of provision including residential homes, day care and domiciliary assistance for children, the old and the handicapped. The great variety of client groups and the assistance offered to them makes it hard to specify any overall objective which these services seek to achieve. In fact, objectives differ according to the group of clients under consideration. Some of these are very specific, such as the statutory requirement to provide for children in need of care, while others, concerning the welfare of old people, are extremely vague. Again, some objectives are laid down in detail by central government whereas others are left to the discretion of local councils.

Some indication of the numbers served by these services for 1978 is given in *Table 7.5*.

Table 7.5 Extent of Provision in the personal social services 1978 (England and Wales)

Form of provision	Numbers
Children in care and boarded out	101 000
Elderly in local authority provided or financed homes	124 000
Receiving one or more 'meals on wheels' (per week)	194 000
Home help attendances (per year)	645 000
Disabled provided with holidays	884 000
Personal aids (telephones, TV etc.) provided for the disabled	375 000

Source: *Social Trends 1980*, HMSO, 1979, *Tables 3.8, 3.12, 3.13* and *8.35*

Evidence exists that the numbers receiving aid in some of these categories may fall far short of those entitled to it. For instance, local authority Social Service Departments frequently have difficulty in identifying the size of the client group simply because the information is not available. They are required to make a register of the disabled but in practice severe problems have been encountered in producing an accurate figure. Social Service Departments also have to deal with groups 'at risk', such as children whose circumstances may be conducive to family violence. The identification of those 'at risk' is very difficult and subject to miscalculation. Differences also exist in the standard of provision in different areas. As a result of all this it is doubtful if there is some minimum level of 'welfare', however this is defined, which these services manage to provide for those who cannot obtain it for themselves.

An area of considerable controversy concerns the appropriate balance between institutional, day and domiciliary care. Some people take the view that institutional care is undesirable because of its high cost and because it tends to reduce the independence of the clients by subjecting them to an organized and inflexible regimen, which seems aimed at meeting their physical, but not their emotional, needs. In the nineteenth century the tendency was to confine everyone needing care to some kind of institution. Nowadays the more common view seems to be that people should be looked after in 'the community' as far as possible.

The main area of political controversy concerns the effectiveness of the 'casework' techniques, involving the development of a personal relationship between social worker and client, which have been traditionally employed by social workers. The notion that the client has something wrong with him that the social worker helps put right has been attacked. From the Left, it is argued that the problem is not the client's personality, but the social structure, which presents some people with insurmountable problems due to their lack of income and opportunities. On the Right the view is frequently held that much social work consists of 'do-gooding' which encourages malingering and dependence.

7.4.5 Social security

The general objectives of this service are to ensure that everyone is insured against the major interruptions of income. In addition, all households with insufficient resources have access to cash benefits to bring them out of poverty and up to a prescribed minimum level. There are three forms of cash benefit. **National Insurance benefits**, covering a wide range of circumstances from maternity to death, are available to those eligible as the result of the payment of National

Insurance Contributions. **Means-tested benefits,** in contrast, are non-contributory, and are only payable to those who can show that their income (and sometimes their wealth) falls below a prescribed level. The main means-tested benefit is Supplementary Benefit which is intended to ensure that all households where there is not a wage coming in are kept out of poverty. **Non-contributory benefits** are those which are available to everyone in a given category. They do not depend on contributions or a means test.

Table 7.6 Social security: expenditure and numbers of clients 1977–1978

Type of benefit	Cost (% of total)	Size of client groups (% of total)
National Insurance benefits		
Retirement Pensions	49.8	36.7
Invalidity and Industrial Disablement Benefits	6.7	3.1
Unemployment Benefits	4.8	2.5
Other: Maternity, Sickness, Injury, Widows and Death	9.5	9.4
Means-tested benefits		
Supplementary Benefits—pensioners	4.1	7.6
Supplementary Benefits—others (unemployed, sick etc.)	10.0	5.6
Family Income Supplement (FIS)	0.2	0.4
Non-contributory benefits		
Child Benefit	5.1	30.8
War and other Pensions	3.4	2.0
Invalidity Pensions: Attendance, Invalid Care and Mobility Allowances	1.8	1.9
Administration and miscellaneous services	4.7	—
	100%	100%
Total of expenditure and client numbers	£13 235m	23 546 000

Source: Adapted from *Social Trends 1980*, HMSO, 1979, *Tables 6.6, 6.9*

As *Table 7.6* shows the main recipients are those receiving pensions. The National Insurance scheme is designed to cater for all interruptions of income although one must qualify for any particular benefit according to complex rules concerning past contributions to the scheme. The clients of the National Insurance scheme come from all income levels of society, although the self-employed are excluded from some benefits and other client categories are disproportionately working class, such as the unemployed, or middle class, such as the retired.

While the National Insurance scheme provides for most of the major interruptions of income, it does have gaps. An example is the lack of provision for one-parent families. Other benefits such as the Death Grant are insufficient to provide for their original objective of paying for a funeral. In addition the overall level of benefits is too low to provide an income up to the Supplementary Benefit minimum for those exclusively dependent on National Insurance benefits.

The Supplementary Benefit scheme has a rather different client profile and a much smaller budget than National Insurance. Because of the use of a means-test as a qualification for benefit the recipients come from the lower income groups. Evidence exists that about one-third of potential clients fail to obtain benefit and to that extent the scheme fails to achieve its objective. A number of other limited means-tested schemes exist which are also subject to low take-up.

The main non-contributory benefit is Child Benefit. While this is an important addition to the incomes of large families it has often been allowed to decline in value through not being adjusted to take full account of inflation.

The overall outcome of these schemes is that a number of peole fail to obtain the state minimum income level, while many more are brought up to, but not beyond it, by the benefits they receive. Most of these however, find it very difficult, or impossible, to raise their standard of living much above this. Those in receipt of a number of means-tested benefits such as free school meals, free prescriptions and FIS, lose their entitlement to these if they get an increase in pay. The result is that they may be no better off; they are caught in the 'poverty trap'. The complexity of the system is also criticized and mentioned as a reason why people often fail to obtain benefits they are eligible for.

7.5 Evaluation

In this section the overall effectiveness of the social services, their economic impact on society and on the living standards of individuals, will be discussed.

7.5.1 Overall effectiveness

The discussion of the organizational structure, role and performance of the individual social services has highlighted a number of general issues. The social services have great difficulty in defining objectives and in measuring the extent to which they are achieved. They frequently have to operate without an exact knowledge of the extent of the needs that they are supposed to meet.

The social services also have to live with the legacy of the past. Particular periods of crisis as well as piecemeal reform have both been important in their development. The fact that they have developed over a long period of time and not in accordance with some overall plan means that their structure is often not well adapted to modern needs. Administrative reorganization has not proved an effective route to greater efficiency as it has been difficult to make changes because of the many groups with a vested interest in maintaining the present arrangements. The considerable geographical variations in the quality of provision in some of the services is also a legacy of the past.

Dilemmas also exist within each service about how priorities should be determined. While the technical problems of deciding priorities are hard enough, there are, in addition, political disagreements about how resources should be used. There is also the question of priorities between services, where decisions have to be made on the relative expenditure on each of the different services. This problem is made more difficult by the fact that expenditure on one service may have implications for another. Improvements in housing or the level of income support for the poor may have effects on health care provision. Expenditure on health care may increase demands for retirement pensions by causing a rise in life expectancy. Educational achievement is likely to be affected by health and housing conditions.

The problems of determining priorities and of implementing them are, therefore, very complex. They occur no less at the mundane level of a choice between residential or community care for a pensioner, for example, than at the level of the global distribution of resources between services. The problem of coordinating the different services in an effective way is exacerbated by their different administrative structures. Variations in the degree of central or local control, in the number of tiers in the administrative hierarchy and in the extent of control by elected representatives or appointees all create problems. Nor are the boundaries of the various authorities controlling services usually coterminous.

7.5.2 Economic impact

The social services make considerable demands on economic resources. Social security, with the biggest budget, has a low wage bill and is mainly a means of distributing transfer incomes to those entitled to them, rather than providing services. Education, second in total spending, has the highest wage bill but also accounts for substantial purchases and transfers. Health makes the greatest demands on the private sector for capital spending, such as hospital building, and current purchasing, such as drugs, although its total budget is below that of social security and education. Housing spends a high proportion of its budget on purchases, such as house building, with a substantial transfer element through rent subsidies. The personal social services have the lowest budget, but nevertheless staff costs are greater than those of social security.

The social services differ considerably in the kinds of labour they employ. Both education and health make very heavy demands on highly trained workers such as teachers, nurses and doctors. At the same time, these services, along with the personal social services, also employ large numbers of relatively unskilled, low-paid, often part-time and female ancillary workers.

The effect of the existence of the social services on the workings of the economy as a whole is a matter of some dispute. On the Right, views like those of Bacon and Eltis tend to see the social services as a non-productive burden, reducing the efficiency of the market system. Moderates and radicals, however, tend to argue that the social services improve the working of the market economy, through having a favourable effect on business operation.

One area where the benefits of social service expenditure are disputed concerns its connection with economic growth. Certainly, there is no clear-cut relationship. Evidence from other countries shows that high growth rates are possible whether or not there is substantial social policy expenditure. Some evidence exists that expenditure on education leads to economic growth through increasing labour productivity and through the application to business of increases in the stock of knowledge.

Whether or not social policy leads to growth, moderates and radicals stress that it increases the efficiency of labour. Unemployment Benefits and health care help to maintain working efficiency and indeed this was one of the earliest justifications for these policies. In addition Child Benefit may reduce the pressure for higher wages as it provides income support for the hardest pressed families. Those on the Right argue that the availability of benefits for the families of those on strike constitutes an encouragement to industrial action. Moderates and radicals hold that the availability of a range of benefits in cash and kind may reduce working class insecurity and working class militancy.

It is difficult to estimate whether the level of aggregate demand is affected since, while social service expenditure creates demand for goods, it also involves reductions in real disposable income, through direct and indirect taxation. Social policy does, however, have a minor counter cyclical effect as it provides income for some of the unemployed during a recession and thus may help to keep up the level of aggregate demand.

Those adopting a right-wing view argue that social policies affect the incentive to work, both by reducing the rewards of work through income taxation, and through providing cash benefits to those not working. The available evidence on incentives is, however, inconclusive. There is no firm evidence that entrepreneurial incentives are affected by the existence of social policy though it is claimed on the Right that high levels of public expenditure reduce 'business confidence'.

Turning from the economy as a whole to the impact of the social services on the living standards of individuals, a similar pattern of disagreement is to be found. Those on the Right and in the Centre tend to adopt the Consensus view that the social services are financed by the better off to the benefit of the poor. This view rests on the assumptions that social policy expenditure is financed by progressive taxation and that this expenditure disproportionately benefits the poorer members of society. Those holding a Conflict view question both these assumptions. They argue not only that many taxes, such as value added tax (VAT), excise duties and vehicle licences, are not progressive, but also that the opportunities for income tax avoidance and evasion, especially through fringe benefits, go mainly to the better off. They also point out that the system of tax allowances for such things as mortgage interest payments yields disproportionate benefits to the same people. They argue that social policy expenditure, especially on education and social security, mainly benefits the better off since students tend to come from middle class families, the members of which also tend to draw pensions for longer because of their greater life expectancy. Those who take the opposing view might point to the fact that VAT is not levied on some items that make up a high percentage of the expenditure of the poor, such as food, fuel and public transport, and that the income tax regulations are steeply progressive. They would point to the fact that many services are aimed at the poor such as Supplementary Benefits, FIS, subsidised local authority housing and Unemployment Benefit.

It is extremely difficult to evaluate these two views partly because there is disagreement about whether or not tax reliefs should be counted as benefits. If they are, then the extent to which real incomes are seen as being vertically redistributed (from the better off to the poor) is reduced. Family size is also important. Larger families receive substantial benefits in cash and kind and as working class families tend to be larger there is some evidence here of vertical distribution. It may be, however, that most of the redistribution is horizontal, that is, within income bands, rather than between them. This is because both income and expenditure taxes are paid mainly by those in work, whereas benefits in cash and kind go disproportionately to the young and the old and others unable to work. In a sense the effect of the social services is to redistribute real income so that it is spread over a person's whole lifetime as shown below in *Figure 7.1*.

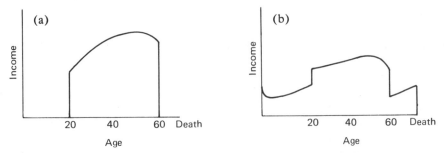

Figure 7.1 The impact of the state on command over resources. (a) Gross employment income (typical pattern). (b) Net employment income plus social service benefits minus indirect taxes (typical pattern)

7.6. Conclusion

Throughout the discussion of the social services stress has been put on the differing views that are taken about their development, their effects and their purposes. These are briefly summarized in *Table 7.7*. Some indication of the range of views found across the political spectrum is given at the bottom of the table.

While the views of any individual on the social services will obviously not fit exactly into one or other of these categories they do indicate coherent viewpoints to which people's actual opinions tend to approximate. This demonstrates that questions concerning the origins, nature and performance of the social services are not simply academic issues which can easily be answered in an objective and dispassionate way. Of course, it is necessary to attempt to do this, but it should also be remembered that the political views and the theoretical frameworks employed, particularly the variant of a Consensus or a Conflict approach that is adopted, will be likely to colour the results obtained and the interpretation given to them.

Table 7.7 Social services and political ideology

	Conflict view Left	Consensus views Centre	 Right
View of key factors in development	Pressure from below. Ruling class attempts to reduce economic and political conflict.	Humanitarianism and social conscience. Growth of knowledge of social conditions.	'Creeping socialism.' Increasing power of the 'Left'.
View of effects	Increased labour discipline. Reduction of class conflict. Horizontal redistribution. Little real benefit to the poor.	Increased labour efficiency. Greater social integration. Some vertical and horizontal redistribution. Considerable benefit to poor.	Reduced incentives. Burdens private sector. Increased dependence on state. Substantial vertical redistribution. Overgenerous provision for poor.
Desired purpose	Economic equality.	Equality of opportunity.	Maintenance of inequality.
Range of views found within political parties			Conservative
		Liberal and Social Democrat	
	Labour		

Guide to further reading
General

Baugh, W. E. (1973). *Introduction to the Social Services*. Macmillan, London. A useful, mainly factual account of the social services.

Gough, Ian (1979). *The Political Economy of the Welfare State*, Macmillan, London. A Marxist approach with useful material on the development of the welfare state and the present situation.

Hill, Michael (1980). *Understanding Social Policy*, Blackwell and Robertson, Oxford. Contains chapters on each of the five services, with a focus on policy-making.

Marsh, David (1974). *The Welfare State*, Longman, London. An account written mainly from a Consensus standpoint.

Subsections
7.2

Fraser, Derek (1973). *The Evolution of the Welfare State*, Macmillan, London. Useful source for details of development of the social services, especially Chapters 7–9.

7.3

Brown, R. G. S. (1975). *The Management of Welfare*, Fontana-Collins, Glasgow. Very detailed on administrative structures, but useful for reference.

7.4

Marsh, David C. (1979). *Introducing Social Policy*. Routledge and Kegan Paul, London. Contains chapters on each of the social services.

7.5

Sleeman, J. F. (1973). *The Welfare State*, George Allen and Unwin, London. Chapter 7 is very good on the economic impact of the social services.
Field, Frank, Meacher, Molly and Pond, Chris (1977). *To Him Who Hath*, Penguin, London. Chapter 9 contains a discussion of the redistributive effects of the welfare state.

Exercises

Review questions

1. Which services have grown most rapidly in the postwar period?
2. List the factors involved in the development of the social services.
3. What part did war play in the development of the social services?
4. What features do the organizational structures of education, housing and welfare have in common?
5. What aspects of education are subject to political debate?
6. What is the difference between the National Insurance scheme and the Supplementary Benefit scheme?
7. What is the poverty trap?
8. Outline the argument that the social services increase labour efficiency.
9. What are vertical and horizontal redistribution?

Application and investigation

1. Update *Table 7.1* using *Social Trends* and National Income statistics. Comment on changes since 1978.

2. Find out the present Supplementary Benefit rates and calculate them as a percentage of average incomes for different household types (*see Social Trends* for this data).
3. Examine press coverage of social services in the past fortnight. Classify the coverage according to the perspective it appears to adopt.

Projects

1. Examine the view that the social services and the tax system benefit the poor at the expense of the rich.
2. Select one social service and identify the major social, economic and political changes by which it is being affected. Describe how the service is likely to change as a result.

The context of business

In Part B the distinctiveness of the four major business sectors was emphasized. In Part C the focus will be upon the range of environmental, or contextual, influences affecting all business sectors. Chapter 8 will describe those aspects of society shaping the attitudes and behaviour of producers and consumers. Chapter 9 will focus upon the changing political and governmental context within which business operates while Chapter 10 will focus on the major legal influences on business. Chapter 11 will be concerned with the major international economic transactions between Britain and the rest of the world and their impact upon business and society. Finally, Chapter 12 will speculate about future trends and developments in business and society.

Chapter 8

The social context of business

8.1 Introduction

This chapter will discuss those aspects of social structure relevant to an understanding of business in society. In particular the social determinants of man's behaviour as a producer and a consumer will be examined. In order to understand these, the nature of work, and the patterns of inequality which result from the organization of economic activity, will be looked at. The changing forms of community and the role and nature of values will also need to be discussed. The previous five chapters examined the nature of the British economy and the distinctive features of its different sectors. In this chapter the nature of the society within which these economic activities take place is outlined.

Modern British society is characterized by an economy based on the production of goods in large organizations employing advanced technology. The population lives mainly in towns and cities and enjoys a relatively high standard of living. The changes that brought this about began about 1760 when the pace of economic change began to increase and set in motion the overall transformation of society known as the 'industrial revolution'.

The term 'revolution' is used because of the rapidity and extensiveness of the changes brought about by the development of industry. While these changes originated in the economy their impact transformed many other aspects of existence, such as family life, politics and even religion. The development of industry also constituted a revolution because it ushered in an era of rapid economic and social change.

Up until this period the way of life of most people would change little during the course of a normal lifetime; now change is constant and often abrupt.

The greatest social innovation of the industrial revolution was the invention of the factory. By bringing large numbers of workers into a single building the manufacturer secured a number of advantages.

- Mechanical sources of power could be used.
- Larger and more complex machinery could be employed.

- Specialization of work could be achieved through the division of labour.
- The workforce could be more closely controlled.
- The costs of transporting raw materials and finished goods could be reduced.

As a result, the domestic system, in which simple machines in the home were used to produce goods, was gradually destroyed by competition from the low-cost products of the factories. Starting in the wool and cotton textile industries, these methods gradually spread. Industries such as shipbuilding and iron manufacture adopted factory methods of production and the size of firms, as well as the general level of technology employed, grew. The 1840s saw the appearance of the first really large-scale enterprises with the growth of the railways. These heralded the era of the giant joint-stock corporations which now dominate the British economy. By 1880 the process of Britain's transformation from a mainly rural society based on small-scale production into an industrial, urban society had been largely completed. Developments since then have been, by comparison, evolutionary, rather than revolutionary. The society produced by these changes has many characteristic features. For the purposes of this book the following areas have been selected for discussion because of their importance for an understanding of the way people behave as consumers, producers and citizens.

- Occupational structure and the nature of work.
- Management, unions and industrial conflict.
- The form and extent of inequalities in society.
- The different communities in which people live.
- The nature of the values and beliefs which people hold.

8.2 Work in modern society

8.2.1 Occupational structure and the nature of work

The term 'occupational structure' refers to the distribution of people between different kinds of occupations. As there are several hundred different occupations a way is needed of classifying them into a limited number of types. The Registrar General distinguishes six socio-economic groups (SEGs) according to the type of work done, although identical or similar classifications are frequently used by other government bodies, market research agencies and social scientists. They give a general indication of the nature of the work and the educational level of members of occupations, as well as their status, that is, the esteem in which an occupation is held. There is, however, considerable overlap in incomes between categories. Generally these are higher, the higher the SEG. The average incomes of junior non-manual workers, however, are about the same as those of semiskilled manual workers.

Table 8.1 shows the distribution of working men and women between the SEGs. Differences between men and women are marked. Men make up about 63% of the workforce and the majority work in manual occupations. There are few female skilled manual workers. Most working women are in routine office work or are semiskilled manual workers. About 40% work part-time. Men's hourly wage rates are on average 50% higher than women's.

Table 8.1 Men and women in the labour force 1977

Socio-economic group		All (%)	Men (%)	Women (%)
I	Professional	16.0	22.5	6
II	Employers/Managers			
III	Junior non-manual	31.3	17.5	53
IV	Skilled manual	27.0	39.0	8
V	Semiskilled manual	17.3	13.0	24
VI	Unskilled manual	8.4	8.0	9
Total		100	100	100

Source: *Social Trends 1980*, HMSO, 1979, *Table 5.9*

The occupational structure has been subject to considerable changes over time. These result from alterations in the demand for labour in the economy. Changes in the pattern of output, and in the methods used to produce it, are reflected in changes in the nature of the labour force. A number of general trends can be identified.

Increased scale. Employing organizations in all sectors have increased in size and most employees now work in large organizations. One result has been the growth of specialized management roles. Large enterprises invariably require a complex managerial division of labour with a hierarchy of control and the provision of specialized services such as accounting, legal advice and research and development. The coordination and integration of these functions is normally achieved by requiring everyone to adhere to known rules and procedures governing the way work is carried out. In a word, the management of large organizations has become bureaucratic. As a result, there is an increased demand for those who work in administration. At the higher levels, managers and a variety of specialists are needed, and at lower levels, there is a mass of clerks and typists to produce and process documents.

Technological change. Equally important has been the general increase in technological sophistication which has brought new sources of energy, such as electricity, gas, oil and nuclear power; new forms of machinery; and new products. As technology has advanced it has progressively allowed the replacement of more and more complex kinds of labour.

A number of different levels of technology can be distinguished as shown in *Table 8.2.*

Table 8.2 Levels of technology

	Level of technological sophistication		
	Low	*Medium*	*High*
Type of equipment	Hand tools, simple machine tools	Linked machine tools	Automated and semi-automated
Type of worker	Craftsman	Semiskilled operative	Technician
Type of organization	Craft workshop	Assembly line	Continuous process production plant

In general there has been a move towards the use of more sophisticated technologies in all sectors of the economy. Large numbers of scientists and engineers and many kinds of technician are today in employment. In general, the newer the industry the greater the number of scientifically trained employees; examples are aeronautics, nuclear power and computers. In addition, large numbers of people are employed in the education of scientific and technical workers.

Amongst manual workers, the general effect of technology has been to reduce the number of unskilled heavy labouring jobs as these are generally the easiest to mechanize. The work of highly skilled craftsmen has also been reduced in importance as a result of the development of forms of automatic control in, for example, toolsetting. In some areas even semiskilled manual work is being replaced by robotics. The microprocessor is at present beginning to be applied to various aspects of the labour process. It is possible that its major applications will be in those areas of work which at present are most labour-intensive, such as retailing and office work. This, however, is only the latest in the long line of technological innovations which have been a permanent feature of the economic system since the advent of modern industry.

State employment. Employment in the public enterprise sector is dominated by declining traditional industries such as coal, railways and steel and it is possible that employment in these areas is somewhat greater than it would have been without nationalization. Other nationalized industries, such as electricity, make considerable demands on technical and scientific skills.

The social services have been associated with two of the major changes in the occupational structure. The first is the growth of the 'new professions' such as teaching, social work, nursing, and the paramedical occupations, such as radiography. The second is the expansion of low-paid work for women, involving domestic tasks such as cooking, cleaning and laundry. In addition, large numbers of administrative workers are employed to execute the business of the state in central and local government. The stringent requirements of public accountability and the extraordinary complexity of the range of government business mean a very heavy administrative load.

8.2.2 Interpretation

The interpretation of the general trends at work in the changing occupational structure is the subject of a controversy which fits neatly into the Conflict–Consensus dichotomy.

Those adopting a Consensus view suggest that the general level of occupational skill required is increasing and claim that the increase in non-manual jobs supports this view. They also suggest that amongst manual workers the average level of skill has risen. They claim that the most advanced forms of technology, such as 'continuous process' production, which is found in oil-refining and chemical industries, will gradually supersede traditional manual work and replace it with the responsible task of monitoring and controlling the production process. It is suggested that these kinds of jobs will come to predominate in the future. Technology is seen as taking the drudgery out of manufacturing work, while the growth of the tertiary sector of the economy is seen as expanding the numbers of intrinsically satisfying jobs performed in pleasant working conditions.

The Conflict view puts more emphasis on the idea that technology has replaced skilled manual jobs with machine-minding. The expansion of white collar work is seen as mainly involving an increase in the numbers of low-paid routine jobs. The general level of skill required of the workforce is not seen as having increased, although a minority of highly skilled and trained white collar workers is required. Advanced technologies such as process production are seen as substituting one form of boring and meaningless work for another. The social service sector is viewed as an area of employment utilizing a great deal of low-paid and unskilled labour, as well as expanding the numbers of professional jobs. According to the Conflict view, the more science and technology is incorporated into the labour process, the less skill and knowledge are required of the ordinary worker.

8.3 Management, trade unions and industrial conflict

8.3.1 Management

The everyday distinction between 'management' and 'workers' reflects a real division of authority which occurs whenever people are employed. There are those who manage and those who are managed. Management is the function of controlling the overall direction taken by the organization. The problem faced by management is to ensure the pace, continuity and quality of production.

In the early phase of industrialization a major difficulty was that the workforce was unused to, and often opposed to, the disciplines of industrial work. The owners were concerned to achieve voluntary acceptance of their authority. This involved developing an ideology which justified and explained their authority. The doctrine of *laissez-faire* was eagerly adopted by the expanding class of industrial capitalists because it justified their authority as key figures in the market system. Up until about 1850 this 'entrepreneurial ideology' was the form in which capitalists and their spokesmen justified their authority. It stressed the right of owners to control all aspects of the enterprise because their capital was at risk and they could best be counted on to protect it.

Around the middle of the nineteenth century a rather different set of justifications of authority within the enterprise began to emerge. The development of much larger enterprises, along with the use of limited liability shareholding as a form of ownership, resulted in the appearance of managers who were not owners of the enterprises in which they worked. A new 'managerial ideology' emerged which stressed expertise and professional skill rather than ownership and the rights of property, as a basis for authority. This ideology has remained the dominant justification for managerial authority.

Management has had to develop means to ensure that it remains in control of the enterprise. Three main channels have been used by managements in their attempts to control the workforce. The first involves using the system of pay and incentives to raise productivity. The second involves using technology and the division of labour to prevent employees from controlling the work process. The third involves using a variety of means to promote loyalty to, and dependence on, the employer.

It is difficult to generalize about the overall methods utilized by management in the last 100 years but they have usually involved some permutation of these three approaches. Individual firms or industries have always been exceptions to the general trend, however, and under the pressure of exceptional events such as war, practices have often changed very rapidly.

An important twentieth century development has been the appearance of academic 'theories' of management which have tended to promote one or other of these three approaches. 'Scientific management', or 'Taylorism', first appeared in 1899 in the book *Principles of Scientific Management* by F. W. Taylor. For Taylor, the solution lay in a clear division of labour, scientific selection and training of workers, tight discipline and a carefully designed payment system. Taylorism has been immensely influential, having given birth to work study, job evaluation and ergonomics. Taylorism sees the worker as a human machine who can be made to work at maximum productivity, to the benefit of himself and his employer, if the correct principles are applied.

Another influential current in theories of management is 'human relations', developed in the 1920s by Elton Mayo and his associates. This portrays the worker as motivated by a 'logic of sentiment' and claims that the social relations which develop amongst groups of workers in personal contact are a major determinant of their behaviour. As social relationships are a key factor, management needs to develop a sensitivity to the social needs of the workers and to employ appropriate styles of supervision in order to generate worker interest and commitment. 'Human relations' has been immensely influential, particularly amongst personnel managers, in whose training it is widely used. Its effects can be seen in the provision of facilities for employees, such as canteens and social clubs. It is the theory underlying most attempts to persuade employees of large organizations that their employers have a personal concern for their welfare.

In the postwar period there has been an enormous growth of management literature and a proliferation of approaches. In the main, however, these consist of variants of either the 'scientific management' approach or the 'human relations' approach.

On the 'scientific management' side there has been great interest in redesigning management structures on a more scientific basis. The growing number of management consultants is evidence of this. There has also been the development of new forms of payment systems such as 'measured day work', designed to create a closer link between effort and reward.

On the 'human relations' side there have been proposals for greater employee participation. It is hoped that this will increase the loyalty of workers to employing organizations. There have also been attempts to increase employee commitment by trying to make work more interesting, through 'job enrichment' and 'job enlargement'.

These two approaches, 'scientific management' and 'human relations', are not necessarily alternatives. Organizations sometimes employ elements of both, and fashions in management, at least as demonstrated by the literature produced for managers, tend to fluctuate between the two. It is interesting to note that many industrial enterprises in the past seemed to employ 'scientific management' for their manual workers and 'human relations' for their white collar workforce. Nowadays, the methods of scientific management are increasingly being applied to office work.

The attraction of these theories for managers is that they suggest that it is in their power to maximize labour productivity through the use of managerial strategies based on the right approach. They are both Consensus approaches in that each assumes that the interests of workers and employers are not opposed, and that all that is necessary to reconcile them is the application of the right principles. Management strategies may, of course, be a potent influence on the attitudes of workers. However, these are also strongly affected by the resistance of workers to managerial attempts to control all aspects of the work process. This resistance is generally channelled through trade unions.

8.3.2 Trade unions

The main objective of a trade union is to protect and improve the pay and conditions of its members. In contrast to most Western nations, Britain has a large and unified trade union movement. In 1978 there were 112 unions affiliated to the Trades Union Congress (TUC), with a total of 12.1 million members. Trade unionism has a foothold in nearly every part of the economy and in many sectors the workforce is overwhelmingly unionized. Indeed, in many workplaces union membership is made compulsory through the 'closed shop'. For many workers, unions represent an alternative source of authority to that of management. Unions also play a major part in the political process, both through providing financial support for the Labour Party, and through engaging in negotiations with the government of the day.

The precise origins of trade unions are unclear. They certainly existed on a local basis in the late eighteenth century, when members of a trade would meet regularly, usually in a public house, in order to discuss matters of common interest. Despite being illegal, many local unions developed in the first two decades of the nineteenth century. After 1824, when they were legalized, there was a rapid growth, culminating in largely unsuccessful attempts to set up national confederations in the period 1828–1834.

The first national unions to secure long-term viability developed amongst skilled workers in the mid-nineteenth century. These were unions of craftsmen and they used relatively high subscriptions to provide welfare benefits for their members. They did not normally pursue a militant policy, preferring to negotiate a strong market position for their members through the provision of long apprenticeships. They had a strong organization based on a full-time staff with policy conducted according to carefully drawn up rules. In the late 1880s the rather slow growth of unionism amongst the unskilled suddenly accelerated with a series of successful disputes involving unskilled workers such as the dockers and the gas workers.

While total union membership has risen since 1890, this growth has not been steady as is seen in *Figure 8.1*. The rapid growth in the period 1910–1920 was largely due to the influence of World War I, during which the government attempted to secure worker cooperation for the

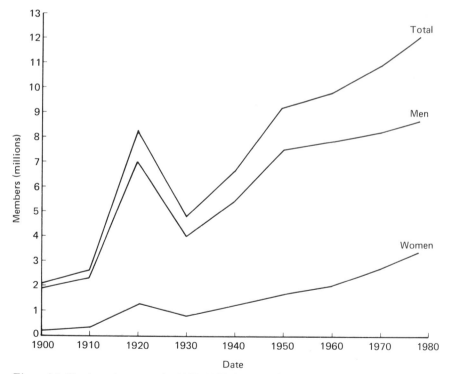

Figure 8.1 Trade union growth, 1900–1978 (men and women)

war effort through involving trade unions in the process of economic decision-making. This also occurred in World War II, helping to explain the increase in the period 1940–1950. The reduction in membership in the interwar period was due to the failure of the 1926 General Strike, the subsequent anti-union measures of the government and the weakness of unions during the depression.

The postwar period has seen a steady expansion of union membership and a majority of the workforce are now union members. About one-third of all union members are non-manual workers. They are concentrated in the public sector, where about 80% of employees belong to unions. Unionism among private sector non-manual workers is, however, expanding rapidly. The increased scale, mechanization and standardization of office work in industry and commerce is a factor here. There has also been a reduction in the opposition to unionism of private sector employers.

Figure 8.1 shows that the number of women trade unionists has been increasing rapidly since the last war. This has partly offset the fall in the number of union members in declining industries such as mining and the railways.

Britain has a very complex union structure with several different types of union as indicated in *Table 8.3.*

Table 8.3 Types of trade union

Type	Characteristics	Examples
General	Semiskilled and unskilled workers in many industries	Transport and General Workers Union (TGWU)
Multicraft	Craftsmen in many industries	Amalgamated Union of Engineering Workers (AUEW)
Industrial	All or most manual workers in an industry	National Union of Mineworkers (NUM)
Craft	Craftsmen in a single industry	Amalgamated Society of Locomotivemen, Engineers and Firemen (ASLEF)

Different kinds of trade union perform different functions for their members. Craft unions often seek to maintain long-established craft privileges and differentials against the encroachment of non-skilled workers. General unions, given the diversity of their memberships, tend to concentrate on wages. The attitude towards unionism in different industries and occupations also varies. At one extreme there may be an 'instrumental' attitude in that the union is simply seen as the most effective available means of improving pay and conditions. On the other hand the attitude may be 'solidary' in the sense that the union is the focus of strong emotional bonds which unite those who perform a particular occupation. It has been suggested that this kind of unionism, which is associated with older industries such as mining and dockwork, is in decline because of the decline of employment in these areas.

Trade union structure is related to industrial structure. Because Britain was the first country to develop modern industry most of her industries went through a phase of small-scale production, when craft unions tended to be formed, before reaching a phase of mass production, when larger unions of semiskilled workers developed. The very diversity of British industry also led to fragmentation of union structure and the result was a very large number of separate unions. In 1900 there were 1323, but mainly as a result of amalgamation, this had gone down to 112 by 1978. The separation of the unions for skilled and unskilled workers which developed in the nineteenth century remains in part today and represents an important, although declining, division within the working class.

There are definitional problems in determining the number of trade unions, as some organizations that perform trade union activities, such as pay bargaining, do not call themselves unions and are not affiliated to the TUC. This is true of certain professional associations such as the British Medical Association which represents doctors. It is arguable whether these organizations are different in principle from unions. In fact, they share an important characteristic with craft unions in that they restrict entry by long periods of training. Even if they are not fully and exclusively trade unions they certainly perform union functions.

The role of trade unions at the workplace varies. In some industries, particularly in the public sector, bargaining over pay and conditions is undertaken solely at national level. In others, such as the engineering industry, national agreements merely create the framework within which local bargaining takes place. In this case shop stewards, who are unpaid officers of the union, are more likely to undertake a prominent role in union affairs.

Throughout this century two important changes have taken place in industrial relations. First, bargaining has become more centralized, with many employees having their pay and conditions determined by national negotiations between trade union leaders and employers' associations. Secondly, the state has become more involved directly as an employer and indirectly through incomes policies and arbitration.

8.3.3 Industrial conflict

The relationship of employer and employee always contains the potential for conflict because of the possibility of disagreement over wages and working methods. In situations of conflict each side tries to impose its viewpoint on the other through bargaining or through the use of sanctions. Managements may use lockouts, disciplinary action or even dismissal, when disputes arise. On the part of the workforce, conflict may be individual or collective. When conflict takes an individual form it can involve absenteeism, labour turnover or industrial sabotage. Where it takes a collective form it normally, but not always, involves trade unions. It may consist of a work-to-rule, an overtime ban, a sit-in, a work-in, or a strike of some kind. Strikes are 'official' if they are supported by the relevant union, or 'unofficial' if they are not. They may be 'constitutional' if they follow an agreed 'disputes procedure', or 'unconstitutional' if they do not. At one extreme there are strikes which involve the entire workforce of an industry for weeks or even months; at the other, there are 'downers' where a small group of aggrieved workers down tools in order to speed up the solution of some pressing problem.

The number of strikes, and the number of workers involved, varies considerably from year to year, partly because of the changing economic and political environment. Britain's strike record is not wildly different from that of other countries. In the decade up to 1977, Canada, Italy and the USA on average lost rather more working days per thousand employees, while Belgium, France, Japan and Ireland lost rather less.

In common with other countries, industrial disputes in Britain tend to be concentrated in certain industries such as mining, docks, shipbuilding, iron and steel, vehicles and engineering. Strike-prone industries are likely to have the following characteristics which help to create the conditions for industrial disputes.

- A large number of employees in each plant.
- A predominance of impersonal, bureaucratic forms of authority.
- A labour force living in communities where the industry is the major employer.

8.3.4 Evaluation

The nature of management, labour and industrial conflict are subject to different interpretations when seen from a Consensus or a Conflict viewpoint. In the Consensus view harmony is seen as the norm. It sees management as undertaken for the joint benefit of owners, clients and employees. The job of management is to ensure the efficient organization of work and to foster a cooperative attitude on the part of the workforce. Serious industrial conflict is seen as unnecessary in present conditions where collective bargaining and the peaceful settlement of disputes through negotiation are provided for. Where industrial disputes do occur they may be viewed either as a result of poor communications or as the work of a minority of 'militants' or 'wreckers' attached to out-of-date class attitudes. The state is seen as a generally impartial referee, operating to smooth the path of good industrial relations.

In the Conflict view industrial strife is seen as the norm. It views the role of management as the extraction of the maximum output at least cost. In order to do this, control of the labour process is denied to the workforce through a form of work organization which reduces the need for skill. The provision of welfare services for employees is seen as an attempt to manipulate them. Trade unions are seen as organizations which attempt to protect living standards against the attempts of employers to keep labour costs down. Management is involved in an attempt, sometimes successful, to prevent open conflict, although this is always likely to break out. Where disputes do occur they reflect the fundamental incompatibility of the interests of labour and capital. The state is seen as supporting management and the owners of private industry through professing to act impartially while actually siding with the employers.

8.4 Inequality in modern society

8.4.1 Wealth and income

The work people do and the rewards they receive from it are major determinants of inequality in society. Much industrial conflict occurs over the issue of the level of rewards for work, and this is also a major theme of political debate. It is often held that there have been substantial reductions in inequalities of income and wealth during this century. Considerable inequalities remain, however, particularly in the distribution of wealth, although the share of the very rich has decreased slightly. This indicates a redistribution amongst top wealth holders, probably due to sharing of family wealth amongst children to avoid death duties. Present-day inequalities of income and wealth are shown in *Table 8.4*. While both wealth and income are unequally distributed, the inequalities in the distribution of wealth, and income from wealth, are far greater than inequalities in the distribution of income from employment. The highest incomes consist mainly of investment income and profits. About 70% of the incomes of the top 20% income recipients were from these sources.

Table 8.4 indicates that the effect of income taxation is to reduce inequality of incomes. It is likely, however, that the Inland Revenue figures used as a basis for the comparison underestimate both the wealth

Table 8.4 Distribution of income and wealth 1976–1977

Share taken by	Income Before tax (%)	After tax (%)	Wealth (%)
Top 1%	5.4	3.5	24.9
Top 10%	25.8	22.4	60.6
Bottom 50%	24.5	27.6	5.6

Source: Adapted from *Royal Commission of the Distribution of Income and Wealth, Report No. 7.* HMSO, 1979, *Tables 2.4, 2.6* and *4.3*

and the pretax incomes of those in the higher groups. Where income comes from profits, or self-employment, it is easier to avoid taxation than it is where income earned from employment is taxed by PAYE. In addition, the table does not show the full value of largely untaxed fringe benefits, such as company cars, school fees and private health insurance, which tend to be much greater at high income levels.

The general pattern of rewards from different occupations has not changed much this century although there has been some reduction of the relative incomes of the higher professions. The relative income of routine non-manual workers has also fallen and now lies between that of skilled and semiskilled workers. Incomes are determined by ownership of property and by occupation. Those who own substantial property have very high incomes, those in professional and managerial jobs have high incomes and low incomes are received by manual workers and routine non-manual workers.

8.4.2 The impact of the state on inequality

The state, through the taxation of income and the provision of services, has a major effect on the overall pattern of inequality. Attempts that have been made to estimate the net gains and losses for different income groups seem to show a considerable degree of redistribution. The groups with the lowest original income, receive a much higher income, when the value of all benefits in cash and kind, plus the impact of taxation, are considered. However, if the value of tax reliefs is included in the calculation of benefits, the overall levelling effect is reduced as tax reliefs are most valuable to the rich. In addition, within any income group, larger families will receive the bulk of the benefits and pay less tax, so that not everyone benefits equally within each group.

The impact of taxation on the distribution of wealth is difficult to estimate. There have been loopholes in all attempts to tax capital, and massive inequalities of wealth remain.

8.4.3 Secondary inequalities

Inequalities of income and wealth are reflected in the distribution of opportunities to obtain such things as education, good health and a long life, and in differences in expenditure on the consumption of such items as housing, consumer durables and leisure. Inequalities of this kind are sometimes termed 'secondary' inequalities in contrast to the 'primary' differences in income and wealth from which they stem.

Educational achievement is very unequally distributed. Members of higher SEGs tend to have higher qualifications than members of lower groups. The majority of manual workers have no educational qualifications at all. There is also considerable sexual inequality in education, with women obtaining far fewer qualifications than men at degree level and 'A' level, despite reaching a similar standard at 'O' level. The child of professional parents is 15 times more likely to go to university than the child of unskilled manual workers. Despite the massive expansion of higher education this differential has not been substantially reduced. Children from better-off families thus obtain more costly higher education, at the taxpayer's expense.

Considerable inequality exists in housing. Those in the higher SEGs more frequently own their own houses, which are larger and more valuable, while those in the lower SEGs tend to live in local authority or private rented accommodation. The worst housing is found in the private rented sector where the poorest people are most likely to live.

Perhaps the most dramatic indicator of inequality concerns the risk of disease and death. Those in the lower SEGs tend to have a shorter life. Unskilled manual workers are nearly 60% more likely to die before the age of 65 than professional workers.

Table 8.5 Survival rates and life expectancy by socio-economic group (men)

Socio-economic group	Number dead by age 65 per 1000 alive at 15	Future life expectancy at 15 (Years)
I Professional	225	57.2
II Employers/managers	234	57.0
III Junior non-manual	273	56.0
IV Skilled manual	293	55.7
V Semiskilled manual	307	55.1
VI Unskilled manual	357	53.5
All	288	55.6

Source: Adapted from *Occupational Mortality 1970–1972*, HMSO, 1978, *Table 8A*

The pattern of fatal disease also varies between groups and it is interesting to note that some diseases kill fairly evenly while others are heavily concentrated amongst manual workers, especially the unskilled.

There is also evidence to show that the lower SEGs suffer the highest rates of chronic and acute disease and have higher rates of infant and maternal mortality. These differentials result primarily from the greater dangers found in the working environment of manual workers. They are also related to inadequate diet, poor housing and smoking, which are more frequent among manual workers.

Consumption expenditure of all kinds is closely related to SEG. This affects a person's income and creditworthiness, and his chosen pattern of consumption. The way people spend their money depends on the 'life-style' they adopt. Life-style is an aspect of status. The kinds of goods people consume reflect the kind of person they wish to be seen as. Groups with a very high status generally adopt a life-style that others are unable to emulate because of its cost. They live in expensive houses, wear expensive clothes and drive expensive cars. The life-style adopted by lower SEGs is sometimes an attempt to emulate that of their social superiors. Others, however, may deliberately adopt a life-style which differs from that of higher status groups in order to symbolize their rejection of the values that these groups stand for. Various forms of youth subculture involving unusual forms of dress and behaviour are common examples. Regional differences also exist in consumption patterns, and different kinds of community may have their own distinctive life-style.

The ownership of consumer durables, including refrigerators, freezers, washing machines and hi-fi equipment, is unequally distributed. The possession of goods of this kind makes a major contribution to the standard of life enjoyed. The possession of labour-saving household goods reduces the drudgery of housework and the possession of various means of home entertainment increases the quality of home life. In general, the poor spend a higher proportion of their incomes on the necessities of life such as food and fuel and a lower proportion on durable household goods and transport.

Considerable differences exist in the area of leisure expenditure. The better-off spend more on recreation, holidays and meals out. They spend more time on leisure and their activities are more varied. Leisure activities are also affected by the kind of work people do. Those with stimulating and creative jobs often use their leisure time to follow up activities related to their work. Architects, for example, frequently have leisure activities linked to art and design. Those doing physically arduous work, or subject to continuous discipline, such as miners or seamen, often devote their leisure to activities as far removed from work as possible.

A major determinant of patterns of consumption is the ease with which people can gain access to various goods and services. Private transport is especially important. Car owners have greater access to low-price retail outlets such as out-of-town hypermarkets. They also have more access to various commercially provided leisure and recreation facilities. The ease with which people can use the social services, particularly educational and health facilities, is also affected. Car ownership is closely related to income. Those who do not own cars, especially if they are also poor, tend to have a more limited set of opportunities to obtain goods and services from both the private and public sectors.

Inequalities exist, therefore, in all aspects of life and life-style. The pattern of these inequalities shows great stability over time and while the taxation and expenditure policies of the state have modified the patterns in a number of ways the overall framework of inequality has remained the same in most essentials. The economic role performed by an individual as a producer is the major influence on the opportunities he has in the role of consumer.

8.4.4 Classes in modern Britain

While inequality is of importance in understanding patterns of consumption it is also the foundation of the division of society into different social classes. These classes may form the basis of major divisions which have a significant impact on industrial and political life.

There are few societies which are not divided into various layers or strata. In some the strata are categories such as nobleman, freeman or serf, which have different legally defined rights and duties. In British society, however, there is formal equality based on universal civil and political rights. Legal equality is, however, quite compatible with the existence of social classes. A social class is simply a group of people who share a similar economic position and who as a result exhibit many other similarities of attitude and behaviour. The class structure is normally seen as made up of three classes: a working class, a middle class and an upper class.

The working class. The working class is made up of all employees and their families who normally carry out manual work or routine non-manual work. The routine non-manual workers are included in the working class because their income and opportunities are generally less favourable than those of skilled manual workers. In addition, many are women, married to manual workers. Most members of this class are born into it and remain in it. The chances of moving out of the working class are greatest for the children of skilled manual workers and routine non-manual workers.

We are justified in referring to these people as a class because of the many attributes that they share. The jobs performed by working class people are likely to have a number of distinguishing characteristics.

- A high element of routine.
- Little control by the worker over pace, scheduling and methods of work.
- Little authority exercised over others.
- Few educational requirements.
- Work involving operating a machine.

Those who perform these jobs are likely to have low incomes, few fringe benefits, few educational qualifications and a relatively low chance of good health and a long life. Members of a class not only share similar conditions of work and material opportunities, but they also have a tendency to hold similar views. This 'subjective' aspect of class is demonstrated in two main ways. First, most people objectively classified as working class would describe themselves in this way. Secondly, working class people seek to exert some power and influence through the organizations to which they belong or support. For many working class people these organizations are trade unions and the Labour Party.

While members of the working class have many features of life in common there are also important differences which exist within it. First, there are differences in status. The longstanding division between skilled and non-skilled workers is one aspect of this. Another is the division which arises because non-manual workers may consider white collar work to be a superior activity, while many manual workers consider that the 'real' work they do should provide them with a higher status. In addition, status differences exist based on race and ethnic background. Black people, regardless of their occupation, are generally assigned a low status. The second area of difference, which can also be related to the first, concerns political values. A large minority of working class people do not support the Labour Party. Many of these work in small enterprises and do not belong to trade unions. In addition they are likely to live in rural areas or small towns. Variations in the nature of work and community, therefore, lead to important divisions within the working class.

The middle class. As its name suggests, the middle class lies between the upper class and the working class, although the boundaries are not clear cut. Incomes are normally higher than those found in the working class. Most members of this class are born into it. Certainly most children of middle class parents become members of the middle class as adults. However, because the class is expanding due to changes in the occupational structure and because of its relatively low average family size, the middle class also recruits members from the working and upper classes. The pattern of geographical mobility of this class is interesting. Some members, often those attached to family businesses, tend to stay in the area where they were brought up; others, especially employees of large private and public sector organizations, tend to move frequently as they progress up the promotion hierarchy. Middle class occupations and members of the middle class are likely to have the opposite characteristics to those given above for the working class.

The middle class may be divided into three segments according to the source of income. Middle class income may come from fees for work performed, profits from entrepreneurial activity or salaries from employment. This produces three groups, as shown in *Figure 8.2*.

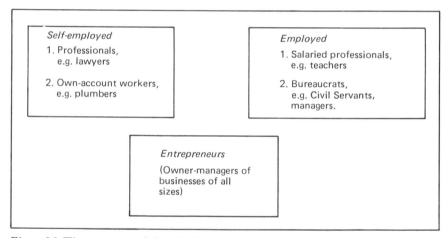

Figure 8.2 The structure of the middle class

There is considerable variation within the middle class. Educational levels vary, with the highest average levels found amongst the professionals, both salaried and self-employed. The greatest range of incomes is found amongst the entrepreneurs and the self-employed. The most marginal entrepreneurs and own-account workers have very low incomes. The highest incomes are found amongst the entrepreneurs, although a few self-employed professionals, such as leading lawyers, may also be highly paid. The range of incomes of salaried employees is generally rather less.

Important differences in status also exist. Professional jobs tend to have a high status even if, as with nurses, the level of income is low. Non-professional own-account workers tend to have a low status because of their association with manual work. Non-professional salaried employees and entrepreneurs tend to have a status related to the size of their incomes.

In view of the considerable diversity within this class the members exhibit a surprisingly high degree of similarity in their political views, which are predominantly Conservative. They are also likely to perceive themselves as middle class and many seek to pursue and protect their interests through the membership of various organizations. Several hundred professional associations of varying degrees of size and importance exist, to which middle class employees and self-employed professionals belong. There are also large numbers of trade associations, some catering for those in particular lines of business, such as the Confederation of Retail Tobacconists, and some for businessmen in general, such as Rotary Clubs or Chambers of Commerce. Other members of the middle class may belong to trade unions. This is particularly true of public sector employees amongst whom larger numbers of non-Conservative voters are to be found.

The upper class. The upper class consists of those who own considerable wealth and who are therefore not substantially dependent on income from their own labour even though they may engage in economically gainful activities. The wealth owned may be land, housing, financial assets, industrial and commercial capital, or very often some combination of two or more of these. The upper class recruits new members from amongst commercial and industrial capitalists. The British upper class has continuously absorbed those who have accumulated great wealth. Full membership of this class, however, is not simply a matter of money but involves acquiring a particular style of life. The majority of members of this class are born into it. This is particularly true of landowners, some of whom belong to families whose wealth has been established for centuries. A section of the hereditary aristocracy, which is largely found in this group, has special legal privileges including membership of the House of Lords. Members of this class share a number of characteristics. They tend to have been educated at fee-paying schools. They tend to marry members of the same class and they tend to find work in a number of limited areas. An important minority of the very rich live solely from their income from property and adopt the life-styles of a 'leisured class'. In this they are sometimes joined by wealthy 'celebrities' from the world of entertainment. However, the majority of members enter business, the professions or the public service. Those who enter business tend to be found more in the financial sector than in manufacturing. Those who enter the professions and public service tend to be found in the Church, the Law, the Armed Forces and the Civil Service. The majority of those in leading positions in business, commerce, finance, the Church, the Civil Service, the Army and the Judiciary are from upper class backgrounds. People from the same background are also prominent in the leadership of the Conservative Party.

It is not possible to draw a precise dividing line between the upper levels of the middle class and the upper class. What is clear, however, is that a small group of families, persisting from generation to generation, holds a disproportionate share of national wealth and of positions of authority.

8.4.5 Theories of class structure

There are three separate approaches to understanding the overall nature of the class structure in Britain. One approach, associated with a Consensus view, sees differences of status as the major focus of inequality in our society. This is the functionalist theory of stratification, so called because it argues that inequality is necessary and useful because of the functions it performs in helping society to operate smoothly. This theory suggests that those occupations which are most vital to the existence of society—positions of leadership and responsibility—will have the highest status, and the highest material rewards. The status of all occupations will form a hierarchy with the position of each depending on its generally recognized importance. As a result the ensuing economic inequalities are based on a consensus that they are acceptable and indeed desirable.

There is no doubt that evaluations of status are a factor in inequality. While the law provides for the equal treatment of all, people are often treated differently according to the evaluation which is made by others of their status. High status individuals generally receive more favourable treatment than those with a lower status: they tend to receive more deference and more respect. Evidence exists that if people are asked to rank occupations according to their 'importance' then they usually put them in the kind of order found in the Registrar General's classification with professional/managerial jobs at the top and unskilled manual work at the bottom.

According to the functionalist view, society is made up of a number of 'social classes', each composed of occupations of a similar type with a roughly similar status. It is suggested that there is considerable social mobility, with many people occupying a different occupational status from that of their parents, and others moving from one class to another in the course of their working life. The system of stratification is seen as fluid and open, with individuals free to find their own level through the occupational system.

In contrast, the radical view is an example of the Conflict approach. It stresses that class differences arise from the ownership or non-ownership of capital. It holds that the owners of capital exploit the majority who are forced to sell their labour in order to live. Between capitalists and workers is a small middle class of professional people and those in position of authority who share some of the economic privileges of the owners of wealth by virtue of the services they perform for it.

This viewpoint sees little evidence of social mobility and suggests that families with wealth tend to pass this on to their children while those from working class families tend to have little chance themselves of escaping from the working class. The class structure is seen as relatively 'closed' with the upper class occupying a position of dominance. The acceptance of the class structure by working class people results from the manipulation of their beliefs. This produces a 'false consciousness' in which people are unaware of their real interests.

An intermediate view, lying midway between the Conflict and Consensus approaches is commonly found in the literature on stratification. While it gives little prominence to the ownership of wealth as a factor in stratification it does suggest a major division between manual and non-manual workers with the former making up a 'working class' and the latter a 'middle class'. Little discussion of an 'upper class' takes place. This view sees a degree of inequality as acceptable provided it can be justified. It suggests that while there is general agreement on the hierarchy of occupations, the possibility of a limited form of conflict is not ruled out, especially in industrial relations. The class structure is seen as relatively open, and becoming more so, with considerable social mobility between manual and non-manual socio-economic groups. It suggests that while inequalities generally have diminished there is also evidence of the persistence of inequality of opportunity. The place occupied by an individual is determined jointly by his family background and occupational achievement. This view is often associated with the notion that class conflict is becoming less severe. The three approaches are summarized in *Table 8.6.*

There can be no doubt that substantial inequalities exist in the UK. However, the significance of these inequalities is open to different interpretations. In the Consensus views they are seen as the reflection of the needs of a complex society to ensure that important roles are performed while in the Conflict view they are seen as evidence of the exploitation of the majority by a wealthy and powerful minority.

Those who take a Conflict view stress the influential role played by the upper class and see the working class as making up the vast majority of society, including all routine non-manual workers and some professional and managerial workers. Class inequality and class conflict are seen as having continuing importance. Those who take the

Table 8.6 Different views of class structure

| | Conflict | Consensus | |
	Radical	Intermediate	Functionalist
Cause of stratification	Capitalist system	Functional necessity	Functional necessity
Nature of strata	Groupings related to ownership/non-ownership of capital (e.g. capitalist and workers)	Groupings of those with similar type of work (e.g. manual/non-manual)	Groupings of those with similar occupational status (e.g. Registrar General's classification)
Extent of social mobility	Low	Medium	High
Relations between strata	Class conflict	Limited conflict	Interdependence

Intermediate or the Consensus view are more likely to see the working class as a contracting group because of the increasing numbers of non-manual workers. They are also likely to believe that class conflict is declining in importance as a result of the reduction of class inequalities. These different viewpoints reappear in the study of other areas of social life, such as community and ideology, as later parts of the chapter will show.

8.5 Communities in modern Britain

While a knowledge of social inequality is basic to understanding modern Britain it has also to be remembered that a variety of different ways of life are found here. In different locations there are distinctive traditions and patterns of behaviour. In the main these ways of life have resulted from the process of industrialization which has led to the growth of industrial cities and transformed the countryside. However, the survival of aspects of a pre-industrial way of life is also significant.

8.5.1 Patterns of settlement

A distinctive characteristic of industrial cities is the way in which different social groups are located in different areas of the city. The general pattern is that there is an area of shops, offices and places of entertainment at the centre. Around this is found the 'inner-city' which is often a run-down, partially derelict area containing small private terraced housing, some local authority accommodation and many large old houses divided into rented flats. Further from the city centre there is often a working class residential area consisting of small houses, owned or rented, with a relatively long established population. On the fringes of the city are found the middle class suburbs, with larger houses, usually owner-occupied. Many cities also have large peripheral council estates. Most cities also have an 'industrial zone' where industry is concentrated in a segment of the city, around and within which there is also a strong concentration of working class housing.

Industrial cities have usually experienced a similar pattern of growth. As the population of the city expands, middle class people move to new areas of housing on the outskirts. The housing vacated by them is taken over by working class people. Thus, some working class people now live in solid terraced housing built for the Edwardian lower middle class, while others live in flats, in the substantial dwellings of the Victorian middle classes. Over a long period, therefore, areas change their character, with middle class districts eventually housing a working class population as the middle classes move further out to the suburbs. An interesting new twist to this pattern has been given in recent years by the trend towards middle class people moving back to the inner-city through the improvement of older housing, which sometimes involves returning a multi-occupied house into a single dwelling. This process has been termed 'gentrification'.

The similarity of the pattern found in different cities, which first developed in the last century and which is still visible today, resulted from the existence of a largely free market in land and housing. The most desirable locations became the most expensive and were monopolized by the better off. Those without resources to buy, had to rent, and also had to live close to their place of work. Thus, the poor tended to live near the industrial areas, while the better off commuted from the suburbs.

Not all industrial towns grew in this way. In some cases, particularly where only a single economic activity was feasible, the settlements ceased to expand as soon as the local industry had reached its peak size. Mining villages and some textile towns are examples. In addition, there are many towns in predominantly rural areas which are mainly involved in providing goods and services for the surrounding area and lack a substantial manufacturing base. Many of these old market towns have pre-industrial origins and lack the characteristics of a typical industrial city.

Today land and housing are no longer in an entirely free market and the state has an influence over how and where communities develop. Town planning influences whether land should be used for agriculture, industry or housing. In general, industry is now located in areas designated for that purpose alone, while 'green belts' restrict urban growth. Slum clearance has led to massive removal of older housing in the inner-city and working class residential areas. About a third of all households are now in local authority housing. Council housing is usually built in the form of large estates, either in the areas where slum clearance has taken place or on 'green field' sites on the outskirts of the city.

Early observers of industrialization frequently drew a contrast between the teeming life of the industrial city and the slower pace of existence of the rural and small town life of pre-industrial society. As a result of industrialization, however, rural life has been extensively transformed as agriculture has become mechanized. While agricultural employment has continued to fall, the amount of capital employed and the level of output have increased considerably. Traditional methods of agriculture survive in only a few remote communities. The countryside has also become 'urbanized' and, increasingly, villages in the vicinity of towns and cities are attracting an urban middle class population in the form of commuters, retired people and owners of second homes.

8.5.2 Types of community

The nature of any community is largely determined by its social class composition, which in turn influences the standard of living of the population. However, the standard of living is also affected by access to particular types of work and housing, and to publicly and privately provided goods and services. Along with these 'objective' differences are found differences of a 'subjective' kind, such as distinctive local subcultures. These involve a set of values and beliefs associated with a particular kind of work, or with geographical and cultural isolation. Many descriptions of different kinds of community exist and the following accounts illustrate some of the most important.

The **traditional village** is the remote rural community with considerable continuity of population, based on agriculture, usually with a sharp social divide between farmers and labourers but with a high degree of acceptance of inequalities of status. Access to such services as shops, educational and medical facilities is often poor. Family relationships tend to be male dominated with considerable emphasis given to family life and contact with relatives. Local custom and tradition may be a strong influence on behaviour. These kinds of community are becoming increasingly rare.

The **commuter village** is a rural community found in the vicinity of urban areas. It includes farmers and farm labourers as in the traditional village, as well as a number of middle class residents who do not work in the village. Social differences often rest on the distinction between locals and newcomers, rather than on class. The farmworkers and their families are frequently restricted in their access to services. This kind of rural community is becoming increasingly common.

Many **country towns** are found in predominantly rural areas. They tend to have a relatively stable population and a variety of employment, usually in small-scale enterprises. In the absence of large numbers of industrial workers, the local middle class of shopkeepers and professionals often forms a widely accepted local elite. These towns are usually well provided with conveniently located services and facilities. There is a fairly traditional pattern of family life with considerable importance given to kinship. Increasingly, however, these towns are changing due to the establishment of modern industries and the influx of newcomers this involves.

Suburbia is the normal community of the middle class. All towns have their suburbs while larger cities have several, some more exclusive than others. A defining characteristic of the suburb is that it is situated away from the area of employment. It is often also relatively remote from various services, although access is usually eased by high levels of car ownership. Community identity is reflected in widespread support for clubs, societies and churches. There is often considerable uniformity in values, reflected by a high level of support for the Conservative Party.

The term **'urban village'** has been used to describe long-established or 'traditional' working class communities. The term 'village' is used because of the close-knit community. They are usually based on a single predominant occupation. They may be physically isolated, as in a pit village, or part of a larger city, as with London's dockland. In these communities people live amongst their workmates and a strong sense of solidarity against those in positions of authority is often found. Because these are declining communities, they often lack modern facilities and services. The stability of the area is usually reflected in strong kinship links and a traditional family structure. Local customs and traditions in the field of leisure are also a feature. These traditional working class communities are in decline as the mainly heavy industries on which they are based are run down.

The term **'new working class'** has been used to describe working class communities based on modern, expanding, high technology industries. The new towns and what were, until recently, the expanding industrial areas of the South and the Midlands, typify this type. These communities contain large numbers of people who have migrated in search of higher wages and a better life. They often lack the strong community links of the traditional working class areas. Since people have moved away from the friends and relatives they were brought up with, a more 'privatized' or 'family-centred' life has developed. This has also involved a more equal and shared life between married couples.

It has been argued that this is likely to become the dominant type as the 'traditional' working class community declines.

The term **'inner-city'** is used to describe deteriorating areas found close to the centre of cities. Many 'traditional' working class communities in areas of industrial decline are becoming inner-city areas. The inner-city contains a mixed population. Some are transient, such as students and young middle class couples living temporarily in flats, while there are others who are unable to find accommodation elsewhere, such as blacks. Employment in these areas is falling due to factory closures and the creation of new jobs on peripheral industrial estates. Ethnic divisions and a low level of political participation are often present. Both retailing and social service facilities are frequently inferior to those found in the suburbs. Housing conditions are especially bad and sometimes made worse by the failure of local authorities to redevelop areas cleared of 'slums', and by such 'improvements' as urban motorways, which are usually routed through these areas. These areas also contain concentrations of poverty, deprivation and petty crime. The problems of the inner-city have been a major focus of political concern in the last 15 years.

8.5.3 Conclusion

Many kinds of community exist in Britain. These differences arise from differences in class composition, occupational structure, family life and kinship, the standard of services and facilities, and the nature of local customs and traditions.

The effect of industrialization has been to increase the numbers living in urban communities and to transform rural life. It has also led to the increased residential segregation of social classes. Communities change primarily as a result of economic changes which result in the expansion of some industries and occupations, and the communities based on them, and the decline of others. This leads on a national scale to the decline of some regions and the expansion of others. On an urban scale it often means the development of pockets of severe deprivation, particularly in the inner-cities, as a result of the decline of central-city working class employment. The changing pattern of business in society is the underlying cause of changes in community life.

8.6 Values and society
8.6.1 Changing values

In modern society values change rapidly. Established standards are called into question as people search for ways to adjust to the rapid economic, political and social changes which confront them. Values also come under challenge through a widening of people's experience. Industrialization destroyed the stable, largely self-sufficient and encapsulated world of rural and small town communities. People were brought into contact with rapid economic change involving massive shifts of population and new social and political movements. Today, Britain is subject to varied and powerful international influences affecting all areas of life.

Numerous attempts have been made to identify the major ways in which the process of industrialization affects values. The term 'rationalization' has been used to describe the way in which behaviour moves away from being based on tradition and becomes based on a rational calculation of how best to do things. This process is seen to be at work in all areas of life outside the purely personal spheres of family and friendship. The growth of large-scale organization and the increasing stress on efficiency are seen as a reflection of this.

The term 'secularization' has been used to describe the decline in religious belief and observance. Religion comes to play a smaller and smaller part in life and its place is taken by a reliance on scientific knowledge as a means of understanding man and his place in the world. As a result, morality is no longer based on absolute standards.

Traditional patterns of authority are also changing. Increasingly, people demand that authority is justified on the grounds of its beneficial effects rather than simply being accepted unquestioningly.

The impact of these changes may be seen in every area of life. In the economy, the changing nature of work has resulted in a decline of the traditional craft ethic of pride in work skilfully performed. The Puritan belief in hard work and simple living, which played a part in the early development of capitalism, has given way to a more hedonistic outlook.

In politics, the dominant nineteenth century values of individualism and self-help have been challenged by the growth of state intervention in the form of the social services, the managed economy and the spread of socialist ideas. Political authority is no longer able to rest on the idea that a traditional elite has an automatic right to rule.

The standards used to judge family life have also changed. People now see a smaller family as desirable. Relations between men and women in the family are becoming more equal, leading to a sharing of family tasks and authority. Child-rearing practices have changed, with more emphasis being given to the rights of children.

In the area of life-style there is also continuous change. Fashions in clothing, facial appearance, diet, furnishings and decorations, music, literature and active leisure pursuits, all change rapidly. Leisure is becoming more family-centred as higher living standards allow increased comfort in the home. Recreations are becoming more active as knowledge of, and concern about, health increases.

These changes in values, affecting different areas of life, have considerable implications for the future role of business in society. On the basis of new values, man in his role as producer, consumer and political participant may, in the future, make new demands and create new circumstances to which organizations will have to respond, as the final chapter will show.

8.6.2 Influences on values and beliefs

The question of how people acquire values and beliefs is tied up with the fundamental disagreement about the nature of society contained in the Consensus and Conflict viewpoints. Both approaches agree that it is through socialization that people learn the values, beliefs and skills necessary to perform roles. The earliest form of socialization occurs in the interaction between a child and its parents, and many aspects of personality are acquired very early in life along with language and knowledge of relationships. As a child grows it becomes subject to more varied influences. Those of its friends, other adults and school all play a part.

Socialization is a life-long process. New knowledge, skills and standards of judgement and behaviour, or values, are continuously acquired. Direct personal experience is a major influence on attitudes and values. Through the work that a person does, he is exposed to a particular set of influences. Many occupations have a 'culture'—a set of ideas and beliefs—which new recruits acquire. Work also provides experience of authority, as a superior or a subordinate, which affects a person's outlook. The same effect may arise from membership of an organization, such as a union or professional association.

Work largely determines the level of status possessed by a person. It may determine his income and thus the kind of housing he is able to afford. Both status and income will determine the kinds of influences that are encountered amongst people he or she mixes with socially. In addition, the community in which a person lives may foster a particular set of values and beliefs.

The Conflict and Consensus views differ in their explanation of how people acquire their values and beliefs. The Conflict view sees this as a process whereby the upper class and their supporters have a disproportionate influence, whereas the Consensus view portrays people as choosing their own viewpoints.

According to the Conflict view, those in authority in all the major institutions of society are likely, implicitly or explicitly, to lend support to the *status quo*. The Monarchy, leading figures in the Church, the Civil Service, the Armed Forces, the Judiciary, and industry and commerce, are all seen as proponents of a similar viewpoint. However, these views meet with resistance from some working class people. It is suggested that the everyday experience of authority and economic exploitation at work helps to create opposition to the views on work and unionism promoted by the wealthy and the powerful. Where well established working class communities exist and where trade unionism is strong, an alternative view of reality is likely to be found. This alternative view will probably involve a 'them–us' attitude to authority, and a willingness actively to oppose employers and governments when it is felt to be necessary. This opposition is seen as a reflection of class conflict in that it expresses a basic opposition between upper class and working class interests.

The Consensus approach stresses the diversity of viewpoints amongst those in positions of authority and tends to decry the idea that a single viewpoint is promoted by them. It is more likely to stress the political neutrality of the Monarchy, the Judiciary, the Armed Forces and the Civil Service. It stresses the diversity of outlooks found amongst groups and individuals and denies that attitudes are likely to polarize on the basis of class membership. Where particular occupational groups do develop a strong opposition to the government or employers, this is seen as a result of special factors, not as a normal outcome of a conflict of interest between labour and capital.

The influence of the mass media has been the subject of particular disagreement between proponents of the Consensus and Conflict viewpoints. The Consensus view generally sees them as a source of ideas and opinions of all shades, through which the recipient is able to obtain useful information as well as entertainment. This view stresses the diversity of opinions which are put forward and claims that everyone has an equal chance to make his voice heard. Free speech and freedom of publication are seen as a guarantee of a free society. The information obtained allows the recipient to make informed judgements about matters of social and political interest. It is argued that while the mass media have some impact on opinions, people are generally left to make their mind up about issues and that public opinion reflects what people choose to think, not what they have been persuaded to believe.

The Conflict view sees the output of the media as giving a one-sided version of reality in which the values of the upper class are given special stress. This view suggests that the media, perhaps unconsciously, construct a favourable view of the existing organization of society and portray all but the mildest criticism as perverse and destructive. Ownership of the press is concentrated in the hands of a few newspaper magnates and their papers generally select and slant the news in order to promote a right-wing political viewpoint. It is also suggested that television, in its news and current affairs reporting, adopts a similar pattern. The outbreak of a strike is always 'bad news on the industrial front' regardless of its cause, while a return to work is always 'good news', regardless of the terms on which it takes place. The Conflict view claims that the mass media have a substantial impact on opinion in the direction of promoting support for, or acquiescence in, the *status quo*.

8.7 Conclusion

In examining the social context of business, three themes have consistently emerged. The first is the pervasiveness of change. While its pace has varied from time to time and from place to place, it has affected all areas of life. The second is the interconnectedness of the different facets of society. Developments in technology, for example, may transform the occupational structure, leading to changes in both community and family life. In all this, however, it is clearly changes in the economic organization of society which ultimately have the most impact. Thirdly, it has been shown how, in many areas, it is possible to adopt different perspectives in the interpretation of events.

The kind of work people do, the standard of living they enjoy, the kind of community in which they live and the ideological influences to which they are exposed all help to determine their political behaviour. An understanding of the social context is important not just for the light it throws on the way people behave as producers and consumers. It also influences the nature of political conflict and the activities of the state— matters which are taken up in the following chapter.

Guide to further reading
General

Reid, Ivan (1977). *Social Class Differences in Britain*, Open Books, London. A good source of data on many aspects of inequality.

Ryder, Judith and Silver, Harold (1978). *Modern English Society*, 2nd edn, Unwin, London. Covers many of the issues discussed in this chapter.

Subsections
8.1

Hobsbaum, E. J. (1971). *Industry and Empire*, Penguin, London. Chapters 3 and 6 give a classic account of the industrial revolution.

8.2

Braverman, Harry (1974). *Labour and Monopoly Capital*, Monthly Review Press, London. Chapter 20 provides a Marxist discussion of the nature of work.
Routh, Guy (1965). *Occupation and Pay in Great Britain 1906–60*, Cambridge University Press, Cambridge. Chapter 1 contains an extended account of the changing occupational structure.

8.3.1

Salaman, Graeme (1979). *Work Organisations*, Longman, London. Chapters 8 and 9 give an informative analysis of management strategies.

8.3.2 and 8.3.3

Hyman, Richard (1972). *Strikes*, Fontana/Collins, Glasgow. Conflict approach to industrial relations.

8.4.1–8.4.4

Westergaard, John and Resler, Henrietta (1976). *Class in a Capitalist Society*, Penguin, London. Covers all the areas of inequality discussed in this chapter, in some detail.

8.5

Pahl, R. E. (1971). *Patterns of Urban Life*, Longman, London. Contains material on urbanization (Chapter 2) and urban ways of life (Chapter 5) as well as other relevant material.
Newby, Howard (1979). *Green and Pleasant Land?*, Penguin, London. Chapter 5 is a well researched account of modern rural life.

8.6

Golding, Peter (1974). *The Mass Media*, Longman, London. Chapter 5 gives a short account of the impact of the mass media on people's values.

Exercises

Review questions

1. Why is factory production more efficient than the domestic system?
2. In what kinds of jobs are women most commonly found?
3. What are the different levels of technology?

4. How has the growth of state employment affected the occupational structure?
5. What are 'entrepreneurial' and 'managerial' ideologies?
6. What effect has war had on trade union membership?
7. What are the different forms of industrial conflict?
8. What effect does taxation have on inequalities of income and wealth?
9. Why do the various socio-economic groups have different death rates?
10. Explain how status and life-style are related.
11. What are the typical characteristics of working class jobs?
12. What are the three segments of the middle class?
13. How do the Marxist and functionalist views of class structure differ?
14. How do 'traditional' and 'commuter' villages differ?
15. What is 'the inner-city'?
16. Explain the term 'secularization'.
17. How do Conflict and Consensus views of the mass media differ?

Application and investigation

1. Obtain up-to-date figures on strikes in different industries. Discuss whether they fit with past trends.
2. Obtain figures for the growth of union membership amongst different types of employees since 1960. What trends can be observed?
3. Use the latest edition of *Social Trends* and the *General Household Survey* to find up-to-date information on secondary inequalities. Comment on any significant changes from the figures given here.
4. Examine the various national daily papers and note the political perspective they promote. Obtain figures for their circulation. To what extent does the information you have collected support a Conflict or a Consensus view?

Projects

1. Examine the view that class inequalities have not altered substantially this century.
2. Read Chapters 1 and 9 of the following book:

Beharrell, Peter and Philo, Greg (1977). *Trade Unions and the Media*, Macmillan, London.

Use the ideas in these chapters to design a small research project on bias in press or TV coverage of business and industrial relations. Report on your results.

Chapter 9

The political and governmental context of business

9.1 Introduction

For most of the nineteenth century, government regulation of business was limited as was the provision of public services. Parliament was controlled by an upper class made up of landed and commercial interests which were committed to a minimal role for the state. Businessmen were consequently free to expand at home and were provided with protected markets in the colonies. The political and governmental context within which business operates has, however, changed profoundly since then.

In this chapter, two major aspects of the contemporary political and governmental context of business will be described. First, the significance for business of political phenomena such as elections, parties, ideologies and pressure groups will be examined. Such political phenomena shape the constraints, opportunities and resources affecting business. Secondly, the expansion of state activity and the increasingly close relationship between the state and business interests will be analysed.

Before describing these changes, however, it is important to restate, as a central theme of this book, that the facts do not speak for themselves. They are open to different interpretations reflecting the Consensus and Conflict views of society which lead to very different interpretations of the relationship between business, politics and government. In the Consensus view, political and economic power is widely dispersed. In the Conflict view, however, economic and political power still resides with the upper class. Whilst the Consensus view stresses that the state is not controlled by one class or interest, the Conflict view emphasizes that the economic power of the upper class allows it to determine political events. Not surprisingly, therefore, these two views lead to different interpretations of political phenomena, such as elections, parties and pressure groups, and also of the changing role of the State.

9.2 Elections and political parties

9.2.1 The development of the electoral system

Until well into the nineteenth century the right to vote and stand for election was limited to property owners, thus ensuring the political dominance of the upper class. The extension of these rights to all adults was a gradual process. It proceeded in stages from 1832, and not until 1948 did all adults have equal political rights. At each stage there was opposition from many in the propertied classes to the extension of rights to those lower down the social hierarchy. Similarly, the political rights of women were contested, and not until 1928 could they vote on the same basis as men. Nevertheless, those with a Consensus view believe that the extension of equal political rights ensures that ultimate power in Britain rests with the people, not with a wealthy minority. Those with a Conflict view, however, stress that the extension of rights was granted only reluctantly by the propertied classes. Nor do equal political rights guarantee social and economic equality. The apparent fairness of the electoral system may indeed legitimize (make more acceptable) economic and social inequality. It may deflect the struggle for social change into peaceful and largely unproductive parliamentary channels. In the Conflict view, therefore, elections are an important means of changing society, but they must be supplemented by direct action.

9.2.2 Elections and the party system

Free elections provide the ultimate form of public control over governments. At elections, the voters can pass judgement on the performance of the government and the promises of the opposition parties. Fear of defeat at the next election also encourages governments to take account of public opinion between elections. However, even those with a Consensus view admit that elections are a very limited form of public control. They are infrequent and do not permit a clear expression of public opinion on particular issues or policies. Nor do the electors determine the candidates or policies at elections but merely select among those offered by the parties. Moreover, the UK electoral system of simple majority, or 'first past the post', is criticized as unfair. The proportion of votes won by each party is not reflected in the proportion of seats it gains in Parliament, as *Table 9.1* shows in the case of the 1979 General Election. Smaller parties are penalized by this system, especially where, as with the Liberals, their votes are thinly spread over the country. The two main parties, however, benefit greatly. One of them usually wins an overall parliamentary majority and forms a government. Yet no postwar government has won a majority of the votes cast, and it may even happen, as in 1951 and February 1974, that the party with the most votes does not win the most seats.

Table 9.1 The 1979 General Election

Party	Total vote	Percentage of total electorate	Percentage of votes cast	Percentage of seats won
Conservative	13 697 753	33.3	43.9	53.4
Labour	11 509 524	28.0	36.9	42.2
Liberal	4 313 931	10.5	13.8	1.7
SNP	504 259	1.2	1.6	0.3
Plaid Cymru	132 544	0.3	0.4	0.3
Nat. Front	191 267	0.5	0.6	0
Others	971 512	2.4	2.8	2.0

Electoral systems cannot be judged only on arithmetical grounds, however. They must also be judged by the kind of party system and government which they produce. The British electoral system sustains the two-party system, and since the war, has usually produced a government with a clear parliamentary majority. An assessment of the electoral system must therefore take account of the party system in the UK.

Britain is unusual in that since the war there has been a disciplined two-party system. In contrast, most other Western nations have multiparty systems and, consequently, coalition governments. The distinctive features of the UK party system are that:

- an overwhelming majority of seats in Parliament are won by the Conservative and Labour Parties,
- a government is formed exclusively from the Labour or Conservative Parties, although it may be in a minority or have only a small parliamentary majority,
- party discipline is strong, with MPs voting according to party lines, thus allowing a single party to govern even with a small majority or when in a minority.

These features, especially the first two, did not apply consistently to British politics prior to 1945. It was not until the late nineteenth century that the many parliamentary groups coalesced to form the Liberal and Conservative Parties. The extension of the franchise to the working class and the growth of class consciousness and the trade union movement gave rise to the Labour Party in the early years of this century. In the interwar period, Labour displaced the Liberal Party as the main opposition to the Conservatives, and for much of this period there was no clear two-party system. Furthermore, all-party coalition governments were formed during both world wars and during the economic depression of the 1930s.

In historical terms, therefore, the two-party system is of recent origin and is certainly not inevitable. Indeed, the percentage of votes won at general elections by Labour and Conservative Parties combined has fallen from 97% in 1951 to 81% in 1979, when only 61% of those entitled to vote actually voted for the two main parties. Support for the two major parties is, therefore, increasingly uncertain, and voters have shown rising support for the Liberals in England, and for Nationalist or Regionalist parties in Scotland, Wales and Northern Ireland.

The electoral system and the two-party system which it sustains have important consequences for the economy. The electoral and party systems have been criticized by those with a Consensus view for exaggerating political conflict and creating economic uncertainty. The 'first past the post' system leads to the alternation of Labour and Conservative governments based on only small changes in votes between the parties. Governments do not gain the support of a majority of voters yet usually gain a sufficient parliamentary majority to implement their policies. Each party, therefore, is said to undo the policies of its predecessor and introduce its own. The result is frequent alteration of government policies in key areas such as industrial or regional policy. Furthermore, the prospect of forthcoming elections encourages govern-ments to change their policies to please the electors. For instance, tax cuts or increases in public spending may be announced before an election regardless of their economic consequences.

Those with a Consensus view stress that these frequent policy changes associated with the two-party system do not adequately reflect public opinion and create great uncertainty for businessmen and those in the public services. Various proposals have been advanced to reduce this alternation of governments and insulate the economy from political uncertainty. Some Consensus theorists, for example, advocate the introduction of proportional representation at elections to ensure a closer correspondence between the votes and seats won by parties. It is hoped that such a change would encourage the emergence of a multi-party system, and lead to centre-ground and moderate coalition governments. It is claimed that such changes would ensure that public opinion is reflected more faithfully than under the present two-party system. The changes are also intended to lead to greater continuity in government policy.

In the Conflict view, however, there is too little rather than too much political change. The alternation of parties in government has not led to fundamental changes in government policy. Those with a Conflict view see both Conservative and Labour Parties as following policies that sustain the present economic system. Whilst Consensus theorists stress the short-term changes in government policy, those with a Conflict view stress the long-term continuity of policy. Supporters of the Conflict view hope to see political conflict intensify and political control over the economy increase. They hope that the Labour Party and trade unions will intensify the struggle to change society, using political and economic disruption as well as electoral and parliamentary methods.

9.2.3 Party origins and interests

The major parties have different origins, draw their supporters from different sections of society and have close connections with different economic interests. These factors influence what the parties say and do, whether in government or opposition.

The Labour Party was created in the first two decades of this century by an alliance of trade unions and socialist groups with often divergent ideas. Its initial aim was merely to ensure that working class interests were represented in Parliament. Only in 1918 did the Party commit itself to the overtly socialist objective of securing the 'common ownership of the means of production, distribution and exchange'. The commitment of the Party, and especially its leaders, to this objective has, however, often been more symbolic than real: a useful means of cementing Party unity but not something which should greatly influence the Party when in government. Furthermore, since its origins, Labour, and especially its leaders, have favoured gradual change by parliamentary methods rather than by civil disobedience or by using the economic power of the trade unions for political purposes.

The Labour Party was, and still is, a coalition of diverse elements. It consists of affiliated trade unions, usually with limited economic objectives, together with various socialist groups, the Cooperative Party and an elite of professional and increasingly middle class politicians who lead the Party. The link with the trade unions is especially important. They provide 80% of the membership and national level income of the Party and have 89% of the votes at annual party conferences. They also sponsor a substantial number of Labour MPs: 132 out of 268 after the 1979 election. The actual influence of the unions on Labour policy should not be exaggerated, however. They are frequently divided amongst themselves and consider politics as secondary to their economic role. Also, Labour governments have often followed policies, such as cutting public spending, regardless of trade union opposition, and there has often been bitter conflict with the unions when Labour governments have imposed pay restraints. Nevertheless, Labour's reliance on trade union support and working class voters gives a distinctive emphasis to its policies.

The link between the Conservative Party and particular interests and classes is less clear-cut. Even more than the Labour Party it claims to be a national rather than a class party. The modern Conservative Party was created in the mid-nineteenth century and was originally a party predominantly of the landed interests. As it evolved, it gained the support of the business, professional and managerial classes and a substantial section of the working class. Consequently, it also is a coalition of interests, ideologies and groups.

Although the Party does not have such direct links with business as Labour has with the unions, nevertheless, the indirect links are very strong. Most of the Party's national level income derives from company donations. A survey of the largest companies in 1979, for example, discovered that the political donations of 445 companies totalled over £2.5 million. Over 60% of this total went directly to the Party, with the remainder going to pro-Conservative bodies such as Aims, a free enterprise propaganda body, the Economic League, an anti-union body, and various regional industrialists' councils. Although not formally affiliated to the Party the general effect of such bodies is to boost the Conservative cause. Likewise, there is no direct sponsorship of Conservative MPs, but an overwhelming proportion of them are drawn from businessmen, managers, the professions and landowners. Business interests such as retailers, financiers and manufacturers are, however, frequently in disagreement and they rarely present united views to the Party leaders. Also, Conservative governments have sometimes followed policies, such as price control, which have been opposed by businessmen.

Each party clearly has distinctive origins and links with particular interests and classes. The parties also have distinctive patterns of electoral support. In comparison to most Western nations, class is an exceptionally important influence on how British people vote. In other Western countries, such as the USA, and the states of the EEC, class has far less effect on voting, and region, religion or race are of great importance. In Britain, however, the link between class and party allegiance is strong, but not overwhelming, as *Table 9.2* demonstrates.

As with all opinion polls the exact percentages need to be treated with caution, but their general message is consistent with most academic research into voting and class in Britain. The importance of class voting is clearly evident, especially in the professional and middle classes (A and B) and white collar workers (C1). Among the skilled working class (C2) voting along class lines is less evident, but among the semiskilled, unskilled and poor (D and E) it is stronger. It should be remembered, however, that in 1979 the Conservatives gained substantially in classes

Table 9.2 Class and voting in the 1979 General Election

| | Class (Institute of Advertising Practitioners' classification) | | |
	ABC1	C2	DE
Percentage of voters	35	34	31
Conservative	59	40	34
Labour	22	42	51
Liberal	16	15	11
Swing to Conservatives since previous General Election (Oct. 1974)	0	10.5	9

Source: *New Statesman*, 18 May 1979, from Market and Opinion Research International Polls

C2, D and E, thus weakening the link between class and voting. When Labour wins, as in 1974, the link is much stronger.

The link between class and party allegiance is not overwhelming as the 1979 election illustrates. It is, nevertheless, very strong and when combined with the ties which the parties have with the unions and business, it gives party politics in Britain a distinctive class flavour. Those with a Consensus view, however, wish to minimize this. Class is regarded as outdated and divisive and it is suggested that parties should be concerned with the interests of the whole nation not just of particular classes. To those with a Conflict view, class inequality is inherent in capitalism and the class struggle should be intensified through political and economic action. The Labour Party should therefore adopt an explicitly working class position. These differences of opinion about class reflect the deeply rooted ideological divisions found within the parties. For parties in Britain are not merely electoral machines, or vehicles for particular interests. They are also vehicles for political ideas and ideologies.

9.2.4 Parties and ideologies

As has been suggested throughout this book the major ideological division in British politics is not that between the Labour and Conservative Parties. Within each party there are several ideological groups and factions. Within the Labour Party, for instance, there are important differences between the right-wing Manifesto group and the left-wing Tribune group. Similarly, within the Conservative Party, there are right-wing groups, like the Monday Club, and left-wing groups, like the Tory Reform Group. There is consequently much common ground between the parties, with most MPs in both parties being **centrists or moderates**. In each party there is, however, an alternative ideology. In the Conservative Party that alternative is right-wing **individualism**, whilst in the Labour Party it is left-wing **radicalism**.

The individualists. Individualism is derived from the nineteenth century Liberal, or *laissez-faire*, belief in market forces and individual initiative. Individualists believe first and foremost in the freedom of the individual from state and other restrictions. The individual's freedom, or liberty, to pursue his own self-interest is believed to be the basis of political freedom and economic prosperity. Individualists believe in equal legal and political rights but stress the value of social and economic inequality. It is seen as an incentive to greater effort and initiative. In the long term, therefore, social and economic inequality is believed to lead to greater prosperity and freedom for all.

The growth of state intervention in society is viewed by individualists as a threat to both liberty and prosperity. Government economic intervention distorts the workings of the market and restricts the freedom of consumers and businessmen. Similar arguments are used against the growth of social services and the pursuit of social equality. They are said to encourage idleness, undermine incentives and impose a heavy burden on the economy. Indeed, it is individualists who most often make the distinction between the 'wealth-creating' private sector and the wealth-absorbing, and essentially parasitic, public sector. To individualists, therefore, the state's social and economic interventions are self-defeating. For individualists, there can be no halfway house between capitalism and totalitarianism. There have been persistent demands since the war from pressure groups, political parties and public expectations, for ever more government intervention. Unless these pressures are resisted, individualists foresee a society where everything is regulated by the state and everyone is dependent on the state.

The solutions to Britain's problems offered by individualists are varied, but they reflect the common themes of 'less government' and 'more freedom'. It is accepted that government intervention is sometimes necessary to remedy market imperfections or to provide a safety net for those in greatest need. In general, however, individuals, groups and businesses should be left alone to pursue their own self-interests.

Individualism was the dominant ideology in Britain throughout the nineteenth century and up to the 1940s. Since the late 1960s these ideas have become widely accepted once more. The last two Conservative governments have embarked on individualist policies immediately after gaining office in 1970 and 1979. When faced with rising unemployment or high inflation, however, postwar Conservative governments have usually resorted to inteventionism. Whatever ideological preferences they started with, most Conservative governments have become moderates, albeit reluctant ones.

The moderates or centrists. Moderates occupy the centre ground of British politics and are to be found in all major parties. Their approach to problems appears pragmatic compared with the more explicitly ideological approaches of individualists and radicals. Nevertheless, their approach is based on a Consensus view of society and is as much an ideological stance as individualism or radicalism.

Moderates or centrists believe in using the power of the state to regulate economic and social affairs. Following Keynes and Beveridge they wish to use this power to increase prosperity, reduce inequalities and so minimize social discontent. Among Conservatives there has always been support for such state intervention. Not all Conservatives believe in the virtues of unrestrained free enterprise. Many have stressed its inefficiencies and social costs. Such Conservatives, often referred to as being in the 'Tory' tradition, argue the case for a mixed economy and a substantial measure of social welfare provision. Their ideal is a middle way between capitalism and socialism. Labour politicians generally need no convincing of the unfairness and inefficiency of free enterprise, but most of them believe in moderate and gradual change. Such moderate Labour politicians are often referred to as 'Social Democrats'. Although there are differences between Tories and Social Democrats these are outweighed by their shared commitment to the Consensus view.

Centrists in both parties hold similar views on the need to manage the economy. They advocate Keynesian demand management supplemented by whatever specific interventions are required by the circumstances, for instance, in prices and wages, or industrial location. They are pragmatic about economic intervention and optimistic that governments can manage the economy without the traditional socialist remedies of nationalization or stringent economic planning.

The basic elements of capitalism, such as the profit motive and private ownership, are accepted by moderates. They believe, however, that the worst features of unrestrained capitalism can be eliminated by moderate trade unionism, state regulation of business and the provision of public services. The private sector remains, though, as the major source of prosperity and as an important bulwark against excessive state power. Centrists too are aware of the dangers of an all-powerful state.

Centrists put great trust in progressive taxation and the social services to reduce the inequalities that cause social unrest. Policies that free people from poverty or ill health are not viewed as threats to freedom, as they are by individualists, but as extensions of freedom. Social Democrats do, of course, put more emphasis on reducing inequality than do their Conservative counterparts. But they are alike in supporting equality of opportunity, that is, allowing everyone an equal chance to compete in life, rather than ending social and economic inequalities. Moreover, greater equality is to be achieved primarily through faster economic growth rather than through large-scale redistribution of income and wealth. Faster growth provides higher living standards and permits higher state spending. To moderates, therefore, progress towards equality must be heavily dependent on economic conditions.

During most of the postwar period governments followed Moderate policies. Conservative governments of the 1950s and 1960s, especially those of MacMillan (1957–1963) and Home (1963–1964), extended welfare provision and followed increasingly interventionist economic policies. In the 1970s the Heath government reverted to such policies after 1972, and piecemeal interventionism was the major feature of the policies of the Labour governments of Wilson (1964–1970, 1974–1976) and Callaghan (1976–1979). By the late 1970s, however, individualist ideas, in the form of monetarism, were becoming influential once more, even in Labour ranks.

The radicals. Radicalism is the most left wing of the three major political ideologies in Britain and draws much of its inspiration from Marxist critiques of capitalism. Radicals are to be found on the left wing of the Labour Party, among trade unions and among revolutionary parties. Radical ideas have become increasingly common in Labour circles because of disillusionment with the performance of recent Labour governments.

Radicals reject the capitalist system and wish to transform Britain into a socialist society. They believe that the ownership of economic assets is the basis of economic and political power. Under capitalism, private ownership predominates and this leads to great inequalities and the exploitation of workers by a wealthy capitalist class. The interests of these two main classes are therefore inevitably at odds and class conflict exists. Radicals believe the conflict should be settled to the advantage of the majority at the expense of the minority. Unlike moderates, therefore, they welcome class conflict and seek a fundamental redistribution of power and wealth. Radicals also believe that capitalism, even in the form of the mixed economy, is inherently unstable and wasteful. Radical economic policies are, therefore, claimed as necessary to reverse Britain's economic decline.

The transformation from a capitalist to a socialist society is to be achieved primarily by an extension of public ownership and state planning of the economy. Radicals reject the optimistic view of the moderates that the economy can be controlled through Keynesian and *ad hoc* interventions. Public ownership is claimed to be the only really effective form of economic control. Radicals also advocate more democracy and participation, at work and in the community, so that people have more control over decisions affecting their lives.

Radicals view the other two ideologies as legitimizing class inequality. Individualists are seen as offering an explicit justification for inequality, while moderates are seen as maintaining class rule by removing some of the harsher features of capitalism without tackling the root cause of inequality, which is the private ownership of economic assets. Radicals wish to redistribute power, wealth and opportunity so that any remaining inequalities are based on 'social justice' rather than luck, inheritance or power. In contrast to the individualist view that freedom and equality are incompatible, radicals believe that freedom is incomplete without social, economic and political equality. In contrast to moderates, they advocate strongly redistributive and egalitarian policies.

Conclusion. The division of political opinion into individualist, moderate and radical ideologies throws useful light on the differing views about the relationship between the economy, the state and society. When considered together with party origins, interests and supporters, the division makes it easier to understand the motivation behind the proposals and actions of politicians and governments. Politicians are not, however, influenced only by political ideas or a desire to favour particular interests or classes. When in government, they encounter unexpected problems which may deflect them from their declared intentions. Politicians' reactions to the problems will, nevertheless, be influenced by their ideologies. In 1976, for example, when faced by the demands of the City and the International Monetary Fund (IMF) during a financial crisis, moderate Labour ministers reluctantly accepted the imposition of monetarist policies. A minority on the Left, however, saw the crisis as an occasion for much more radical policies. The actions of governments are, therefore, shaped, but not dictated, by circumstances, for circumstances may be interpreted in different ways.

9.3 Business interests and governments

9.3.1 The pressure group system

Elections and political parties allow citizens to exercise influence over governments. Citizens also influence governments by joining or supporting pressure groups, which are organizations seeking to influence governments but which, unlike political parties, do not wish to take over the formal power of government.

A distinction is often drawn between **interest** groups and **cause** groups. The former, such as trade unions, employers' associations or the Royal Automobile Clubs (RACs) represent the sectional and material interests of their members. Cause groups, such as the Royal Society for the Prevention of Cruelty to Animals (RSPCA) or Friends of the Earth, form around shared attitudes, rather than material interests. Although the distinction between the aims of groups may become blurred in some cases, for instance, trade unions have broad social and political as well as material aims, it is nevertheless a useful distinction. Differences in aims are often associated with differences in group methods and ultimate effectiveness.

In seeking to influence governments, pressure groups may work through public opinion, Parliament, political parties or direct consultation with government. Frequently they work through several of these channels.

Through mounting public campaigns, groups hope to put pressure upon governments by securing widespread public and media support. Campaigns using demonstrations, public meetings, advertising and so on are, however, difficult and expensive to sustain, especially for cause groups which rely mainly on unpaid workers. They are, moreover, a very indirect way of influencing governments.

The influence which Parliament and political parties have over government policy makes them natural targets for pressure groups. Groups frequently ply Members of Parliament of all parties with circulars and information presenting their views. Many business interests also retain MPs as parliamentary advisors or spokesmen. Most groups, however, avoid a close identification with any one party because of the internal disagreement this can cause, and because the group may be penalized when another party is in government. The links which unions and businessmen have with the major parties nevertheless ensure that these economic interests are represented at the highest levels of party policymaking. They are well placed to secure legislation they favour. The value of parliamentary and party representation is, however, limited, as most MPs feel their first loyalty is to party rather than pressure group.

For cause groups, these public and parliamentary channels may be essential. In contrast, interest groups use them mainly in support of direct consultations with ministers and officials, or if consultations have been unsuccessful. Prominent businessmen and trade unionists often have personal access to ministers and officials. Much contact between economic interests and government is, however, conducted through 'peak' organizations, like the Trades Union Congress (TUC), Confederation of British Industry (CBI) or Retail Consortium. Peak organizations can represent the views of a whole business interest and employ full-time staff to maintain regular contact with their Civil Service counterparts.

Direct consultations between pressure groups and government take many forms. Draft proposals of government policy will normally be circulated to key interest groups, consultations will continue as proposals pass through Parliament and groups will be consulted about the impact of policies. Groups are also likely to be involved in administering policies on behalf of government. It has also become increasingly common for people representing business interests to become part-time members of government-appointed bodies. These may be advisory bodies, such as Royal Commissions; consultative bodies, such as the National Economic Development Council (NEDC); or executive bodies, such as the Manpower Services Commission (MSC). Such institutionalization of contact between groups and government, complements, but does not displace, the extensive informal consultation which takes place.

9.3.2 The representation of economic interests

Most accounts of how economic interests exert political influence tend to emphasize the importance of organized and visible pressure groups, such as unions or employers' associations. This is, however, far too narrow a focus. Some interests, such as the City, are not organized as a visible pressure group but nevertheless possess great influence. The influence springs from the normal workings of the economic system rather than from overt political action. This section is, therefore, structured around an examination of the major economic interests in Britain, rather than the particular organizations which represent them. This approach makes it easier to identify the hidden as well as the overt influence which they possess.

There are three major economic interests which need to be considered: **Capital**, **Labour** and **Consumers**. The distinction between Capital, those who own and control enterprises, and Labour, those whose income derives from selling their labour, is fairly clear. Consumers may, however, in their roles as producers, also be part of Labour or Capital, although the basis of their political influence is different. In this section, the political methods and relative influence of these three key interests will be examined.

Capital. The interests of Capital are not homogeneous nor are they represented by a single pressure group. For instance, there is frequently conflict between the political demands of small, national and multinational firms. Of particular political importance is the contrast between industry and the City. The latter traditionally favours *laissez-faire* and monetarist policies. Such policies, however, frequently harm industry in the short term. Although opposed to government intervention in general, therefore, industrialists may welcome particular interventions which benefit industry, such as subsidies or import controls. Whatever the differences between industry and finance, however, they have a common interest in preserving an economic system based on private property and the pursuit of profit.

There are important differences between the political methods of industry and the City. Industrialists have long been organized in trade associations, although of late, the importance of peak organizations, such as the CBI and Retail Consortium, has increased. Such organizations operate through the normal pressure group channels. Their economic importance ensures such groups have direct access to government, and contacts are often institutionalized by representation on various government agencies.

The interests of the City are not primarily represented through such obvious pressure group methods. Although many banks have now joined the CBI, the City is not really organized as a formal or visible pressure goup. Yet, as argued in Chapter 5, the City is probably the most important economic interest shaping government economic policy. Its influence is brought to bear informally through the Bank of England which expresses, and usually supports, the City's views in government circles. The City also expresses its opinions to the government through the financial markets. Financiers may express their dislike of government policies, especially those of Labour governments, by selling sterling and precipitating a crisis on the foreign exchanges, as in 1967 and 1976.

In the Consensus view the need to 'retain the confidence' of industry and finance, including international bodies such as the IMF, acts as a valuable discipline on governments. Governments, especially Labour governments, are forced to moderate their policies and are prevented from imposing too much of an economic burden on the productive private sector.

Those with a Conflict view, however, claim that Capital, both industrial and financial, has a 'hidden veto' over government policy. This stems from the private ownership and control of key areas of the economy. Governments are therefore dependent on 'business confidence', and even Labour governments are forced to adopt policies acceptable to business, even though they may be the opposite of those in the Party's election manifesto.

Conflict theorists also claim that Capital has other advantages denied to Labour and Consumers. First, Capital is said to have great 'cultural' power, that is the power to shape people's ideas and beliefs. It has succeeded in presenting private enterprise, inequality and a Consensus view of society as normal and benevolent, when in fact, they benefit mainly the rich. In gaining widespread acceptance of its views through education, the media and the apparently democratic political system, Capital limits political debate to safe issues. Radicalism, on the other hand, is portrayed as extremist, abnormal and disruptive.

Those with a Consensus perspective deny these claims. Freedom of expression and the independence of the mass media are said to ensure wide and open debate. A variety of opinions, including many critical of Capital, are put before the public who are free to choose those which seem most sensible.

The power of Capital is also said by radicals to be bolstered by the class, educational and family links between those in the higher reaches of industry, the City and the state. The continued dominance of a public school and Oxbridge-educated elite obtains in most branches of the state, notably the Judiciary, the Armed Forces and the Civil Service. Such personal links do not mean that the state slavishly follows business opinion. In the Conflict view, however, they ensure easier access to government by businessmen and increase the likelihood that government and businessmen will have a common outlook. The practice of former Civil Servants and ministers, including those in Labour governments, moving into top jobs in industry and the City is seen as disturbing evidence of this common outlook. These close links and common outlook also mean that any radical ministers will encounter opposition within the state from Civil Servants, the Judiciary and possibly the Armed Forces.

It is suggested in answer to these charges that the importance of common family, class and educational background is exaggerated, for they do not determine attitudes and behaviour at work. Instead, the professional integrity and impartiality of public servants are asserted. It is admitted, for instance, that Civil Servants are not necessarily passive and may hold strong opinions in conflict with those of ministers. Conflict may also arise from Civil Servants fulfilling their professional duty to give often unpalatable advice to radical ministers. Despite these areas of potential conflict, however, it is claimed that Civil Servants normally give loyal service to the government of the day. Similar claims are made that judges interpret and apply the laws of the land impartially regardless of political considerations. In the Consensus view, therefore, the advantages of Capital are not significant and do not guarantee its domination of government.

Labour. Whilst the power of Capital stems from its control over major areas of the economy, the basis of the political power of Labour is both narrower and more visible. It is based on the essentially negative power of trade unions to disrupt the economy and undermine governments' key economic policies, especially incomes policies.

The political stance of trade unions is, however, ambivalent. Their links with the Labour Party give them a continuing interest in politics and special influence over Labour policy. Yet, British unions have been far more concerned with securing immediate economic gains through collective bargaining with employers than with working through political channels to change society.

In advancing their interests politically, unions have never limited themselves to party political channels. They have also used public campaigns, demonstrations and selective strikes, notably when opposing either wage controls or anti-union legislation. With these important exceptions, when they believed their basic rights were threatened, unions have usually avoided open conflict with governments. Indeed, like industrialists, they have become increasingly drawn into direct contact with governments and have secured representation on many government-appointed bodies.

Radicals believe that the unions have failed to use their full power of disruption to secure political or economic change. They have shown excessive respect for constitutional procedures, and too narrow a concentration on collective bargaining, both of which play into the hands of Capital. Unions are therefore seen by radicals as passive and essentially negative in their attitude to politics, only exerting themselves when their basic rights are challenged.

On the Right, by contrast, union power is seen as excessive and in need of legal restriction. Increasing union militancy and a willing-ness to 'hold the country to ransom' by strike action are said to have greatly increased union power in the 1970s, which reached a peak during the period of the Social Contract. Awareness of union power imposes a powerful constraint on government policy. Union influence is said to be especially strong on Labour governments, but even Conservative governments are believed to adapt their policies to retain union cooperation. Moderates are less concerned to curb the power of unions by legal restriction. Instead, they wish to secure the cooperation of unions in determining and implementing government policy.

Consumers. Consumers are those who use the goods and services of both public and private sectors. Just as their economic power comes from the ability to withdraw custom so their political power comes from the ability to withdraw votes. Consequently, groups such as old age pensioners or those with mortgages are courted by the major parties. Pressure from consumers accounts at least partly for the expansion of public services and regulation of business. As has been suggested, however, the electoral and party systems are very crude methods of registering public wishes.

Consumer groups did not come into national prominence until the 1950s, when the Consumers' Association, which now has 600 000 subscribers to its magazine *Which?*, was created. Consumer groups, however, lack the resources and sanctions of producer groups such as unions and employers. Significantly, consumers are more likely to have to resort to campaigns and parliamentary lobbying as they rarely have the access to governments possessed by producer groups. In recent years, there has, however, been a spontaneous growth of groups representing the consumer interest. Some groups, such as the Campaign for Real Ale, have been launched by consumers themselves. Others are cause groups organized on behalf of groups such as the aged or the homeless. A feature of many of these newer cause groups is their increasing willingness to use disruptive action to express their views. In some cases local authorities have undertaken public participation exercises, notably in town planning, to discover the views of consumers and the community, while in the National Health Service (NHS) and nationalized industries there are organizations representing consumers created by statute.

In the Consensus view consumers already have considerable power through the mechanisms of the market and political democracy. Nevertheless, the growth of the consumer movement is generally welcomed as securing a better balance between producers, consumers and the state, as long as consumers adopt peaceful and constitutional methods. In the Conflict view, however, business interests are dominant in society and attempts to sponsor consumer participation in the public services are usually viewed as token gestures which give little real power to consumers. Consequently, aggressive consumer and community groups are welcomed as means of mobilizing the people against the combined power of business and its allies in the state.

9.3.3 Evaluation

In general, those with a Consensus view believe that competition between the multiplicity of groups and interests ensures a reasonable dispersion of political power. Unions may be too powerful but they are not all-powerful and must do battle with many other groups and interests. The world of pressure groups and interests looks very different from a Conflict perspective. Capital is seen as the dominant interest, possessing advantages denied to other interests. Although power appears to be dispersed to the Consensus theorist, it appears highly concentrated to the Conflict theorist. Moreover, the exercise of power by businessmen is not only seen in overt pressure group activity. It is also inherent in the ownership and control of economic assets which are said to give them immense, if hidden, power over the state.

9.4 The state and business

9.4.1 The growth of the state

The emergence, since the mid-nineteenth century, of a mass electorate, political parties and pressure groups has greatly altered the political environment of business. The same period has also seen the growth of the state.

The state in the nineteenth century has often been labelled a 'nightwatchman state'. Its main function was the maintenance of order and protection of property. It did not regulate the economy nor provide extensive social services. Such a state matched well with the prevailing individualist ideology of *laissez-faire* and self-help. Over the last century, however, the extended responsibilities of the state have led to a massive growth in the size of the public sector and of public spending. The acceptance by postwar governments of a responsibility for managing the economy and the extension of the public enterprise and social service sectors shows how far the state has moved from a purely nightwatchman role. *Figure 9.1* shows these changes over the century, as measured by rising public spending, and *Figure 9.2* highlights the recent growth of the public sector, as measured by its rising labour force.

As previous chapters have indicated, it is easy to identify the factors associated with the growth of the state but less so to determine their relative importance. Moreover, there are strong political disagreements about the origins and significance of this growth.

Some commentators stress the importance of economic growth, experienced by all Western nations, as a contributor to state expansion. Rising private spending, for instance on cars, brings about rising public spending on roads, traffic regulation and so on. It is also said that the rising tax revenues, generated automatically by economic growth, finance a growth in the public sector without recourse to unpopular higher taxation. Nor should the importance of the interwar depression or the state's success in managing the economy in wartime be overlooked.

Political and social trends also contributed to the growth of the public sector. The rise of the Labour movement, competition between the parties and among pressure groups all served to push up public spending. So too did pressure within the government from public officials committed to the extension of their services. Moreover, public attitudes have changed over the century. The population has grown and people have gradually increased their expectations of the level of state provision.

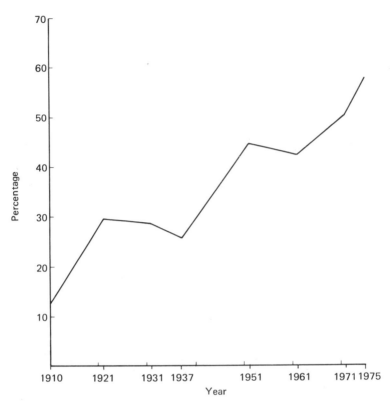

Figure 9.1 The growth of the state—public expenditure as percentage of GNP

Source: Gough, Ian (1979). *The Political Economy of the Welfare State*, p. 77, Macmillan, London

There are, however, strong disagreements about whether the nature of the state has changed substantially. Consensus theorists believe the state has changed fundamentally. It is said to have assumed a positive responsibility to promote economic and social welfare through intervention in society. Britain is now claimed to be a welfare state with a mixed, rather than a capitalist, economy. By contrast, those with a Conflict view believe that the state still works to further the interests of the middle and upper classes. These classes are said to make greater use of many public services. They also gain indirectly from government economic and social policies which secure working class support for the present economic order. To Conflict theorists, therefore, the state has not changed fundamentally. Its main function is still seen as the maintenance of order and the protection of property, although this is achieved through far greater intervention in society than in the nineteenth century.

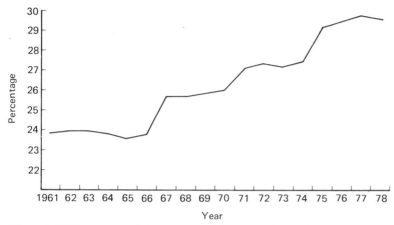

Figure 9.2 The growth of the state—public sector share of total employed labour force

Sources: *Economic Progress Report*, February 1980, HMSO; Semple, Matt, 'Employment in the public and private sectors 1961–1978,' *Economic Trends*, November 1979, No. 313, HMSO

9.4.2 The institutions of the state

The state possesses unique powers of legislation, taxation and coercion. In the UK these powers are vested in Parliament from which all public authorities derive their powers, although EEC membership creates new sources of legal authority outside the country.

Three broad types of state or public authority can be distinguished. First, there are central government departments controlled by ministers and staffed by Civil Servants. Secondly, there are local authorities controlled by councillors and staffed by local government officials. Thirdly, there are state agencies created to carry out a single or narrow group of functions or services and controlled by appointed boards. The existence of so many public authorities means that the modern state is not only very large but is increasingly complex, heterogeneous and potentially fragmented.

Central government. The Cabinet has been the major decision-making body in central government since the monarch ceased to dominate government in the eighteenth and early nineteenth centuries. Since then the legal supremacy of Parliament has been undisputed, and the power of the Cabinet rests on its control over Parliament, especially the House of Commons.

The government is normally drawn from the majority party in Parliament and consists of about 20 senior politicians, who are members of the Cabinet, and about 80 junior ministers. All ministers are accountable to Parliament, individually, for the performance of their departments, and collectively, for the overall performance of the government. They must appear in Parliament to explain and defend government policy, and they need the continued support of Parliament to remain in office. If, as happened to Labour in 1979, a government loses a vote of confidence in the Commons, it is expected to resign. More normally, a government with a majority governs with the approval of Parliament and gets its legislative proposals endorsed. The government has, however, to pay a price for this approval. It must subject itself to the daily criticism and scrutiny by MPs, in questions and debates, and to more detailed investigations by all-party Select Committees of MPs which specialize in particular areas, such as foreign affairs or industry and trade.

The Opposition maintains a constant campaign to embarrass the government and put its own ideas before the public. In addition, ministers are subject to private lobbying from their own MPs whose votes keep them in office. When the government lacks a majority, as from 1974 to 1979, the power of Parliament is correspondingly increased. Despite the government's normal control over Parliament, and the tendency to decide policies in consultation with economic interests, it is still argued, especially by those with a Consensus view, that Parliament is far from powerless and helps to keep the government in touch with public opinion.

Within the government, the Cabinet, under the leadership of the Prime Minister, has the key responsibility for deciding government policy and coordinating the work of the departments and other public authorities. The position of the Prime Minister as party leader and chief publicist of government policy provides the incumbent with unique opportunities to influence the direction of that policy. So too does the Prime Minister's power of patronage, which includes the selection of ministers, the chairmen and members of many public authorities and the right to recommend individuals for Honours. The Prime Minister also possesses the normal powers of any chairman, to influence the agenda and conduct of meetings, and to determine the use of various committees and subcommittees to investigate particular matters. The use of these powers will vary according to the incumbent's personality, style of leadership and standing in the party and country. Although these powers put the Prime Minister in a unique position, their use is circumscribed by the need for all Prime Ministers to retain party and Cabinet unity.

The structure and operations of the Cabinet have evolved considerably over this century to meet the increasing burden of work. During most of the period of the 'nightwatchman state' the government was small enough for all ministers to be members of the Cabinet. So limited was the work of the Cabinet, moreover, that all key decisions could be determined by the full Cabinet in a fairly informal manner. Since then, the scope of government has increased as has the number of ministers so that a ministerial hierarchy has emerged and only the most senior ministers are in the Cabinet. In addition, more of the Cabinet's work is now conducted in small committees of ministers, usually supported by parallel committees of Civil Servants. At any one time there are probably between 20 and 25 standing Cabinet Committees dealing with the recurrent issues, such as foreign affairs or economic policy. A number of *ad hoc* committees will also be in existence, dealing with particular matters of topical interest. The full Cabinet, usually meeting twice a week, still, however, retains the final power of government approval.

As a result of these developments the full Cabinet is not primarily concerned with initiating policy or establishing overall priorities, with the exception of the annual exercise to determine public spending plans. Instead, it is mainly concerned with responding to crises outside government, reacting to initiatives from the departments and acting as the final court of appeal on interdepartmental disputes. Consequently, central government departments operate with a good deal of freedom, especially in non-financial matters.

Central government departments or ministries vary considerably in the type of work they do. They can be divided into those with direct responsibilities for public services, such as Defence, Education and Health; those, namely the Cabinet Office, the Treasury and the Civil Service Department, which coordinate respectively overall policy, finance and personnel; and those ministries for Scotland, Wales and Northern Ireland responsible for a wide range of services in those areas.

In carrying out their responsibilities, departments come into regular contact with the representatives of various interests. The Department of Employment, for instance, works closely with unions and employers, the Department of Education and Science works with local authorities and teacher's unions and the Department of Transport works with road hauliers, motorists' organizations, motor manufacturers and so on. It frequently happens that the relationship becomes so close that departments become spokesmen for such interests rather than considering the broader public interest. When this happens the specialization of departments and the pressure of interests make government more fragmented.

It is a distinctive feature of British central government that it rarely executes its own policies. With a few notable exceptions, such as defence, taxation and social security, the implementation and often the determination, of government policy is decentralized to other public authorities. This decentralization takes place on either a **territorial** or a **functional** basis. Where there is territorial decentralization, power is vested in public authorities responsible for particular areas of the country. Local government is the main form of territorial decentralization and the primary reason given for such decentralization is the democratic justification that local people should be allowed to govern themselves. Functional decentralization involves vesting responsibility for services in specially created state agencies, established separately from central and local government control. The nationalized industries and NHS are examples of functional decentralization, and the main justification given for this type of decentralization is essentially managerial. It is claimed that certain public services need to be insulated from political interference to allow the maximum managerial freedom.

Local government. There are just over 400 county and district authorities in England and Wales, each under the control of elected councillors. This has been the fastest growing part of the public sector since the war and by the late 1970s UK local authority expenditure amounted to almost 20% of the Gross National Product (GNP) and its labour force 12% of the national labour force.

These authorities must, however, operate within powers given by Parliament and under the supervision of central government departments. Moreover, local authorities are heavily dependent on central government grants, which constitute half of their income, and have borne the brunt of public spending cuts since the late 1970s. They are not, however, mere agents of central government. They have an independent source of income from the rates and possess considerable discretion in the provision of services, as shown by the variations in levels of services among authorities.

Local government services in England are provided both by County and District Councils, although the division of services between them varies according to the type of authority. In the Metropolitan Counties, which cover the six major conurbations outside London, most of the services, especially the social services, are provided by the Districts, which may be large cities such as Birmingham or Manchester. In the Shire Counties, which cover the rest of England, most services are provided by the County rather than the Districts, which are often relatively small. London has a unique structure somewhere between the Shire and Metropolitan models.

Local authorities are essentially providers of social services. Many local government services nevertheless affect commercial enterprises directly or indirectly. Firms benefit from the provision of economic infrastructure, such as roads, and from the protection provided by the fire and police services. In addition, local authorities frequently try to stimulate the local economy by encouraging firms to set up or expand within their boundaries. Sites, buildings and in some cases loans at attractive rates may be offered to firms to create or protect local jobs. Local authorities also have important regulatory duties in areas such as Planning, Environmental Health and Consumer Protection which constrain businesses.

Control over local authority services is exercised by committees of councillors responsible for particular services, although ultimate power rests with the full Council. As in central government strong tendencies towards fragmentation and departmental rivalry exist. Moreover, local authorities need to coordinate their services with those of many other state authorities. Local authorities are not the only state authorities operating locally, for in addition there are local offices of central government departments and an increasing number of functional agencies.

State agencies. Many public services or functions are delegated to state agencies created by statute outside central or local government control. They have been variously named '*ad hoc* authorities', 'Quangos' (quasi autonomous national governmental organizations) or simply 'fringe bodies'. Unlike local authorities, such agencies are under the control of people appointed by ministers rather than elected by the people. They are usually responsible for a single function, such as gas, or a narrow range of functions, such as water, sewage and sewerage, compared with the more multipurpose local authorities.

Estimates of the number of such specialist agencies vary, from around 300 in official estimates, to three times that number in unofficial estimates based on wider definitions. Whatever estimates are used, there has clearly been a proliferation in recent years of government-appointed commissions, committees, panels, boards and so on. They have been used for a variety of executive, advisory and consultative purposes. The archetypal appointed state agency is the public corporation structure used to manage the nationalized industries. These agencies have also been used for:

- providing public services on a non-commercial basis, as do the NHS and the Manpower Services Commission (MSC),
- regulating business activity, as do the Monopolies and Mergers Commission or various Pay and Price Commissions,
- promoting business activity, as do the National Enterprise Board (NEB) and various Research Councils.

The traditional justification given for this alternative to central or local government provision of services is the need to insulate certain services from political, especially party political, interference. It is claimed that the degree of autonomy granted is more conducive to efficiency, initiative and impartiality than would be control by national or local government. At the same time, it is claimed that ultimate answerability to minister and Parliament is ensured.

A more recent justification is the need to involve key interests in making and implementing government policy. By appointing representatives of affected interests to the boards of state agencies, governments aim to secure their expertise and cooperation. The changes affecting the Department of Employment in the 1970s illustrate both of these justifications. Many of the Department's functions have been delegated to agencies such as the Health and Safety Commission, the MSC, and the Advisory Conciliation and Arbitration Service. In each case the new agencies are removed from the direct control of ministers and established under boards made up of representatives of the CBI, TUC and other interests.

Even further removed from direct political control are those organizations operating in the private sector and under Company Law, but which are wholly, or partly, owned by the state. The mixed enterprise, or shared public and private ownership, is not new. The number of such mixed enterprises has, however, grown considerably since the 1960s. This has occurred partly through the state's acquisition of 'lame duck' companies, partly through the entrepreneurial activities of the NEB created by Labour, and partly through the 'privatization' policy of the Conservatives. Such mixed enterprises are not government agencies but nevertheless fall within the ambit of the state.

The proliferation of state agencies and fringe bodies has not been without its critics. It is claimed, most notably in the case of the nationalized industries, that an acceptable balance between independence and accountability has not been found. On a more ideological level right-wing critics condemn the proliferation of state agencies as a hidden growth of the state. It is claimed that their expenditure and performance are not properly scrutinized by Parliament. Moreover, critics on both the Right and the Left maintain that the power of ministerial appointment, officially estimated in 1978 as 8000 paid and 25 000 unpaid appointments, is open to considerable abuse. Despite attempts by the Conservatives to abolish some of these bodies on coming to office in 1979, with 290 being abolished during the first year of office, some ministers created new ones to cope with ever-increasing demands on their departments.

9.4.3 State regulation of business

Much of the work of state authorities is directed towards regulating and influencing business. Even individualist supporters of the free market accept that some degree of government intervention is necessary. To moderates and radicals of course, there is need for much greater intervention.

As previous chapters have shown, modern governments have used an extensive range of instruments to influence economic events. In this section the range of economic instruments will be reviewed and classified and the relationship between economic instruments and political ideas explained. The range of economic instruments is set out in *Figure 9.3*. At one extreme public ownership and economic planning permit direct and detailed control over business. At the other extreme monetary and fiscal policy provide only very indirect and general control. They affect the economic conditions in which firms operate but firms are still free to make their own decisions in the light of market conditions. Between these two extremes governments influence businesses through various forms of persuasion, promotion and regulation.

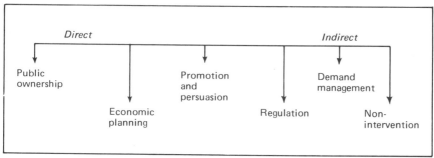

Figure 9.3 State regulation of business

In choosing among these alternative economic instruments, governments also make political choices. They are opting for more or less government control over economic life. The choice will be determined by circumstances to some extent, but it will also reflect the individualist, moderate or radical leanings of politicians and officials. In describing each form of economic control, therefore, it is necessary to point out its political as well as its economic implications.

Non-intervention. Non-intervention has its roots in *laissez-faire* economics and the political ideology of individualism. Today, of course, no government can disengage itself from the economy so completely as its nineteenth century predecessors—if only because of the scale and economic importance of the public sector. Contemporary non-intervention therefore means that government intervention is by general rules rather than specific involvements.

Since the late 1970s this has been attempted by reliance on monetarist policies and the abandonment of interventionist industrial, pay and prices policies. In principle, monetarism is the most indirect, limited and non-discriminatory form of state regulation of the economy. By creating the right conditions for the free market to operate, monetarists claim there is no need for governments to resort to more interventionist economic instruments.

Demand management. Demand management has its roots in Keynesian economics and is an essential element in the strategy of the moderates. It involves governments in managing the economy by manipulating the aggregate level of demand. By altering levels of government spending and taxation, demand is expanded or restrained as appropriate to counter the effects of slumps and booms. Government intervention is therefore limited to a few key economic variables. Governments do not directly control the decisions taken by firms, and the free market system is not abandoned but merely guided by Keynesian techniques of 'fine tuning'.

Although demand management is the antithesis of monetarism they are alike in two important respects. First, they are both very general, indirect and non-discriminatory forms of economic intervention. Secondly, they both accept the need for a strong independent private sector.

Throughout the 1950s, demand management was the dominant form of economic intervention. Since the mid-1960s, and especially in the 1970s, Keynesian techniques have proved inadequate for dealing with problems of low growth, inflation and even unemployment. Nevertheless, Keynesianism has a strong political appeal to moderates as a middle way between unrestrained free enterprise and socialist planning. The limitations of demand management, however, have forced moderates to use more direct and discriminating economic controls.

Regulation. Both monetarists and Keynesians willingly supplement general interventions with some detailed controls over business activity. Even in the mid-nineteenth century regulations were imposed on business, for example, the Factory Acts (1833–1853) governing hours and conditions of work. Since then, the extent of regulation and inspection of business activity has grown enormously. Today, there are extensive regulations defining the rights and duties of investors, employers, employees and consumers. There have also been attempts to legislate for the social and environmental consequences of business activity, for instance, in the control of atmospheric pollution.

Many of these regulations create an orderly framework necessary for the conduct of businesses and are acceptable to individualists. Centrist-dominated governments, however, have gone much further and regulated central economic matters such as wages, dividends and prices, often creating special state agencies for the purpose.

The large body of government regulations affecting business clearly imposes limits on the use of private property. These limits are nevertheless quite compatible with a free enterprise or mixed economy. Alternatively, regulations could be extended as part of the creation of a planned economy. It is this latter possibility of 'creeping socialism' which frequently makes discussions of technical regulations matters of great political controversy.

Promotion and persuasion. Although regulation of business may be very effective it is essentially a negative and restrictive form of economic intervention. In order to achieve many policy objectives, therefore, governments intervene positively to provide support for specific economic activities. For example, policies to encourage investment or exports depend largely on governments' powers of promotion and persuasion. Governments have to work with and through the private sector in order to achieve their objectives. Not surprisingly, therefore, postwar governments have usually sought the cooperation of unions, employers and other interests, and close relations frequently develop between sponsoring ministries and their clients.

Governments also provide direct assistance to business. Many public services, such as road-building and water supply, are geared closely, though not exclusively, to promoting general economic development. Direct financial assistance to firms, through investment allowances, grants and subsidies, may however, allow the government to be even more discriminatory. Financial assistance has been given to promote particular regions, such as Scotland; industries, such as agriculture; firms, such as British Leyland (BL); or projects, such as Concorde.

Governments have used promotion and persuasion in a piecemeal fashion since the 1930s. In the 1960s and 1970s, however, reliance on them increased significantly as governments sought to stimulate the supply side of the economy left untouched by demand management. Many of these policies are anathema to individualists for they are believed to distort the workings of the market. Both moderates and radicals, however, see them as supporting and smoothing the operations of the market, although they disagree over whether this is desirable.

Economic planning. Economic planning is central to the antimarket ideology of radicals. In a fully planned economy the state sets output targets for industries and directs labour, capital and materials to achieve them. Britain came nearest to this from 1940 to 1945 when the economy was planned to support the war effort. In peacetime, such planning has been considered by individualists and centrists alike as incompatible with private enterprise and political freedom.

It is, nevertheless, possible to distinguish two forms of economic planning which were adopted in the 1960s and 1970s, although neither was pursued vigorously or consistently. One form of planning, favoured by moderates, involves the government, employers and unions reaching agreement on the future development of the economy, and on the policies to be adopted to stimulate the growth of the economy as a whole, or of particular sectors. The agreement is not binding and does not involve any direct government control over firms. It is expected, however, that by reducing uncertainty about the future, business confidence and investment will be stimulated. The other form of planning, favoured by radicals, involves increased state control over business, so that investment can be directed and planned to achieve an industrial revival. This is to be achieved through extending public ownership and imposing planning agreements on large companies covering their major policies. As a means of regulating business, therefore, economic planning becomes scarcely distinguishable from public ownership.

Public ownership. This is the most direct and complete form of state control of business. Although Conservative governments have nationalized concerns, they have done so reluctantly. The Labour Party, however, has been explicitly committed to public ownership of the 'means of production, distribution and exchange' since 1918. Despite this, Labour governments have been reluctant to nationalize profitable companies. To radicals, public ownership still has a special appeal. They view it as the only effective way to regulate business and to redistribute power and wealth. All other forms of economic control leave untouched the private ownership of economic assets which radicals see as the cause of social injustice and economic decline. In contrast to individualists, who are totally opposed to public ownership, and moderates, who are pragmatic about it, believing each case should be considered on its merits, radicals advocate large-scale nationalization.

Conclusion. There are several general comments which can be made about this range of instruments available for the government to regulate business and the economy. First, although described separately, they are often used in combination, or in succession. The industrial policies of the Labour governments of the 1970s, for instance, involved a combination of public ownership, planning, promotion and persuasion, and regulation. Conversely, one objective may be pursued using a succession of different instruments. For instance, pay restraint has been attempted at different times using regulation, persuasion and monetary controls. Secondly, forms of intervention are likely to change with circumstances. The displacement of Keynesianism by monetarism as the economic doctrine followed by governments in the 1970s demonstrates the point. Finally, it must be remembered that the selection of a form of intervention is not like selecting the right tool from a toolbox. Each form of intervention carries with it political as well as economic consequences. Governments' political ends will therefore influence the economic instruments they select. In particular, the selection will reflect beliefs about the desirability of private ownership of economic assets and of state intervention in the economy. It is appropriate, therefore, to finish this chapter by summarizing the different views about the nature of the state and the political role of business.

9.5 Evaluation: democracy or class rule?

There are clearly divergent views about the relationship between business, the state and society, which reflect the Conflict and Consensus views. In the Consensus view, political power is widely, though not equally, distributed. Civil and political rights, such as freedom of speech, association and movement, and the right to vote are available to all. Elections and political parties, whatever their deficiencies, ensure the views of the public are expressed. Particular interests, such as labour, capital and the consumers, have their say, as do a multitude of interest and cause groups. It is argued, therefore, that there is a free play of political forces, and no one interest or class can dominate. Britain may have been controlled by a capitalist and landowning upper class in the nineteenth century, but now, it is argued, the interests of all are safeguarded. It is believed, moreover, that the aspirations of these various classes and interests are compatible. Politics should, therefore, be conducted peacefully through democratic channels and in a spirit of compromise and bargaining.

The state has a crucial role to play in the Consensus perspective. It is the guardian of the national interest against powerful sectional forces. It arbitrates between conflicting groups, regulates business and economic interests, and redistributes power and wealth through taxation, public ownership and the social services. Consensus theorists frequently argue that particular interests, whether labour or capital, are allowed too much licence by the state, but overall they are optimistic that the state has sufficient powers to curb them. Furthermore, the multiplicity of state organizations is claimed to increase the responsiveness of the state. By fragmenting state power in this way checks and balances are built into the state machinery. No element of the state can dominate all others and the variety of elements provides many points at which the public can apply pressure. In the Consensus view, therefore, the state is kept responsive to the needs and wishes of the people.

From the Conflict perspective things look very different. Political power is believed to be concentrated in the hands of a dominant capitalist class. This class, which consists of those who own and control industry and finance, has the support of the more prosperous professions and many senior public officials who are linked to it by family and educational background and a shared outlook. Its ideas are the dominant ideas in society and the need to 'retain business confidence' bolsters its control over the state. The existence of democratic rights is not insignificant and has forced the capitalist class to make concessions to working people. To Conflict theorists, however, the conclusive evidence of the power of capital is the continuation of capitalism despite its injustices and inefficiencies.

The state is not, therefore, seen as neutral in the Conflict view. It is rather seen as sustaining the capitalist system. It is seen as removing the worst excess of capitalism in order to defuse radical working class opposition to the existing order of society. Whatever party is in government, Conflict theorists believe that the capitalist class is the dominant influence on its policy. While in the Consensus view, therefore, the state is believed to control business, in the Conflict view the opposite is thought to be the case. Moreover, the dispersal of power between many state authorities is seen as far less significant than in the Consensus view. Because the state as a whole works to sustain capitalism the exact distribution of power within it is seen as relatively unimportant.

Although Conflict theorists are critical of the present operations of the state, they believe that its power could be used to alter society radically. This would involve not only large-scale public ownership to undermine capitalist ownership but also an intensification of the class struggle through trade union, as well as political, action.

It is not possible to evaluate two such different views on the political and governmental context of business exclusively by recourse to empirical evidence. Not only is evidence interpreted differently but, more significantly, their supporters appeal to different evidence. The Consensus view rests heavily on what is visible: civil rights, elections, parties, organized interests, the growth of the state and so on. On such evidence it is claimed Britain has changed fundamentally since the nineteenth century and, whatever its deficiencies, is a democratic society. In contrast, the Conflict view rests on what is not visible and what does not change: hidden biases, invisible power and the continued existence of capitalism. Clearly, the selection and investigation of relevant facts, as well as their interpretation are strongly influenced by the perspectives on society which people hold.

Guide to further reading
General

Miliband, Ralph (1973). *The State in Capitalist Society*, Quartet Books, London. An excellent Marxist account of British politics.
Rose, Richard (1980). *Politics in England: An Interpretation for the 1980s*. Faber and Faber, London. A useful text on most aspects of British politics.
Sked, Alan and Cook, Chris (1979). *Post War Britain, A Political History*, Penguin Books, London.
Smith, Brian (1976). *Policy Making in British Government*, Martin Robertson, London. Part IV summarizes succinctly the two perspectives on politics and government.

Subsections
9.2.1–9.2.3

Pulzer, P. G. J. (1975). *Political Representation and Elections in Britain*, 3rd edn, Allen and Unwin, London. Summarizes much of the evidence and argument about elections, voting and the party system.
Rose, Richard (1974). *The Problem of Party Government*, Macmillan, London. Covers most aspects of parties in detail.

9.2.4

Barker, Rodney (1978). *Political Ideas in Modern Britain*, Methuen, London. Chapter 7 provides a summary of recent political ideas.
Castles, F. G., Murray, D. J., Potter, D. C. and Pollitt, C. J. (Eds) (1976). *Decisions, Organisations and Society*, 2nd edn, Penguin Books, London. The extracts from Anthony Crosland in Reading 19 represent the Social Democratic ideology within the Labour Party.
Holland, Stuart (1975). *The Socialist Challenge*, Quartet Books, London. Chapter 1 is a useful introduction to the Radical ideology in the Labour Party.
Behrens, Robert (1980). *The Conservative Party from Heath to Thatcher*, Saxon House, Farnborough. Reviews the major divisions within the contemporary Conservative Party.

9.3

Richardson, J. J. and Jordan, A. G. (1979). *Governing Under Pressure*, Martin Robertson, Oxford. A general review of pressure groups.
Keegan, W. and Pennant-Rea, R. (1979). *Who Runs the Economy?* Temple Smith, London. Chapter 4 gives a good journalistic account of the major interests influencing economic policy.
Westergaard, John and Resler, Henrietta (1976). *Class in a Capitalist Society.* Penguin Books, London. Part 3 provides a Marxist account of inequality of political power and of the nature of the state.

9.4

Kempner, T., Macmillan, K. and Hawkins, K. (1976) *Business and Society*, Penguin Books, London. Chapter 4 analyses the increasing state control over business activity.
Thomas, R. E. (1976). *The Government of Business*, Philip Allan, Oxford. Most aspects of relations between government and business are covered in Chapters 2, 7 and 8.
Gough, Ian (1979). *The Political Economy of the Welfare State*, Macmillan, London. Chapter 3 outlines a Marxist view of the state.
Smith, Trevor (1979). *The Politics of the Corporate Economy*, Martin Robertson, Oxford. Part II provides an interesting interpretation of changing relations between economics and politics and between industry and the state.
Ridley, F. F. (Ed.) (1979). *Government and Administration in Western Europe*, Martin Robertson, Oxford. Chapter 2 by D. R. S. Steel provides an excellent summary of the administrative institutions of the state.
Stanyer, Jeffrey and Smith, Brian (1976). *Administering Britain*, Fontana/Collins, Glasgow. A standard text on the administrative institutions of the state.
Maunder, Peter (Ed.) (1979). *Government Intervention in the Developed Economy*, Croom Helm, London. Chapter 5 reviews government intervention in British industry.

Exercises

Review questions

1. What are the main features of the British two-party system?
2. Describe the consequences of the two-party system for the economy as seen from the Consensus and Conflict viewpoints.
3. What are the major similarities and differences between the origins and supporters of the two main parties?
4. Summarize the major elements of the individualist, moderate or centrist, and radical ideologies.
5. Give examples of economic and social policies pursued by postwar governments which reflect individualist, moderate and radical beliefs.
6. What are the differences between interest and cause groups? Give examples of each type.
7. Compare and contrast the methods used by capital, labour and consumers to advance their interests.
8. Explain the views of individualists, moderates and radicals concerning the relative power of these three economic interests.
9. Summarize the major economic, social and political reasons advanced for the growth of the state.
10. Outline the Consensus and Conflict views of whether the nature of the state has changed fundamentally.

11. Describe the relationship between Parliament and the government, and between the Cabinet and the Prime Minister.
12. Distinguish between the two forms of decentralization used in Britain and give reasons for their use.
13. Briefly summarize the major instruments available to the government to regulate business activity.
14. Which of these instruments are most favoured by individualists, moderates and radicals respectively, and for what reasons?

Application and investigation

1. Use *Table 9.1* on the results of the 1979 General Election, and the results from recent elections in a local authority, to assess the claim that the British electoral system is unfair. How would the major parties reply to this claim?
2. Compare and contrast the policies of the major parties as stated in their manifesto at either a local or a national election. To what extent do these policies seem intended to appeal to particular classes or interests?
3. Use a recent government *White Paper on Public Expenditure* to itemize the major spending programmes and their relative size, and to outline the relative size of the current and capital expenditure of central departments, local authorities and other public authorities.
4. Explain the reasons given by those with a Consensus view for their belief that Britain is a democratic society, and by those with a Conflict view for their belief that Britain is still ruled by a dominant class.

Projects

1. When presenting his budget the Chancellor of the Exchequer usually takes the opportunity to state the overall economic strategy of the government. Outline the economic strategy presented to justify any recent budget, and assess the extent to which it shows the influence of ideological, party political and electoral considerations. How will the budget affect the various classes described in Chapter 8?
2. Select a particular business organization or sector, and assess the extent to which it is assisted and constrained by the state. Describe the methods by which the organization or sector might be able to influence public authorities at local and national levels.

Chapter 10

The legal context of business

10.1 The legal system

All forms of behaviour are governed by rules. Mostly these rules are followed quite unconsciously and the fact that they exist only becomes clear when someone breaks them. Custom, convention and tradition are the sources of the rules that govern most behaviour in everyday life. There are certain rules, however, which are made and enforced by the state. These rules make up the law.

The activities of individuals and organizations take place within a legal framework. In all spheres of existence, from family life to the dealings of business, laws exist to regulate behaviour and to resolve conflicts. The legal system is made up of all these laws along with the organizations and individuals involved in administering them, such as the legal profession, the courts and the police.

The nature of the legal system is the subject of a debate which falls clearly into the Conflict and Consensus frameworks. Broadly speaking, the Consensus view holds that the legal system is a set of rules which works to the benefit of all by preventing unacceptable behaviour and by allowing disputes to be settled fairly. The Conflict view sees the legal system as a further means by which the dominant class maintains its hold over society. Justice is seen as taking second place to class interest.

The basis of legal control is the law. It is usual to make a distinction between criminal and civil law. Criminal law defines those actions which the state will punish by fines or imprisonment. Criminal proceedings are normally brought by the police and proof of the offence has to be 'beyond reasonable doubt'. Civil law lays down rules for the conduct of relations between persons or organizations. Civil proceedings are normally brought by private parties and proof has to be 'on the balance of probabilities'. Successful civil proceedings normally end in awards of damages or an order that the defendant behave in a given fashion.

The development of both the criminal and the civil law has tended to reflect wider changes in society. The emergence of Britain as a trading and commercial maritime power in the seventeenth and eighteenth centuries, and the growth of industrial capitalism in the nineteenth century, were associated with changes in law to regulate new patterns of economic behaviour. The increased demands made on the civil courts by the growth of trade and industry in the last century led to their reorganization in 1875. The breakdown of self-sufficient local communities and the increases in disorder and crime that this involved led to the development of new forms of enforcement of criminal law through the establishment of a modern full-time police force, starting in London in 1829. Industrialization also led to the expansion of new branches of law involving such matters as consumer protection and safety at work. Law and the legal system generally is, therefore, continuously adapting to new economic and social circumstances.

Laws may be made in a number of ways. Acts of Parliament, or statutes, are the major source of law. These documents are normally drafted by lawyers in supposedly precise legal language and are often difficult for the layman to understand. Acts of Parliament can also confer on a minister the right to make detailed regulations himself on the basis of general principles laid down in an Act. These regulations are known as Statutory Instruments and they have the same force as statute law. In practice the meaning of laws often has to be decided by judges, and this may lead to unexpected interpretations of the law.

In Britain, another source of law is the common law. The common law consists of the set of rules of behaviour and procedure established over the centuries by the decisions of judges in particular cases. The doctrine of precedent is important here. It involves deciding cases on the same principles as those governing decisions in past comparable cases. In certain cases, where the application of the law as it stands would lead to injustice, a branch of law known as equity may be employed. Equity has evolved along with the common law, on the basis of precedent and judicial decisions. It permits principles of justice and fairness to be applied where the strict letter of the law would lead to injustice. Statute law takes precedence over common law and equity where there is a clash.

The European Communities Act of 1972 introduced a new source of law in that certain laws of the Communities are now binding in the UK, while Community law can be enforced in the European Court. In theory, where there is conflict with national laws, the Community laws take precedence. In practice, since the Community has no apparatus for enforcing its laws, this may not happen.

The law is administered through the courts. Civil and criminal justice are administered through separate systems or jurisdictions. The courts in each system form a hierarchy with appeals from lower courts dealt with by higher courts. In both jurisdictions the supreme court is the Judicial Committee of the House of Lords. The court system and the judges who preside in different courts, are shown in *Figure 10.1*. As well as the courts shown, there is an Employment Appeal Tribunal and a

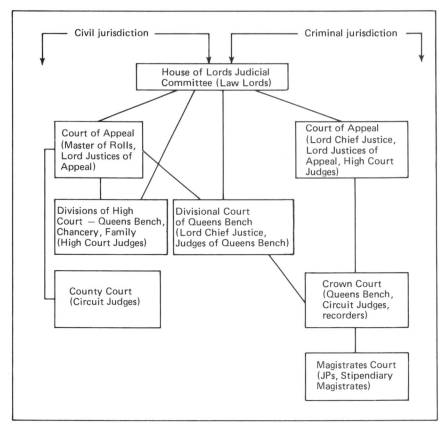

Figure 10.1 The Judiciary and the court system

Restrictive Practices Court, both of which are equivalent in status to the High Court. In addition to the courts there are a great many tribunals which exist to resolve disputes of particular kinds. For example, aggrieved claimants of Supplementary Benefit can apply to a tribunal, while disputes concerning dismissal or redundancy payments may be heard by an Industrial Tribunal. Tribunals generally operate informally and fairly cheaply. While they are not courts in the ordinary sense, appeal to the courts on points of law is often permitted.

Judges for most courts are full-time appointments. However, Recorders in Crown Courts are normally barristers or solicitors who sit for a few weeks each year. There are also about 18 000 Justices of the Peace (JPs) who are not qualified lawyers and who work part-time. As well as manning the courts, judges are often chosen to chair Royal Commissions of Enquiry and Departmental Committees set up by the government to investigate particular issues.

The legal profession is divided into two branches: barristers and solicitors. There are less than 3000 barristers. They have a monopoly on appearing in cases in higher courts and they have their own system of training. Judges are appointed from among their ranks. The court appearances of solicitors, of whom there are about 24 000, are largely restricted to Magistrates Courts. However, they have a near monopoly of 'conveyancing', the legal aspect of house sales, and this, along with giving advice and drafting legal documents, makes up most of their work. Most lawyers, whether solicitors or barristers, work in private practice but a growing minority are employed as legal advisors in business and public sector organizations.

10.2 The legal regulation of business

A number of key aspects of business operation are regulated by law. Many of the relationships which organizations of all kinds enter into, with employees, suppliers, owners and customers, are subject to legal control. Laws governing the following areas relevant to business will be discussed in this chapter.

- The ownership and control of organizations.
- Dealings between organizations.
- Competition and monopoly.
- The employment of labour.
- The rights of consumers.
- Crimes against property.

10.2.1 The ownership and control of organizations

Such organizations as privately owned businesses, trade unions and nationalized industries, have a legal existence which enables them to enter into legally regulated relationships and to be held liable for breaches of the law. The legal existence of organizations is governed by a series of Acts of Parliament. Firms in the private sector are formed in accordance with the Companies or Partnership Acts, which define the rules under which companies may be registered. All companies have to deposit a Memorandum of Association with the Registrar of Companies which states the name, objectives and amount and type of share capital. In addition, each firm will have Articles of Association, which lay down the duties of directors. While the law allows for a number of different types of company, the most important categories are the public company, whose shares may be freely traded, and the private company, whose shares are not freely traded. Shares themselves are simply the form in which the company is owned, and shareholders are therefore the owners of the company. Many small businesses exist as partnerships. Partners not only jointly own the business, but, unlike the shareholders of companies, they have a legal right to engage in its management.

The legal status of organizations in the public enterprise and social services sector is rather different. The legal existence of every nationalized industry and social service is brought about by its own Act of Parliament which lays down rules governing its structure and control. Indeed, in the public sector the extent of legal control is considerable. Under the principle of *ultra vires*, public sector organizations may not normally undertake any activity unless this is specifically approved by the law. This differs from the legal situation of companies that may undertake any lawful action in pursuit of their objectives. The law also defines the legal basis of other organizations. The structure and control of trade unions is regulated under the Trade Unions and Labour Relations Act 1974. Cooperatives have to be registered with the Registrar of Friendly Societies.

10.2.2 Dealings between organizations

In order to carry out the purposes for which they exist, organizations have to make agreements with others which commit the two parties to a predetermined course of behaviour. Agreements have to be made ensuring a supply of the necessary resources of labour and materials and, in addition, customers have to agree to the terms on which the organization provides its goods or services. These agreements are covered by the law of 'contract'.

The law of contract has largely evolved as part of the common law rather than being created by Act of Parliament. It defines the conditions under which agreements requiring two parties to behave in a specified manner may be legally enforced as a valid contract. For a contract to be valid the following conditions must normally apply.

- The terms of the transaction must have been clear, agreed and intended to be legally binding.
- The parties must have the legal right to meet the terms and the agreement must be in a legally accepted form.
- Each side must be providing something for the other.

If one party fails to fulfill his terms of a contract the other may seek damages or an injunction requiring enforcement, through the civil courts. The law of contract allows individuals and organizations to engage in courses of action, the success of which depend on others behaving in a predetermined fashion. Without the law of contract, many of the exchanges underlying the complexity of modern economic life would be too risky to undertake.

10.2.3 Competition and monopoly

The law is extensively involved in regulating the behaviour of firms where competition within an industry is hampered by the small number of firms or by agreements between firms not to compete. The principle of outlawing behaviour that was 'in restraint of trade' grew up within the common law. However, in practice, this mainly served as a legal means of restricting the activities of trade unions. Monopoly or near-monopoly in the supply of goods was not effectively controlled by this area of law. Modern attempts to control monopoly date from 1948. At the present time the Monopolies and Mergers Commission is able to examine cases of monopoly referred to it by the Director-General of Fair Trading.

The Restrictive Trade Practices Act 1956 set up machinery for enforcing the laws against monopoly and restrictive practices. All agreements between firms restricting price, level of output and conditions of sale have to be reported to the Director-General of Fair Trading. If firms wish to continue with the practice they have to argue their case in the Court of Restrictive Practices. So far as retailing is concerned, the Resale Prices Act 1964 outlawed the practice of manufacturers forcing retailers to sell their products at a fixed price. This accelerated the trend towards greater competition in retailing. All restrictive trade practices which prevent, restrict or distort competition are also outlawed by Article 85 of the Treaty of Rome.

10.2.4 The employment of labour

In the last 200 or so years, an extensive body of legislation has appeared which regulates various aspects of the relationship between employers and employees. This relationship is a contract and the common law rules described above apply. In addition, other features of common law apply, such as the duty of employers to behave 'reasonably and responsibly' and the duty of employees to obey 'reasonable instructions' and to give 'loyal and faithful service'. However, the main part of the legal framework is made up of statute law. In this section the following aspects of law are examined: employment law, trade unions, health and safety, discrimination, dismissal and redundancy, and wage regulation.

Since the repeal of the anticombination Acts in 1824, there have been numerous Acts of Parliament and judicial decisions which have affected the legal status and rights of trade unions. Considerable political controversy has occurred over the circumstances in which strikes can lawfully take place and over the legality of various support actions such as picketing, 'blacking' and sympathy strikes. Unions have immunity from civil actions for damages for breach of contract where these occur in furtherance of a trade dispute. The Employment Act 1980, however, imposes some restrictions on the right to picket. Conservative governments have generally attempted to limit the rights of unions, whereas Labour administrations have tended to maintain or expand them. In recent years there has been considerable argument about the 'closed shop', under which all employees in a given workplace are required to join a union. Conservative Party policy is against this practice and the 1980 legislation contains provisions designed to weaken it.

So far as the terms of employment are concerned, all manual workers are entitled to be paid in cash and all employees must be given a written statement outlining the terms of their employment giving details of pay, hours, holidays, sick-pay and notice.

The law is closely concerned with health and safety at work. Various Acts control such matters as sanitary facilities, ventilation and the use of dangerous machinery, although the degree of legal control and the aspects of work covered, vary according to the type of workplace. An overall legislative framework for health and safety is provided by the Health and Safety at Work Act 1974. This Act covers all places of work and it gives the government the right to make regulations concerning health and safety. A Health and Safety Commission exists to oversee the purpose of the Act and there is a Health and Safety Executive to enforce the law. Health and Safety Inspectors can enter any place of work and prohibit or demand improvements in dangerous practices.

Employers are forbidden to discriminate on the grounds of colour, nationality, religion, sex or marital status, under the Race Relations Act 1976 and the Sex Discrimination Act 1975. All cases under these Acts have to be brought by either the Equal Opportunities Commission, in cases of sex discrimination, or the Commission for Racial Equality, in cases of race discrimination. The Commissions may issue non-discrimination notices enforceable by a County Court injunction.

The Equal Pay Act 1970 which came into force in 1975 lays a duty on employers to treat men and women identically in the matter of wages, hours, sick-pay and holidays, where they do 'work of a broadly similar nature' in the same firm, or any other firm owned by the same company.

In addition, contracts of employment have to specify equal pay. This law also complies with Article 119 of the Treaty of Rome.

The Employment Protection (Consolidation) Act 1978 defines the maternity rights of employed women. Under its provisions women may not be dismissed because of pregnancy. In addition, women are allowed to return to their jobs at any time up to 29 weeks after confinement.

The 1978 Act also lays down regulations concerning reasons for dismissal and length of notice. Workers have the right to claim damages for unfair dismissal at an Industrial Tribunal if they are dismissed unfairly. This provision does not apply to members of the Police or the Armed Forces, or anyone who has been with an employer for less than a year. Employers may dismiss workers for misconduct such as disobedience, negligence or incompetence. Where an employee is found to have been unfairly dismissed he will be entitled to compensation and possibly re-instatement. It is also possible for employees to sue employers for the common law offence of 'wrongful dismissal', normally where proper notice has not been given. Workers who are made redundant are entitled to a redundancy payment related to their length of service as long as they have at least 2 years continuous service with an employer.

In certain industries, especially where the workforce is fragmented and unionism is weak, wage levels are determined by a Wages Council set up under the Wages Councils Acts of 1959 and 1979. Since 1975 these Councils may determine not only wages, but also holidays and other terms of employment. Some fifty Wages Councils exist. Employers who do not meet the conditions laid down by the relevant Wages Council are liable to criminal prosecution and to the payment of arrears of wages.

10.2.5 The rights of consumers

The law also gives certain rights to consumers. The common law tradition assumes that it is up to the recipient to ensure that he is getting a fair deal when he obtains goods and services from the public or private sector. Under the common law, consumers injured by faults in goods caused by the negligence of the supplier may obtain damages. In addition, there are a number of Acts covering food products which specify standards of quality. Further legal controls are found in the Fair Trading Act of 1973, which gives the government power, on the recommendation of the Director-General of Fair Trading, to prohibit attempts by suppliers to limit their liability to consumers. The law also regulates information given about goods to be supplied. The Trade Descriptions Act of 1968 makes a 'false trade description' a criminal offence.

The terms on which credit is granted to consumers are controlled by the Consumer Credit Act 1974. Regulations specify the form to be taken by credit agreements and require that the true rate of interest payable is revealed. A 'cooling-off' period of 5 days exists during which the consumer may cancel the agreement where the contract was not signed on the premises of the supplier.

The legal rights of consumers of social services vary considerably. Recipients of National Insurance or Supplementary Benefits may appeal to a tribunal if they believe their entitlement to benefit is not being met. Quasilegal remedies of this kind do not, however, exist for recipients of education and health care. However, Complaints Commissioners, or 'Ombudsmen', have been established to deal with complaints of maladministration in some areas not covered by tribunals, such as health and local government.

10.2.6 Crimes against property

The area of criminal law most relevant to the operation of organizations concerns offences against property. This area of law is relevant because it allows legal penalties to be imposed on those who violate the laws protecting the ownership of property. The Theft Act of 1968 defines theft as the 'dishonest appropriation of property belonging to another with the intention of permanently depriving the owner of it'. Other offences related to theft are: burglary, where theft follows illegal entry; robbery, where theft involves violence; obtaining property or pecuniary advantage by deception; and blackmail.

10.3 Business and the violation of law

The previous section has described relevant aspects of the legal framework. However, not everyone obeys the law and the existence of behaviour violating both civil and criminal law is an important factor in the operation of business. The impact of this unlawful behaviour is influenced by the extent to which laws are enforced and the ways in which the courts treat offenders.

There is some disagreement about the overall effects of legal regulation. One view, which fits the Consensus model, sees the legal system as a neutral mechanism for resolving disputes and regulating behaviour, which works to the benefit of everyone as consumers, producers and citizens. The alternative Conflict view portrays the law and its workings as a device by which the interests of a wealthy and powerful minority are furthered at the expense of the majority of members of society.

10.3.1 Employers, employees and the law

These opposing viewpoints are brought out very clearly in relation to much of the legal regulation of business discussed above. The effectiveness of the laws regulating monopoly and restrictive practices, health and safety, sex and race discrimination, equal pay, minimun wages set by wage boards, and the sale of goods, is a matter of debate. While the law as it stands appears to make clear demands on employers, those adopting a Conflict view suggest that, in practice, loopholes can often be found. In the case of equal pay, for example, this may involve using 'job-evaluation' exercises to define jobs done by women as different and less skilled than those done by men. In addition, it is argued that the extent to which these laws are violated may be very substantial. A study of 200 firms in South-East England in the early 1960s showed 3800 violations of factory legislation in a 5-year period. However, only 1.5% of the violations led to prosecution. Where prosecution is successful, penalties are usually light—an average of £50 in fines in the above cases. A similar pattern is found in relation to other laws affecting employers. Consensus theorists accept the claim made by the authorities that their main aim is to ensure voluntary compliance with the law, not to prosecute offenders. An alternative explanation from the Conflict standpoint is that laws imposing obligations on employers are unlikely to be vigorously enforced by a legal system that is dominated by upper class values. Conflict theorists argue that various laws which appear to protect the rights of employees are ineffective because low penalties give employers an incentive to ignore or evade them, and to treat the chance of prosecution as an acceptable risk to be paid for the benefits of violation. Those taking a Consensus view suggest otherwise, claiming that employees are, if anything, over-protected by a mass of legislation which bears heavily on employers.

Disagreement also exists about the legal position of trade unions. The Consensus view tends to be that their rights are well established and possibly excessive, particularly in relation to their immunity from actions for damages resulting from breach of contract where this is caused by a trade dispute. The opposing view suggests that even where the law appears to grant rights to unions, the judges frequently interpret the law in such a way as to work to their disadvantage.

10.3.2 Business and crimes against property

Organizations are obviously a major focus of crimes carried out for material gain simply because they contain many potential sources of illegal reward in the form of money, goods and financial assets. Various forms of theft, from payroll robberies at one extreme, to petty shoplifting at the other, are a factor that many organizations have to take account of. Indeed, guarding the security of the property of organizations is itself a major business. These forms of theft are usually, but not always, carried out by non-employees. In many organizations, however, considerable amounts of property are removed by those who work for the organization. These crimes can take many forms. Bribery is not uncommon at the higher level of business and may involve considerable sums when large orders are at stake. Fraud may take place whenever the possibility exists of illegally diverting funds. In many organizations theft by employees is common. In retailing it is sometimes referred to as 'stock shrinkage'. Many office workers regularly violate the Theft Act by making unauthorized phone calls, removing office stationary and, if they have the opportunity, falsifying claims for expenses. In some industries a certain level of employee crime is expected and even approved, being viewed as 'perks'. In catering, staff are known to add to their incomes by defrauding customers, thus supplementing the low wages they are paid, at little cost to their employers.

Many offences are committed where financial obligations to the state are involved. At one extreme, some multinational corporations (MNCs) engage in accounting practices of dubious legality, in order to minimize profits made in countries where company taxes are high. At the other extreme, many small businesses evade value added tax (VAT) through the use of cash transactions which are not recorded for tax purposes. Income taxes are also evaded on a very large scale, particularly by the self-employed, but also to a smaller extent by employed people who supplement their incomes by doing jobs 'on the side'. Individuals may also obtain funds to which they are not entitled by defrauding the Department of Health and Social Security (DHSS).

The value of incomes from illegal activities, along with the value of legally made incomes concealed for the purposes of tax evasion, is probably substantial. The term 'black economy' has been used to refer to all those legal transactions which remain unrecorded in the official statistics. This is thought to amount to at least 5% of the Gross National Product (GNP). The Secretary of the Inland Revenue Staff Federation has estimated that, as a result, some £5 billion are lost each year in unpaid income tax. Large-scale illegal business operations also exist, of which the largest is probably the provision of drugs for non-medical use. No one knows the total value of incomes in cash and kind from crime, but it is bound to be substantial, and of course, it is also likely to remain untaxed.

The way in which the laws concerning crimes against property are enforced is again the subject of controversy. Organizations do not always institute proceedings against those who have misappropriated their property. Retailers, especially those catering for high-status customers, frequently avoid prosecuting shoplifters. Many cases of fraud by employees are dealt with internally without involving the law. The Inland Revenue frequently fail to prosecute those who have not met their VAT or income tax obligations, preferring to negotiate payment rather than seek prosecution. Those taking a Consensus view argue that in many cases recourse to criminal prosecution is unnecessary. Where the offender is not a professional criminal, where the offence is considered to be a minor one, or where restitution is promptly offered, then it may be better not to involve the law. Those taking a Conflict view see this as evidence of class bias. They suggest that where middle or upper class offenders are concerned discretion is often exercised to their advantage, while working class offenders are heavily penalized for offences involving small sums. They cite the case of those caught defrauding the DHSS who, unlike those engaged in tax frauds, are very likely to be prosecuted. They also point to the fact that middle or upper class employees obtaining illegal 'perks' are rarely prosecuted, whereas workers who engage in 'pilfering' often are. The Consensus view disputes this evidence of class bias and suggests that where decisions not to prosecute are made, this is done on the basis of the merits of the case.

10.4 Evaluation

The modern legal system is an instrument of great complexity that has a considerable impact on the overall workings of the economic and social system. The function performed by the law is disputed. According to the Consensus view the body of law in existence broadly has the effect of ensuring equality of rights and gives everyone the opportunity to redress legitimate grievances. It also throws the full weight of disapproval and punishment against those whose behaviour violates the common interest in the security of people and property. The Conflict view suggests, on the contrary, that the body of law tends to favour the interests of the wealthy and the powerful and that where the law gives rights to ordinary people, they are often difficult to enforce. It suggests that the law provides legal means for the wealthy to maintain their economic privileges at the expense of other people.

The legal system is not a technical process whereby known violations are automatically followed by legal proceedings consisting of a mechanical application of legal principles. On the contrary, at every stage, from complaint, to prosecution, to judicial decision, choices are made about how to proceed. The law in practice may turn out to be very different to the law in theory.

The Consensus view holds that in general those responsible for enforcing the law, such as the Police, use their discretion fairly and that in their turn the courts offer everyone, in both civil and criminal proceedings, a fair chance to state their case, and a guarantee of a fair decision by the Judiciary. Adequate safeguards against police and judicial misbehaviour are seen to exist in the form of a complaints procedure and the right to appeal.

The Conflict view holds that enforcement agencies are more likely to prosecute working class offenders and that 'white collar' crimes committed by middle and upper class people are seldom prosecuted. The Judiciary is seen as drawn from a socially exclusive minority and to be likely to favour the interests of employers or landlords rather than employees and tenants. The conduct of legal proceedings themselves is seen as favouring the well-off, who can hire the best lawyers. The safeguards of complaint and appeal are viewed as largely ineffective.

A plausible case can be made out for either of these views, depending on the selection and weighting of evidence and argument. Whatever view is taken, however, there is no doubt that the legal structure has a considerable impact on modern business. The law, indeed, forms one of the major constraints within which business has to operate.

Guide to further reading

General

Freeman, M. D. A. (1974). *The Legal Structure*, Longman, London. A good sociological account of how the legal system works, but without much material specifically related to business.

Smith, Peter (1978). *Law and the Legal System*, Sweet and Maxwell, London. A useful description by a lawyer, of the law, especially as it relates to business.

Zander, Michael (1976). *Inequalities before the Law* (D302 Patterns of Inequality, Unit 14), Open University, Milton Keynes. A brief critical account of how the legal system works.

Subsections

10.2.3

HMSO (1978). *A Review of Monopoly and Merger Policy* (Command 7198), HMSO, London.

10.2.6

Titchiner, Lynne and Winyard, Anne (1975). *Consumers' Rights*, Arrow, London. This is written from the consumers' point of view. Chapters 1–3 are useful.

10.3

Chapman D. (1968). *Sociology and the Stereotype of the Criminal*, Tavistock, London. Very useful on class differences in the enforcement of law.

10.4

Griffith, J. A. G. (1977). *The Politics of the Judiciary*, Fontana/Collins, Glasgow. A rare account of the law from a Conflict perspective. Chapter 4 is useful on industrial relations.

Exercises

Review questions

1. What are the various sources of law?
2. What are the differences between solicitors and barristers?
3. What does *ultra vires* mean?
4. Why is the law of contract important to business?
5. How is antimonopoly legislation enforced?
6. What are the legal rights of working women?
7. How does the law protect consumers?
8. What is the 'black economy'?

Application and investigation

1. Discuss any recent proposals to change the law related to business. try and relate these proposals to the political ideology of the Government.
2. Attend the local Magistrates, County or Crown Court. Write a report on how fair the proceedings seemed, using the viewpoints discussed in this chapter.

Projects

1. Examine the arguments and evidence in favour of the view that there is one law for the rich and one law for the poor.
2. Find out how the law relating to labour works in any business organization with which you are familiar. Assess the view that these laws make excessive and unreasonable demands on employers.

Chapter 11

The international context of business

The British economy is one of the most 'open' of all developed economies. A third of the Gross National Product (GNP) is exported, some of the largest multinational corporations (MNCs) are based in Britain and London remains a major centre of world finance. At the same time the UK imports most of its raw materials, half of its food and a growing proportion of manufactured goods, and it has experienced large-scale foreign investment in its industry. British prosperity is therefore profoundly affected by changes in the international environment.

In this chapter the main economic relations between Britain and the rest of the world will be examined. The emphasis will be upon the movement of economic resources in the forms of goods and services (trade), capital and technology (investment and aid) and labour (migration). Descriptions of these movements are by no means value-free. They involve complex economic, social and political judgements. The Conflict and Consensus perspectives used to analyse the domestic context are also therefore of value in analysing the international context of business.

11.1 Britain and the changing international economy

The history of Britain's position in the world this century has been one of relative decline. In 1900 Britain was still the predominant economic and political power because of its early industrialization and large empire. By the 1980s the position has been transformed. No longer an imperial power and with an ailing economy, Britain tries to secure its interests through cooperation with other Western nations in organizations like the North Atlantic Treaty Organization (NATO) and the European Economic Community (EEC). Despite its relative decline, therefore, Britain remains an important member of the community of advanced capitalist nations. As such Britain's world position is strongly influenced by the tensions between the Communist East and the Capitalist West, and between the developed North and the developing South.

The Cold War between East and West has been one of the major features of the postwar world. Although primarily a political and military confrontation it has profound implications for business. It has directly stimulated the arms and aerospace industries, for instance. In addition, overseas trade, aid and investment have all been used by governments as instruments of Cold War foreign policy. Trade embargoes, for example, have been employed against Communist countries, while aid and investment have been channelled to pro-Western countries in Africa and Asia. The Cold War also strengthened the ties between Western countries. NATO was created as a military alliance to meet the perceived threat from the East. Similarly, schemes for European economic union were put forward to strengthen the West in its confrontation with the East.

The end of World War II also saw a concerted attempt to set up a new framework for international economic affairs between Western nations. The Bretton Woods agreement of 1944 established a system of fixed exchange rates between the various currencies, and created the International Monetary Fund (IMF) with powers to advance short-term credits to help nations overcome balance-of-payments problems. The International Bank for Reconstruction and Development, commonly known as the World Bank, was created at the same time to provide investment for longer term economic development. Finally, the General Agreement on Tariffs and Trade (GATT) led to successive mutual reductions in tariffs right up to the 1980s. This framework was based on a mixture of economic ideas. *Laissez-faire* theories lay behind the promotion of free trade through GATT, while the establishment of fixed exchange rates showed a more interventionist, Keynesian approach to economic management.

This framework played an important part in allowing the economic expansion of the 1950s and 1960s to develop. It provided order and stability which encouraged the growth of international trade and investment. It was sustained, moreover, by American economic and military power. By the 1970s, however, this whole system was in a state of disorder. Among Western nations trade rivalries emerged between the USA, the EEC countries and Japan, and the USA lost its previous dominance. The system was also disrupted by the rise of the Organization of Petroleum Exporting Countries (OPEC) and the emergence of the 'Third World', or the South.

Third World countries, many of which are former colonies, are mostly non-aligned between East and West. Their distinguishing feature, with the exception of a few oil-rich states, is their relative poverty. The South has three-quarters of world population but only a fifth of world income.

The economies of Third World countries are inextricably linked with those of the developed, and especially Western, countries. Developed countries look to the Third World for raw materials, markets, investment opportunities and cheap labour. In return, the South relies heavily on aid and investment from the North. This interdependence is especially noticeable in the case of the UK with its extensive trade and investment links with the Commonwealth. Commonwealth countries also receive the bulk of British overseas aid and there has been extensive migration between the UK and the Commonwealth.

In recent years the Third World has become increasingly organized and assertive as the gap in incomes between rich and poor nations has grown. Radical Third World leaders, such as Nyerere of Tanzania and Manley of Jamaica, have been particularly critical of what they see as **neocolonialism**: that is, continued Western control over their economies despite the granting of formal independence. Western governments, Western multinationals and Western-dominated international financial institutions, notably the IMF, are all criticized for exploiting poor countries. Third World countries have become increasingly united in presenting their case for international economic reform. In particular, they want a greater role in the management of international organizations, such as the IMF, and firmer international actions to redistribute the world's wealth. The developed countries, especially the UK, are unwilling to accept such a major change in the international economic order, claiming that the working of market forces will benefit all nations, and that slowing development in the North will harm, rather than help, the South. Relations between North and South consequently remain tense.

The most important change in the South in the 1970s was the emergence of OPEC. In the context of rising world demand and static reserves, the oil-exporting countries were able to form a cartel which successfully raised the price of oil throughout the 1970's. For many Third World countries OPEC's action provides a model of how to challenge the power of the West, whilst for Western countries it emphasizes their vulnerability to united action by Third World countries.

The formation and development of OPEC was but one example of the increasing significance of international economic organizations and trade blocs. Another instance is the EEC, while the European Free Trade Area (EFTA), comprising many non-EEC countries, and the Latin American Free Trade Area (LAFTA) are other examples of trade blocs. The Communist states of Eastern Europe have their own organization, Comecon. The growth of such international and regional trade blocs reflects the growing interdependence of nations, but also shows that many nations have lost confidence in the international economy. Britain's reduced power together with its status as a major trading nation gives it a special interest in such developments which help to reduce some of the uncertainty in the world.

The importance of international organizations, such as the United Nations (UN) and NATO, which deal with the 'high politics' of diplomatic and military matters, has long been recognized. International relations are not, however, limited to such 'high politics'. They increasingly involve 'low politics', such as economic, technological, social and cultural matters. National policies are increasingly influenced by international agreements covering such matters. Indeed, throughout the postwar period, the Western international economic system has been based on international agreements and institutions such as the IMF, World Bank and GATT. Most international organizations are neither as global nor as controversial as these. They are frequently concerned with specialist matters, like the World Health Organization, and are commonly regional, like the European Broadcasting Union, rather than global. Their activities rarely excite public interest but their influence on British business and society is nonetheless real. Nowhere is this more so than in the case of the EEC. It started as a limited form of economic cooperation but is evolving towards an important supranational institution. Because membership of the EEC is one of the most important changes in the UK's international position and an attempt to reverse its decline, it is considered in some detail below.

11.2 Britain and the EEC

11.2.1 The development of the EEC

The impetus for European unity arose from the war and its aftermath. Western European governments saw economic unity as a means of preventing future wars between them and reviving their wartorn economies. The Cold War also encouraged these countries to stand together.

For the 'founding fathers' of European unity the ultimate objective was political union in a fully federal Europe. The methods of integration adopted by governments in the 1950s were, however, much less ambitious. Their approach was 'functional': integration was to be only in selected economic and technical areas or functions. In the longer term, however, some hoped, and others feared, that this approach might pave the way for further integration. Thus, limited and gradual economic and technical cooperations could pave the way for full economic and political integration. This process is illustrated by the way the European Coal and Steel Community (which created a free market in coal and iron and steel in 1962) paved the way for Euratom (which promotes nuclear research) and the broader EEC, which were created in 1957.

The EEC originally comprised six members, grew to nine in 1973 and is expected to grow further in the 1980s as Greece, Spain, Portugal and possibly Turkey secure membership. The economic philosophy of the EEC is essentially a free market philosophy. The central provisions of the Treaty of Rome (1957), which established the EEC, are intended to remove obstacles to the operation of the free market. Members are required to allow the free movement of goods and services, capital and labour within the Community and impose a common external tariff on imports from outside. In addition, members are to refrain from discriminatory practices, such as subsidizing domestic production, which would distort the operations of the market. This approach is justified as encouraging the most efficient use of resources within the Community to the ultimate benefit of all members.

Despite this overall commitment to a competitive market philosophy, there are some limited exceptions. The main exception is the Common Agricultural Policy (CAP) which absorbs 70% of the EEC budget. In contrast to the free market approach in other industries, agriculture is protected by subsidies, guaranteed prices and barriers to imports from outside the EEC. The objectives of the CAP are to make the Community self-sufficient in food, insulate Community prices from world fluctuations and raise the incomes of farmers through higher prices for farm produce. Although successful to some degree in achieving these objectives, it has been far less successful in restructuring and modernizing agriculture and has produced costly food surpluses. From the British point of view the CAP remains the most controversial aspect of the EEC.

The Community has few other common policies and none of such importance as the CAP. A Regional Development Fund and a Social Fund have been established, as has a common Investment Bank. There have also been attempts to agree common policies in areas such as energy, fishing and transport. More significantly, the Community has pledged itself to achieve economic and monetary union. In 1979 the European Monetary System was agreed, by which fixed exchange rates were established between members' currencies, although Britain did not join the system. If this is successful it would be a step towards full monetary union, with a common currency and central bank, and ultimately full integration of the economies and economic policies of member countries.

11.2.2 The effect of EEC membership

Initially the UK was unwilling to join the movement towards European unity. British politicians still saw the country as a world rather than a European power. Rather than join the EEC Britain set up EFTA, which was solely a free trade area with none of the EEC's supranational connotations. Since the 1960s, however, Britain's decline and the success of the EEC convinced UK governments of the necessity of membership. After initial rejection the UK was admitted to the Community in 1973, although transitional arrangements meant that the full impact of membership was not felt until 1978.

It was said at the time of British entry that there would be important economic and political advantages of membership. First, the UK would benefit immediately from freer trade and better access to a market of 250 million people. Secondly, industry would gain from the longer term 'dynamic effects' of membership. Increased competition and the incentive to investment provided by the larger markets would shake British industry out of its decline.

In government publications prior to entry it was, however, stressed that it was impossible to measure the economic effects of membership but that the political case for membership was strong. It was claimed that by joining a large and dynamic trade bloc the decline in Britain's political influence in the world would be reversed. The economic strength of the Community would put it almost on a par with the superpowers in influencing world events, especially economic events. In addition, membership would allow the UK to influence decision-making within the EEC both through participation in EEC institutions and by closer contact with member countries.

The impact of EEC membership on the UK has been the subject of intense and continuing controversy. The immediate economic conse-quences are widely agreed to have been adverse. First of all, there is a large transfer of resources from the UK to the rest of the Community through the Community budget. This arises for two reasons. First, Britain contributes a disproportionate amount into the budget because it imports extensively from outside the Community. The tariffs and levies on these imports are paid into the Community budget and by 1980 constituted almost a quarter of total Community revenue from these sources. Secondly, Britain gets a disproportionately small amount out of the budget because of its small agricultural sector. These two factors meant that by 1980 UK net budget contributions were officially estimated at over £1000 million a year, and likely to grow. Negotiations in 1980 led to a substantial reduction in British contributions in the early 1980s although Britain remains the second largest net contributor despite being one of the poorest Community members. To alter this position radically would seem to require both a major shift in the source of British imports and also in the pattern of EEC spending away from its present agricultural bias.

It was claimed prior to entry that the costs of the Community budget would be more than offset by the 'dynamic effects' on industry and trade. These gains have not, however, materialized. Since 1973 the balance of visible trade between Britain and the EEC has become strikingly worse as EEC companies have penetrated British markets. In contrast, Britain's balance of trade with the rest of the world has deteriorated much less. Furthermore, there has been a large outflow of capital from Britain to the EEC. Although many UK companies clearly benefit from access to the larger market the overall effect has been a loss of national income, estimated by the Cambridge Economic Policy Group at about £3000 millions a year. An additional cost of membership, estimated by several sources at about £300 million for 1980, is borne by the consumers who pay higher food prices than would be paid if Britain bought from the cheapest world sources.

Supporters of the free market argue that in the long run the UK will benefit from membership. Increased competition will raise productivity and efficiency and force Britain to specialize in those goods and services where it has a competitive advantage. In contrast, critics of the free market claim it will aggravate Britain's structural, regional and social problems. Investment, jobs and wealth will increasingly flow to the rich central areas of the Community, making peripheral areas progressively poorer. As it is one of the poorest and most peripheral members of the Community, these tendencies are a special threat to the UK. The threat is officially recognized in the allocation to the UK of over a quarter of all grants from the Regional Development and Social Funds. In addition, by 1979 the UK was receiving a third of all loans from the European Investment Bank (EIB), the Community's investment bank, notably to increase energy supplies. Nevertheless, this assistance is small in comparison to the scale of Britain's regional problems and also to EEC expenditure on agriculture. The assistance therefore moderates, but does not fundamentally alter, the competitive market orientation of the Community.

The argument about Community membership has never been wholly economic. Intense political argument centres upon the issue of national sovereignty, that is, Britain's right to manage its own affairs. Certainly membership involves accepting decisions taken by EEC institutions rather than the UK Parliament. In that sense it involves a clear loss of independence. Defenders of the Community argue, however, that no modern state can be truly independent. Indeed, EEC membership is claimed to make Britain less vulnerable to world conditions. As a trading bloc the Community exerts more influence than its members could separately. It can negotiate advantageous trading agreements with non-EEC countries, for instance, limiting imports such as textiles and steel. As an international organization it can also tackle common problems which face all members, such as the regulation of MNCs. Membership also allows the UK to influence Community decision-making and at times the policies of other member states. Finally, it is said that Britain's independence is still secured as it is free to leave the Community at any time.

Critics of the Community argue that the loss of sovereignty is crucial. The UK is forced to accept decisions of EEC institutions with the minimum of scrutiny by Parliament. As the Community moves towards monetary and economic union, pressure will increase on Britain to keep its monetary and fiscal policies in line with the rest of the Community. Radicals also stress that, while the Community's market philosophy aggravates UK regional and industrial problems, it makes it more difficult for UK governments to adopt interventionist policies to deal with these problems. In particular, import controls, restrictions on capital movements and other interventionist policies favoured by radicals would conflict with the very basis of the EEC.

Clearly, the division of opinion on Community membership remains wide, reflecting different perspectives on the world. Critics of the Community maintain that membership undermines Britain's national interests and sovereignty. In particular, radicals and trade unionists with a Conflict view of society stress the harmful effects of the Community's market philosophy. The supporters of membership, in government, business and the media, share a Consensus view of society. To them the Community and its market philosophy offer great opportunities for the UK. Sovereignty is not so much lost as pooled. The Community is not so much a constraint as a new opportunity. In the rest of the chapter other aspects of the international environment will be examined, especially trade, investment, aid and migration. As with the EEC it will be stressed that those with a Consensus view have a much more benevolent view of these transactions than do those with a Conflict view.

11.3 International trade

11.3.1 The development of international trade

Foreign trade laid many of the foundations of Britain's industrial revolution. Access to foreign markets and supplies of raw materials were vital for the early development of the factory-based textile industries. During the nineteenth century, Britain, the 'workshop of the world', was the principal supplier of manufactured goods to Europe and to the rest of the world, in exchange for food and raw materials.

From the 1840s, British governments espoused the doctrine of free trade: unrestricted, tariff-free imports and exports. This code was highly acceptable to British industry, whose technical prowess was then unmatched. It amounted to the demand that British industry be given unimpeded access to foreign markets.

Belief in free trade was shared by many European governments in the mid-nineteenth century. As industry began to develop in Europe and in America, however, foreign governments began to erect tariffs to protect their home markets from British competition. Another feature of the late nineteenth century was the passing of the technological lead from Britain to the USA and Germany, which were pioneering the new industries of electrical engineering, chemicals and motors.

In response to tariffs and increasing competition, Britain turned increasingly toward the Empire. At the turn of the century, British trade consisted predominantly of selling manufactured goods to the colonies in exchange for food and raw materials. Free trade, however, continued to be official policy, despite the demands by the Tariff Reform Movement that Britain should also put up protective tariffs.

The interwar Depression saw an intensification of protectionism in most countries. In 1931, Britain finally abandoned free trade for high tariffs. Trade with the Empire was, however, declared exempt from tariffs. This was known as Imperial Preference. As has been noted, the postwar world economy was characterized by a concerted attempt by Western nations to restore free trade and international economic cooperation. The IMF was established, as a source of credit for countries with payments deficits. Exchange rates between currencies were fixed, in the belief that this stability would assist trade. The GATT was also signed. In addition the USA supplied massive funds to Europe and other areas, through the Marshall Aid programme, to restore their economies.

World trade expanded rapidly during the 'long boom' of the 1950s and 1960s, especially trade between the developed economies. The trade of the Third World grew rather more slowly, as the prices of the basic commodities which they exported remained low. Certain Third World countries succeeded, however, in moving into manufacturing. These newly industrial countries', such as Taiwan or Hong Kong, offered the advantages of low wage rates and political stability which were frequently taken up by foreign-based MNCs.

11.3.2 Britain's international trade

Britain's share of this expanding world trade has been shrinking. Despite the success of service industries, such as banking, insurance and tourism, Britain has experienced persistent balance of payments deficits. The declining competitiveness of British industry is reflected in the encroachment of foreign competitors onto traditional British markets at home and overseas.

There have also been important changes in the composition and direction of Britain's overseas trade as *Figure 11.1* demonstrates. The

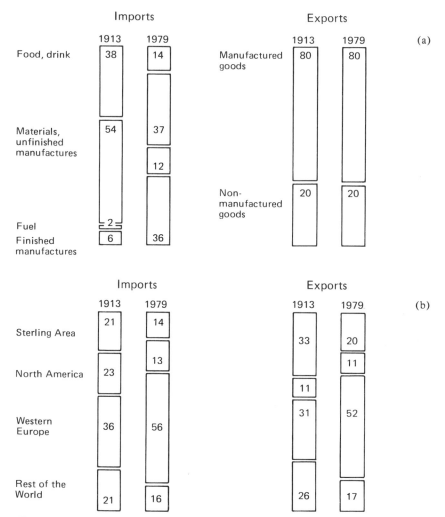

Figure 11.1 UK foreign trade, 1913–1979. (a) Commodity structure (shares, %). (b) Geographical structure (shares, %). Sterling Area is defined as Commonwealth, Burma, Iceland, Irish Republic, Jordan, Kuwait, Libya, Muscat and Oman, South Africa

Sources: 1913 data from *The British Economy, Key Statistics, 1900–1970*; 1979 data from *Overseas Trade Statistics of the UK* (1979), Department of Trade

changing structure of imports is especially significant, with Britain now importing a substantial and growing proportion of manufactures. The changing composition of Britain's trade is of course related to the changing geographical structure of trade, with a swing away from the Commonwealth towards the advanced Western economies.

These and other important changes in Britain's overseas trade are associated with the growth of MNCs. The classic pattern of international trade was between a large number of British firms, operating from Britain, and a large number of foreign firms, operating from their home countries. That pattern no longer obtains. Today, trade is dominated by a relatively small number of firms with plants in many countries. Moreover, international trade is increasingly within, rather than between, firms. These changes in world trade are particularly evident in the case of Britain. Official surveys have estimated, for instance, that in 1976 half the country's exports came from just 87 enterprises, many of them foreign-owned, and that a substantial proportion of exports were to related enterprises abroad, such as subsidiaries or parent companies. The largest exporters to related enterprises were the motor industry (60% of that industry's total exports), chemicals (37%) and metal manufacturing and engineering (29%). Changes in Britain's overseas trade are therefore closely bound up with changes in the pattern of investment into and out of the country.

Britain's trading problems have affected the rest of the economy and have consequently been a major preoccupation of governments. A deficit in a country's balance of payments means that the supply of that country's currency on to the foreign exchange market, where different currencies are bought and sold, exceeds demand. Excess supply generally leads to a fall in price. In the foreign exchange market, a fall in the price of a currency is known as a depreciation. Such a depreciation will theoretically make the country's exports cheaper in terms of other currencies, and its imports dearer in domestic currency. It should therefore help eliminate the balance of payments deficit.

British governments in the 1950s and 1960s, however, sought to avoid a depreciation of sterling because they wished to maintain the stability of the international monetary system. They also felt under obligation to those governments, mainly of Commonwealth countries of the so-called 'Sterling Area', which held large amounts of sterling. To devalue sterling would be to inflict a heavy financial loss upon these friendly countries. In order to maintain the value of sterling, British governments were therefore forced to borrow from abroad and to deflate the home economy, thus creating higher unemployment and depressing living standards. Britain's payments difficulties continued, however, and the pound was devalued in 1967. In the early 1970s, governments abandoned the attempt to maintain a fixed exchange rate, and from 1972 sterling 'floated': it was allowed to fluctuate on the foreign exchange markets according to supply and demand. Sterling fell during the 1970s until North Sea oil and high interest rates pushed it up again, making it harder for UK producers to compete in export and home markets.

11.3.3 Evaluation

The views people hold on international trade are inseparable from their views on the international economy as a whole. Those sharing a Consensus perspective emphasize the 'gains from trade'. They maintain that international trade is preferable to national self-sufficiency. Through international trade, nations can specialize in those goods and services for which they have a competitive advantage. Thus, underdeveloped countries specialize in exporting raw materials and commodities needed by the developed countries. Conversely, Britain and other developed countries specialize in exporting manufactures and providing services such as banking and insurance. By such international specialization the international economy will grow and all nations will benefit. Free trade and an international free market are therefore seen as essential ingredients in Britain's prosperity.

Those with a Conflict perspective stress the unequal distribution of income and power in the world economy. Trade, they argue, is but one mechanism by which powerful Western nations and MNCs exploit the weak. The 'gains from trade' are not distributed according to economic justice or relative contributions to the world economy but according to economic, political and military power. Underdeveloped countries' dependence on raw materials, for example, leaves them vulnerable to fluctuations in world prices, especially when a country is dependent on one commodity. In addition, Western nations may try to prevent the growth of manufacturing in underdeveloped countries, for instance, by limiting imports of manufactures from these countries. The pattern of international specialization and trade is not therefore seen as emerging naturally from the 'comparative advantage' of each country. The pattern is, rather, one which is imposed by powerful Western nations and MNCs to exploit poor nations.

A similar line of argument is applied to British trade with other Western countries. In the Conflict perspective, free trade and membership of the EEC accelerate the decline of British manufacturing industry. They permit foreign competitors to capture British markets and take over British firms. Only a strategy of import controls, restrictions on capital movements and government intervention in industry can prevent Britain's decline and secure her independence.

Clearly, like other aspects of business, international trade is open to very different interpretations.

11.4 International investment

11.4.1 The development of international investment

Britain has a long tradition of investment across national boundaries. There is large-scale investment into and out of Britain, although, on balance, Britain is normally a net exporter of capital. Until 1979, foreign exchange controls were in operation to reduce these outflows, but their abolition, together with EEC membership and Britain's poor economic performance, means that overseas investment is likely to increase.

International investment takes two main forms. **Portfolio investment** involves the acquisition of foreign securities without any control over the management of the enterprise concerned. In contrast, **direct investment** involves the ownership and management of overseas enterprises. This involves not only a transfer of capital overseas but a package of resources including technology, management skills, key personnel and finance.

Throughout the nineteenth century the UK was the major source of international investment. It has been estimated that as late as 1914 UK overseas assets were worth £4000 millions compared with £5500 millions for Germany, France, Holland and the USA combined. UK investment was primarily of the portfolio type in government stocks, railways and public utilities. About half of all British investments were within the Empire.

Since the 1930s and 1940s there has been a change in both the source and type of overseas investment. The USA has displaced the UK as the major source of international investment. Also, the conditions of the 'long boom' of the 1950s and 1960s favoured the growth of direct rather than portfolio investment. Orderly world economic conditions were created, there were improvements in transport and communications and giant US companies were looking overseas for markets. The result was the emergence of a new form of business enterprise: the MNC.

11.4.2 Multinationals and foreign direct investment

An MNC is defined as any company that owns and controls undertakings in more than one country. The earliest MNCs were mainly in the extraction industries, notably oil and minerals, with UK companies being prominent in this search for raw materials. The main postwar explosion of MNCs has, however, been in manufacturing industries, but more recently they have emerged in service industries like banking, insurance and various forms of consultancy.

The most visible feature of MNCs is their size, with many of them having outputs in excess of those of many nation states. Other features of MNCs are their centralized decision-making and tendency to plan their strategies on a global scale, and their concentration in high technology and rapidly expanding industries.

Although MNCs are of worldwide importance—indeed, they are responsible for three-quarters of world trade—they are especially important for Britain. The number of foreign companies operating in the UK has grown markedly since the war. Although only 2% of all manufacturing establishments were foreign-owned in 1975, they accounted for 13% of the labour force in manufacturing and 17% of the output. MNC penetration is particularly marked in some of the more technologically advanced sectors of British industry such as engineering, chemicals, vehicles, and shipbuilding, where foreign participation is over 20%, while in the strategically important North Sea oil and gas fields it is substantially higher. Some two-thirds of these foreign companies are based in the USA and the remainder mainly in Western Europe and, latterly, Japan.

Britain is not without its own MNCs and is second only to the USA as a country of origin for multinationals. Firms such as BP, ICI, GEC and Beechams have plants and subsidiaries throughout the world. It has been estimated that in 1978/79 overseas production accounted for 36% of the total output of the 50 largest UK private sector manufacturing companies. These production facilities are usually intended to serve overseas markets but may also serve the UK market.

11.4.3 The impact of multinationals

The scale and importance of MNCs makes them the subject of great controversy. The controversy is not, however, exclusively about the facts but reflects different values and perspectives about business generally. Foreign MNCs in the UK have been criticized, especially by radicals and trade unionists, on a number of grounds. These include the following.

- Subordinating their UK operations to the pursuit of global profit.
- Concentrating key decision-making, in such areas as investment, pricing and R & D, in company headquarters thus increasing the vulnerability of UK operations.

- Concentrating in depressed areas, such as Scotland and Northern Ireland, thus reducing these regions to 'branch plant economies' vulnerable to changes in corporate strategies.
- Dominating key industries, thus increasing UK dependence on overseas, especially US, technology and goodwill.
- Acting as bad employers, for instance, by pursuing anti-union policies, forcing changes on reluctant workforces and closing plants regardless of the social consequences.
- Using transfer pricing (the prices set on intra MNC transactions which need not be set at market levels) to disguise profits and evade tax liabilities and exchange controls, to charge unfair prices to consumers and to eliminate UK competition.

These criticisms stress the enormous economic and political power of MNCs. They emphasize the great control which foreign and domestic MNCs have over the UK economy and their relative immunity from government control. Critics of MNCs argue that their power is such that it undermines government economic policies and indeed the economic sovereignty of the UK. In addition, the tendency for British MNCs to invest abroad rather than at home is attacked, especially where this investment is intended to supply the British market. Overseas investment is said to deprive domestic industry of much-needed investment, lower its competitiveness and lead to higher unemployment. British MNCs are therefore accused of 'exporting jobs' as well as capital. At the same time it is claimed that British MNC investment in countries with low wages and weak unions is a form of exploitation of poor countries by rich corporations.

MNCs are not without their defenders. Most economists argue that they are a net benefit to the UK. Certainly governments, often with the cooperation of trade unionists, have been eager to attract foreign investment to Britain. Among the benefits foreign MNCs are expected to bring to the UK are the following.

- A package of capital, technology and management know-how, much of which becomes diffused throughout the economy.
- A supply of cheap goods and services.
- Increased prosperity and employment, directly by their investment, and indirectly by their demand for UK components and services.
- Increased prosperity and employment in depressed regions shunned by British firms.
- Higher wages, 'modernization' of working practices and improved working conditions.

In order to secure the benefits and avoid the costs of foreign MNCs, governments have tried to regulate their activities. Any and all of the instruments for regulating business described in Chapter 9 may be used to regulate MNCs. In some cases governments have countered the threat of foreign MNCs by promoting their British competitors. In industries such as aerospace and computers, governments have sponsored domestic mergers or projects as a 'countervailing force' to American competition. Thus, the threat of the foreign MNC is met in the market place. In other cases, such as the motor industry with Chrysler, governments have negotiated agreements with MNCs, seeking assurances on MNC conduct in return for government financial support. It must be said, however, that these assurances are not always honoured. In a few industries, notably North Sea oil and gas, the government has gone further and required some form of state partnership in operations.

As the problems of MNCs are international problems, so halting attempts have been made to find international solutions through such bodies as the UN, the Organization for Economic Cooperation and Development (OECD) and the EEC. In most cases this involves establishing codes of conduct for MNCs. Although such codes give agreed standards for judging MNCs they are rarely enforcible and have had limited effect. Furthermore, whatever the dangers associated with MNCs, governments compete with one another to secure their investment, especially in a period of recession. In general, therefore, the size, flexibility and mobility of MNCs allow them to evade many government controls whether domestic or international in origin.

11.4.4 Evaluation

There is no agreement on the significance of MNCs for the UK or the rest of the world. Judgements are strongly influenced by views of business and market mechanisms in general. In the individualist view the free market produces the most rational division of international labour and the best use of world resources. The MNC is the latest stage in the evolution of business and the most efficient way of organizing business on a world scale. The impact of the MNC is therefore beneficial for the UK both as 'home' and 'host' country.

In the Conflict view of the market held by radicals, MNCs are not viewed so benevolently. They bring substantial economic, social and political costs while the benefits they bring accrue mainly to the rich and powerful. In the case of the UK, MNCs are seen as undermining economic policy and national sovereignty. In the case of the Third World countries, dependence is even greater and multinationals, including those based in Britain, play an important part in perpetuating dependence and exploitation.

Most academics and governments have taken a middle position of guarded optimism between these two extremes. This centrist, or moderate position, is very much a Consensus view. MNCs are viewed as bringing benefits, but there are costs associated with them and therefore a need for regulation. If regulation is too strict investment will be frightened away with a possible reduction in UK and world prosperity. If regulation is selective and flexible, however, those holding the moderate view are optimistic about the net benefits of MNCs. It is clear there is no entirely value-free assessment of MNCs. The facts do not speak for themselves but are open to different interpretations, reflecting different views about the desirability of the private enterprise system.

11.5 International aid

Trade and investment are not the only economic transactions between the UK and the rest of the world. As a former imperial power the UK is a major donor of aid to Third World countries. In the immediate postwar period, however, Britain, along with other European nations, was a major recipient of American aid, under the Marshall Plan. This section will concentrate upon government aid, although there are other donors, such as charities and churches, which often work closely with the government aid agencies.

Governments justify aid to developing countries on grounds both of morality and self-interest. British governments accept that rich countries have a moral obligation to help poor countries to develop their own economies. Aid is also justified, however, on grounds of enlightened self-interest. It is an instrument of foreign policy which allows Britain to support democratic, anti-Communist or pro-British governments. Aid also brings economic benefits to Britain. Much of British aid is 'tied', that is, it must be used to buy British goods and services. Indirect benefits also arise. For instance, overseas students trained in Britain are said to be likely to buy British goods when they return home. Many of these economic benefits of aid are, however, intangible and long term.

11.5.1 The pattern of British aid

British aid is given both directly to other countries (bilaterally) and indirectly through international organizations (multilaterally) such as the World Bank, the UN and EEC agencies. Although multilateral aid has grown as a proportion of aid, British governments still prefer to give bilaterally. This allows control over the destination and use of aid, and makes it easier to secure political and trading advantages for Britain. Bilateral aid is, however, frequently criticized for putting the needs of the donor before those of the recipient.

Aid is given in a number of forms as shown in *Figure 11.2.* Grants and cheap loans are given frequently for specified development projects, such as roads or irrigation and much of this aid is tied. Also, loans, even at cheap rates, may impose heavy debt burdens on developing countries. Loans, which now constitute under 20% of UK aid, can become a trap by which further loans are taken out merely to service existing ones. Aid also takes the form of technical assistance, such as the training of Third World personnel or the sending of British personnel abroad. Finally, food, clothing and medicines are given to meet major disasters such as famines or floods.

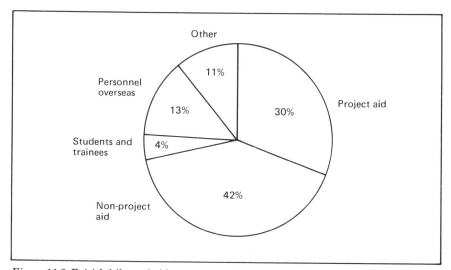

Figure 11.2 British bilateral aid
Source: Overseas Development Administration, 1979

Over a decade ago the UN set a target for the flow of funds to the Third World of 1% of the GNP of developed countries. Of this amount, 70% was expected to come from governments and the rest from private sources. Like most countries, the UK has not reached this target for official aid. Overseas aid is not a priority area in public spending and has suffered cuts along with other areas despite official commitment to the UN target. Public spending plans for government aid from 1980 to 1984, for instance, indicate a smaller rather than a larger aid programme, with a fall from £779 millions (1980/81) to £680 millions (1983/84). Consequently, an increasing proportion of the flow of funds from

Britain to developing countries is from private sector financial institutions. Although this may assist development it also increases Third World indebtedness.

Three-quarters of British bilateral aid goes to developing Commonwealth countries, reflecting Britain's imperial past. When granting independence to colonies successive British governments have offered development aid. Zimbabwe, for instance, received a £75 million aid package on gaining independence in 1980. Such arrangements demonstrate a sense of moral obligation but also reflect the interdependence of British and Commonwealth economies. Commonwealth countries still provide major markets for British companies and supply essential raw materials. Nevertheless, British aid is not limited to the Commonwealth and has been given to strategically important countries, such as Iran and Jordan, for foreign policy as well as commercial objectives.

11.5.2 Evaluation

Overseas aid has done little to reduce the disparities between rich and poor nations and is not without its critics. Although supported by most moderates as a benevolent intervention in the economic process, it is criticized by both individualists and radicals.

In the individualist view aid encourages wasteful spending, the formation of corrupt elites and saps the will of recipients. It is better to rely on market forces and private investment for development, as exemplified by Singapore. Private investment is seen as more discriminating and hard-headed in providing funds. In this view, development in the Third World will only come about by adopting a capitalist approach. By linking Third World nations to the world market it is claimed they can eventually secure the prosperity now enjoyed by the West.

Those with a radical view of the world reject this solution. Rather, they believe the international capitalist system, of which foreign aid is a small part, makes greater the disparities between rich and poor nations. Both bilateral and multilateral aid from Western-dominated agencies like the World Bank and the IMF are seen as giving donors 'leverage' over recipients. Conditions imposed on borrowers by international agencies go far beyond the normal banker's concern to ensure that loans are repaid. Conditional loans are used to force Third World borrowers towards economic policies beneficial to the West and to prevent obstacles being put in the way of Western trade and investment. Typical conditions attached to loans include the abolition of restrictions on trade and investment, deflation, devaluation and reduced public spending—indeed the whole catalogue of monetarist policies. The use of loans as a lever to determine a country's economic policies is not limited to the Third World as British dealings with the IMF demonstrate. In the Third World context, however, radicals claim the leverage is such as to impose a capitalist system on countries that might prefer different systems.

The radical way to economic development for Third World countries is through less dependence on the West. Third World countries are enjoined to adopt radical interventionist and protectionist policies and follow the example of OPEC in using their economic strength against the West. Like individualists, therefore, radicals believe dependence on overseas aid is harmful to Third World countries. The alternatives suggested to reliance on aid, however, reflect a very different view of the world from that of individualists.

11.6 International migration

International migration of labour involves a transfer of economic resources. Mass migration has important economic as well as human consequences and is especially important to the UK with its long history of immigration and emigration.

British emigrants contributed greatly to the economic expansion of North America and Australia, especially before 1914. Similarly, immigrants from Ireland and the New Commonwealth and Pakistan (NCWP) have contributed significantly to British prosperity. Since the 1950s immigration provided a ready supply of labour to meet the requirements of the 'long boom'. Without this supply there would have been labour shortages and severe dislocation in industries like construction, transport, catering and the NHS. Immigration has also produced significant racial minorities. In 1980 it was officially estimated that 3.5% of the UK population are NCWP immigrants and their descendants, and the figure will rise to 5% by 1991. Immigration is therefore of great social and political as well as economic significance, as noted in Chapter 8.

11.6.1 The pattern of immigration

All developed countries of Western Europe have experienced large-scale immigration since the war. Unlike other European countries, which have drawn immigrants and temporary 'guest workers' from Southern Europe, Turkey and North Africa, immigrants to the UK have come predominantly from Ireland and NCWP. Immigration has been caused by the 'push' of domestic poverty and the 'pull' of job prospects and prosperity in the UK. Not all migration has such an obvious economic cause however. Political factors, such as the expulsions of Asians from Kenya and Uganda, have produced unexpected flows of immigrants to Britain.

Since 1962 progressively stricter immigration controls have been introduced to reduce the influx of immigrants. As a result of this, and also because of the declining employment prospects in Britain, the number of immigrants has fallen from over 100 000 a year in the early 1960s to around 40 000 a year by the late 1970s. There has also been a change in the character of immigration. Immigrants in the 1950s and early 1960s were predominantly men seeking work. Now, an increasing proportion of immigrants are dependants joining kinfolk already settled in Britain. In 1978, for instance, such family reunions accounted for 56% of immigrants. Also, immigration controls have been deliberately designed to restrict the number of unskilled immigrants and give preference to those who are skilled or professionally qualified. Although restrictions on NCWP immigrants have been tightened, accession to the EEC allows free movement of labour within the Community. In the long term this may have important consequences for UK immigration and emigration, especially if mutual recognition of educational and professional qualifications is achieved.

Immigrants and their descendants are an important part of the UK labour force. It has already been noted that there are heavy concentrations of immigrants in certain industries. Moreover, they tend to fill jobs with unsociable hours, dirty and dangerous working conditions, low pay and insecurity. In the UK, as elsewhere in the EEC, they fill the jobs that are shunned by indigenous workers. Not all immigrants and their descendants work in such jobs of course: 40% of males and 59% of females are in non-manual jobs. Nevertheless, racial minorities are found disproportionately in jobs with low income and status and a disproportionate number live in the rundown inner-city areas.

11.6.2 Evaluation

Although the importance of immigration is not disputed by those with Consensus and Conflict views of society, they interpret it very differently. Some who share the Consensus view see immigrants as a disruptive and alien element in British society. Those with a more moderate view, however, believe immigration shows the benevolent workings of the market, transferring labour from where there is a surplus to where there is a shortage. The UK is said to have benefited from a cheap and flexible supply of pliant immigrant workers. They carry out essential jobs shunned by British workers, keep down wages and costs and make British industry more competitive. The sending countries also benefit from migration. It acts as a 'safety valve', relieving unemployment and population pressures. The savings which immigrants to the UK remit to their families back home is also important for poor countries. It provides a supply of foreign exchange which can be used to import capital goods needed for development programmes. Finally, the skills which immigrants acquire in the UK are available to the sending countries if immigrants return home. In the Consensus view migration benefits the immigrants, the UK and the sending countries. Their presence here has assisted economic growth both in Britain and in their home countries and given them a standard of living unattainable back home.

In the Conflict view, however, the main benefits of immigration accrue to the upper classes in the UK and in the sending countries. In this view immigrants form a pool of unemployed workers, keeping down wages and increasing profits. In work, they perform the worst jobs for the lowest pay and the lowest esteem. Immigrants are thus the most exploited element of the working class. Furthermore, the divisions between immigrants and indigenous workers are said to weaken the working class and trade union movement to the benefit of the upper class. The benefits to sending countries are also questioned. Migration involves the loss of many of the most ambitious and able members of the labour force in poor countries. It also perpetuates the dependence of Third World economies on Europe. The benefits of immigration depend very much on economic conditions in Europe and on the immigration policies of European governments. In a recession Western governments can stop immigration, thus exporting some of the worst effects of the recession to poor countries. The 'safety valve' effect of migration is also criticised by many radicals for deflecting attention away from much needed reforms and perpetuating the rule of the dominant classes in poor countries.

This divergence between these two views of immigration mirrors the divergence of views over the workings of the economic system. In the Consensus view the workings of the market benefit sending countries, migrants and the UK. In the Conflict view, however, the international market system works to perpetuate inequalities of wealth and power within and between nations.

11.7 Conclusion: alternative perspectives on the international economy

The UK has never been insulated from the outside world. During the nineteenth century when its power was greatest, Britain was able to shape the international environment to its advantage. Pre-eminent in trade and investment and possessing a large empire, Britain was able to dominate the emergent international economic system. Yet international events rarely affected day-to-day life or government domestic policy in Britain. It seemed that Britain shaped the international environment rather than being shaped by it. Following a century of relative economic decline, the UK is no longer so insulated from international events. Pressures for change are more often exerted on the UK from the international environment than ever before.

Today all Western and most Third World economies are closely integrated into the international economic system. There are large-scale flows of goods and services, capital, technology and labour across national boundaries. Consequently nations are more interdependent. Problems in one area, such as the Middle East, may be quickly transmitted throughout the world. The growth of international organizations such as the IMF, World Bank and EEC shows the desire of states to reduce instability in the world economic system.

This closer integration of the national economies into a world system has profound implications for British business and society. Industrial and commercial firms face increasing competition from imports and foreign-owned MNCs, and are presented with new opportunities in foreign markets as exporters and investors. The price and availability of foreign supplies of raw materials and energy are a particular concern. The British financial sector is even more closely bound to the world economy than industry and commerce, for it is a financial centre of world importance. Even British domestic financial markets, such as the gilts market, are profoundly affected by trends in world interest rates. Governments too find that their policies have international implications in fields other than foreign trade, aid and migration. Industrial and energy policies, for example, have required negotiations with MNCs. Moreover, since Britain joined the EEC, governments have found that an increasing range of domestic policies require negotiation with the other members of the Community.

International integration is also strengthening in social and cultural matters. Western culture, fashions and tastes are becoming more uniform. This uniformity is evident in dress, leisure activities, and even in political activity, for example, the active antinuclear lobbies in the USA and Europe stimulate similar campaigns in Britain. The growth of the mass media and international travel, higher levels of education and the activities of firms, have all contributed to the increasing impact of international trends and events on British society.

As this chapter has demonstrated, all these developments are open to different interpretations. In the Consensus view capitalism and the profit motive provide the key to economic prosperity. Thus, in the

Consensus view of the international economic system the benefits of freedom of trade, investment, aid and migration are stressed. Cooperation between governments is needed and is provided through such organizations as the World Bank, the IMF, GATT and the EEC. Such bodies seek to overcome obstacles to the development of the international economy such as monetary instability, slow growth and 'beggar-my-neighbour' protectionist policies. These bodies do not, however, replace international market mechanisms, but rather smooth their operation.

At the heart of the Consensus view of the international economic system is the belief that there are benefits to all who participate in international trade, investment, aid and migration. The interests of the UK are believed to be compatible with those of other nations. Of course, the UK experiences problems arising from its openness to international pressures. Traditional British industries like textiles, shipbuilding and steel which cannot compete internationally are severely affected. However, international competition encourages the transfer of resources in the UK from such uncompetitive and contracting industries to those industries which are more competitive so that in the long term the painful effects of the international market will benefit the UK. In the Consensus view, therefore, it is overwhelmingly in the interests of the British people for the country to be incorporated into the international economic system.

In the Conflict perspective the capitalist system, whether domestic or international, is viewed as unstable and exploitative. The growth of the international economic system based on the pursuit of profit is seen as harmful to the interests of most people in the UK. The benefits of international trade, investment, aid and migration accrue overwhelmingly, although not exclusively, to those who already possess wealth and power. The dominance which MNCs have established over international trade and investment is viewed with particular concern. The MNC is seen as a new and virulent form of capitalism which is beyond the control of governments. Similarly, international organizations like the IMF, World Bank, GATT and EEC are seen as supporting capitalist ideas and exploitation.

In addition, it is argued that inequality is reinforced and increased by international economic transactions. They frequently increase disparities of wealth and power within and between nations. They make Western countries like the UK richer, but at the expense of the poorer countries. Yet within the UK the benefits of international transactions are not equitably distributed. Many British workers may become worse off because of import penetration, the activities of MNCs and large-scale immigration, although many will undoubtedly become better off. In the Conflict view, however, any improvements in living standards are not in the long-term interests of British workers. They deflect workers from the struggle to remove the inequalities of wealth and power inherent in capitalism. In the Conflict view an international economic system based on the pursuit of profit perpetuates and accentuates inequalities within the UK, and between the rich and poor nations of the world.

The Consensus and Conflict views of the world provide very different interpretations of the international context of business. These interpretations complement those of the domestic environment of business. Nor is this surprising, for the Consensus and Conflict perspectives are based on divergent beliefs about the virtues of allocating income, wealth and power through the market mechanism. They are perspectives not only on the world as it is, but as people believe it ought to be.

Guide to further reading

General

Campbell, M. P. (1981). *Capitalism in the UK*, Croom Helm, London. Chapter 6 provides a Marxist critique of international economic relations, with special reference to Britain.

Open University (1976). *Inequalities Between Nations* (D302 Patterns of Inequality, Units 22–24), Open University Press, Milton Keynes. A difficult but useful review of international economic relations using an approach similar to that used in this chapter.

Black, John (1979). *The Economics of Modern Britain: An Introduction to Macroeconomics*, Martin Robertson, Oxford. Chapters 22–24 analyse Britain's overseas trade.

Independent Commission on International Development Issues. (The Brandt Commission) (1980). *North–South: A Programme for Survival*, Pan, London. This Report stresses the interdependence of North and South.

Subsections

11.1

Spero, Joan Edelman (1977). *The Politics of International Economic Relations*, Allen and Unwin, London. Parts 1 and 2 review the major trends in postwar international economic relations, although with an emphasis on the USA.

11.2

Swann, D. (1978). *The Economics of the Common Market*, 4th edn, Penguin, London.
Holland, Stuart (1975). *The Socialist Challenge*, Quartet Books, London. Chapters 12 and 13 criticize the EEC from a radical perspective.

11.3

Lipsey, Richard G. (1979). *An Introduction to Positive Economics*, 5th edn, Weidenfeld and Nicolson, London. Chapters 46 and 52–55 outline the theory of the international economy.

National Institute of Economic and Social Research (1979). *The United Kingdom Economy*, 4th edn, Heinemann, London. Chapter 6 provides a summary of Britain's external trade and payments.

11.4

Hood, Neil and Young, Stephen (1979). *The Economics of Multinational Enterprise*, Longman, London. A thorough review of MNCs, including a useful review of alternative perspective in Chapter 8.

Urry, John and Wakeford, John (Eds) (1973). *Power in Britain*, Chapter 13 by John Hughes examines the growth of US investment in Britain.

11.5

Spero, Joan Edelman (1977). *The Politics of International Economic Relations*, Allen and Unwin, London. Chapter 6 emphasizes the political purposes of aid especially from the USA and multilateral agencies.

Hayter, Teresa (1971). *Aid as Imperialism*, Penguin, London. A radical critique of aid.

11.6

Deakin, Nicholas (1970). *Colour, Citizenship and British Society*, Panther, London. A classic, if dated, account of the consequences of immigration.

Exercises

Review questions

1. List the major changes in the postwar international economy which are most significant for Britain.
2. What are the main political and economic consequences of EEC membership for Britain?
3. Summarize the similarities and differences between the Consensus and Conflict views of British membership of the EEC.
4. What are the main changes in the pattern of UK foreign trade indicated in *Figure 11.1*?
5. Distinguish between the Consensus and Conflict views on free trade.

6. What are the two main types of overseas investment and why has there been a change in their relative importance?
7. Outline the major arguments for and against allowing foreign MNCs to invest in Britain.
8. Why does Britain give overseas aid? What criticisms do individualists and radicals make of overseas aid?
9. Outline the different views on the benefits which arise from immigration into Britain.

Investigation and application

1. What are the major components in the UK balance of payments accounts? Estimate the relative size of these components in any recent year using data published in *The UK Balance of Payments.*
2. Use data from the *Census of Production*, which is summarized in various issues of *British Business* (formerly *Trade and Industry*), to identify the scale of foreign participation in British industry and the changes which have taken place during the 1970s. In which industries is foreign participation most pronounced?
3. Use the latest *White Paper on Public Expenditure* together with data made available regularly by the Overseas Development Administration to discover: the size of Britain's official aid programme; the major recipients of British aid; the major forms of British aid and their relative size; and the major channels through which British aid is distributed.

Projects

1. Compare the extent of foreign ownership of industries in the industrial and commercial sectors with that in the financial sector. Suggest tests which might be used to measure the advantages and disadvantages of foreign ownership. How do those with a Consensus perspective differ from those with a Conflict perspective in their evaluation of foreign ownership?
2. Why has Britain ceased to be the dominant nation in international trade and investment?

Chapter 12

The future of business in society

12.1 Business and the future

The society in which business operates has changed dramatically in the last 100 years. Change is likely to accelerate in the future. Organizations of all kinds are forced to take account of possible changes that will affect their operations. The impact of change on organizations can be assessed by specifying those key areas where it is likely to be strongly felt. These may be usefully dealt with under the headings resources, opportunities and constraints.

Resources. As far as these are concerned, both technology and labour are areas where change might be expected. Organizations of all kinds face a future where they will be required to employ new kinds of technology and a labour force whose attitudes and behaviour differ from those of today. Man's changing role as a producer will confront employers with new kinds of problems in the future.

Opportunities. The pattern of demand for goods and services is dynamic. Changing population structure, changing consumer preferences and changes in markets due to increased or decreased competition all affect the opportunities for effective performance open to organizations. Man's changing role as a consumer will make its mark on organizations whatever pattern the future takes.

Constraints. New types of political and legal regulation are likely to develop in the future. Many organizations are likely to face reductions in their freedom of action as new obligations are imposed on them through regulation at both national and international level. Consumer interests may become increasingly demanding. Some organizations may find their supplies of raw materials more difficult to obtain.

The impact of change on organizations is uneven. For some, the pace of change may be much faster than for others. The extent of change faced will also vary. Some organizations may have to alter their entire mode of operation with great speed while others may be able to cope, with a series of marginal adjustments. All organizations, however, will need to attempt to anticipate the changes that will affect them if they are to be capable of an effective response. This is normally done through planning. Planning is simply the process whereby organizations make provision for the future. The time-scale on which organizations attempt to plan varies. For some, it may be necessary to look no further than a few months ahead. For others, especially large organizations, where investment in new resources may determine their future capacity for several decades, the time-span is much longer.

Planning for the future always involves making guesses about what will happen. It is unlikely that anyone will ever discover a way of making precise predictions about the future course of economic, political and social affairs, for there are simply too many possibilities. However, this does not mean that all speculation about the future is futile. In fact, this form of activity makes up a thriving academic industry known to its adherents as 'futurology'. Such 'think tanks' as the Hudson Institute and the Brookings Institution devote considerable energy to predicting the future development of society. Large organizations in business and government also attempt to cater for expected patterns of change in their long-term planning.

There are two methods which can be used to draw up a picture of the future. The first is to visualize the future as an extension of existing trends of change. The second is to combine the views of experts on different aspects of life, such as the economic, the political and the technological, about how these areas are likely to change. Once again, however, the facts will not speak for themselves. Disagreement exists both about what past trends have been and about how particular aspects of life are likely to change. As a result it is possible to outline a number of different directions in which society could plausibly be seen as moving.

Generally, views which are held about the future depend on how the present and the past are interpreted. Accordingly, the second section of this chapter will summarize the major patterns of change identified in the book. Relevant material in different chapters will be grouped together to give the following four areas of change.

- The economy (Chapters 3–7).
- The social context (Chapter 8).
- The political and legal context (Chapters 9 and 10).
- The international context (Chapter 11).

The third section will outline a variety of possible futures on the basis of Conflict and Consensus interpretations of the overall pattern of change. The fourth section will form the conclusion.

12.2 Change in society

Many different types of change involving business in society have been identified in this book. This section will identify some of the major past trends.

12.2.1 The economy

For the last 200 years there has been a long-term tendency for the productive capacity of the economy to expand. Despite several periods of low or zero growth, on average, the annual rate of increase has been about 2%. A major cause of this has been a fairly steady increase in the quality of the technology used to produce goods and services. New sources of power and new forms of capital equipment have continuously been developed. In the last century this development has increasingly been associated with the growth of scientific knowledge and its application to the production of goods and services in both the private and the public sectors of business. The application of scientific discoveries has also led to the production of many new kinds of commodity, resulting in an increase in the range of goods available for the consumption of ordinary people. As a result, there has been a massive decline of employment in the 'primary' sectors of agriculture and extraction, as well as a tendency for employment to increase in the 'service' sector.

Changes have also taken place in the location of economic activity. In the present century new industrial development has tended to be found in the expanding areas of the Midlands and South East, while the older industrial areas of the North, Wales and Scotland, have declined.

There have been identifiable trends of change in the nature of the organizations which produce goods and services. In all four business sectors, the scale of individual operating units has increased. In the private sector of the economy, the degree of concentration of output has also risen. As a result, the output of many goods and services is dominated by a handful of giant enterprises. While the tendency towards concentration has not proceeded at an even pace, there is no sign of a reversal of the trend. In the public sector this process of concentration has been paralleled over a long period by the growth of centralized control of many services previously subject to a greater degree of local regulation. Over the last century and a half, there has been a noticeable tendency for the involvement of the state in the production of goods and services to increase. The public enterprise sector has expanded considerably, especially during the postwar period. During the present century, the social services sector has also been greatly expanded, although again this has been mainly concentrated in the postwar years. Many services previously provided within the family or the local community are now provided by the state. The present century, and especially the postwar period, has also seen a general increase of state intervention in the economy. As a counterpart of the growing involvement of the state there has been a long-term tendency for taxation to increase. These economic changes are a major cause of changes in the social context.

12.2.2 The social context

A number of trends have affected the working population. Since the late nineteenth century the proportion of heavy labouring jobs has declined and the number of whitecollar jobs has expanded. Professional, scientific and technical occupations have also accounted for an increasing part of the labour force. The length of the working week has declined and holidays have increased in length. The proportion of working women has continued to increase. The greater size and complexity of employing organizations has led, since the mid-nineteenth century, to the development of management roles based on various branches of specialized knowledge, such as accounting. In the same period the number of trade union members has shown a long-term tendency to increase. In the postwar period there has been a marked increase of female and whitecollar union members. There has been a clear trend involving a decline in the number of unions and an increase in their average size. This century, industrial bargaining has gradually become more centralized. More and more employees now have their pay and conditions determined at national level. At the same time the state has tended to become more involved in industrial relations through incomes policies and through intervention in particular disputes and as a large-scale employer.

In the area of social inequality, it would appear that all three classes have derived some benefit from the increase in wealth generated by economic growth. However, this is an area where the precise nature of the trends at work is hotly disputed. Since the start of the last century there has been a steady increase in the urban population. Along with the expansion of industrial employment, this has produced the characteristic urban-industrial way of life of our society. Traditional rural and small-town communities have steadily declined. As a result, many distinctive local and regional cultural characteristics have disappeared and a national culture has emerged. The growth of literacy and the expansion of the mass media have also played a part. Increasingly, people have adopted a materialist view of life. Traditional attitudes have increasingly been questioned. The traditional respect for religion, authority, the family and other social institutions has declined. Scientific and technical knowledge have become the basis for modern society. There has been a perceptible trend towards a more flexible morality and away from an absolute moral code buttressed by religion and custom.

The patterns of change in such areas of life as work, industrial relations, inequality, community and values largely stem from the changing nature of the economic system. In turn, they are closely related to the major trends at work in the political and legal context.

12.2.3 The political and legal context

For the past 150 years a major trend in political life has been the gradual extension of the franchise. This has been coupled with the growth of mass political parties, and this century, with the rise of the labour movement. More broadly, there has been a long-term increase in support for the idea of an active role for the state and a general decline in support for a strictly *laissez-faire* ideology. Another important trend has been the growth in numbers of pressure groups of various kinds and their incorporation into the political system.

The most apparent trend concerning the machinery of government has been the growth in its size. The organs of central and local administration have expanded enormously over the last 150 years, most especially in the postwar period. In the present century there has also been a trend towards the establishment of growing numbers of appointed state agencies. These changes reflect the apparently ever-widening scope of government intervention and the increasing influence of the state machinery on society.

The growth of the machinery of state is part of a more general tendency whereby customary and informal social arrangements are replaced by state-controlled bodies. In the area of law, this has meant the decline of informal methods of regulating behaviour and the growth of official enforcement agencies. The state has also increasingly intervened in various kinds of contract. Particularly in the areas of employment and the sale of goods, the postwar period has seen a growing body of legislation. In addition, there has been a perceptible trend towards improving the legal rights of individuals against large organizations in both the private and the public sector. The areas of life where legal or quasilegal means of resolving disputes exist has been steadily widened by the formation of growing numbers of tribunals of various kinds.

12.2.4 The international context

For at least a century, Britain has been declining relative to many other industrial nations. During this period Britain has moved from being the dominant world economic and military power to being a middle-ranking European power. With the dissolution of the British Empire in the postwar period, links with other European powers have gradually expanded. Britain has become more integrated into the world economy, particularly through expanding links with Western Europe. A growing proportion of British industry is foreign-owned. In addition, foreign competition in markets for manufactured goods has continued to grow throughout this century. Militarily, Britain possesses little capacity for independent action, and increasingly security has been sought through alliances. By most measures of international importance, Britain's progress has generally been downward and internationally the future seems to offer increasing dependence and vulnerability. There is no doubt that massive upheavals are underway in the balance of international economic and political power, as more countries gain political independence and as many of them seek to control their own economic destinies.

12.2.5 Past trends and the future

It might seem to be a simple matter to draw up a picture of the future through an extension of past trends. In practice, however, a great many difficulties arise. First, a very large number of trends may be identified. The list of those identified above is by no means exhaustive. In order to draw up a picture of the future at a manageable level of simplicity, the most important of these trends have to be selected. While some trends are obviously of major importance, there may be debate about the significance of others. Secondly, some trends only appear as such in the very long term. Within relatively short periods of time the continuity of the trend may not be apparent. Moreover, circumstances such as war, or economic recession, create discontinuities in trends. Doubt often exists, therefore, about what is, and what is not, a trend. Thirdly, some trends are of much more recent origin than others. It is not clear how long a pattern of events needs to occur before it can be viewed as a trend. And fourthly, account must be taken of the pace of change described by some trends. It needs to be known whether the trend is slowing or accelerating.

From the above, it should be clear that the selection and interpretation of trends is a highly complex matter, and that rather different views of the future might be drawn up, even starting from what appear to be the same trends. The view that is taken of the future is also influenced by the perspective through which the past and present are viewed. It is not surprising, therefore, that a number of possible futures may be envisaged.

12.3 Alternative views of the future

There is a major division, concerning the shape the future is likely to take, between Consensus and Conflict theories. Consensus approaches generally envisage the future in an optimistic way. The problems of the present will be solved as the major trends in society work themselves out. Conflict approaches generally view the future pessimistically. The problems of the present will be magnified, eventually leading to social breakdown. The two approaches contain a number of variants, each of which envisages a related but different outcome. A few of the more important variants will be discussed.

12.3.1 Consensus approaches

The Consensus approach to the future rests on the belief that advances in science and technology will continue to take place. As a result, the production of goods and services of all kinds will continue to expand and living standards will go on improving. Whatever problems the future brings will be soluble. Within the Consensus framework the major division is between those who view the future with guarded optimism and those who take a superoptimistic view. In addition, a few authors give a pessimistic interpretation.

The guarded optimists recognize that new kinds of problems may develop in the future, but they consider that solutions will be found to them. Domestically, social stability and the lack of support for extreme policies will enable the Moderate viewpoint to prevail in politics. The state will develop increasingly effective forms of economic management to ensure the overall conditions for continued economic progress. Technical solutions will be found to the growing shortages of raw materials and fuels. The stability of the international economic system will increase as the developing countries gradually move toward economic maturity.

Many of the undesirable features of present society will gradually disappear. Business itself will gradually move away from an exclusive concern with the pursuit of profits, to a recognition of wider responsibilities. Working conditions will improve as technology takes over the more unpleasant jobs. Greater productivity will allow hours of work to be reduced and holidays to be increased. While inequalities will remain, they will be of a kind that are acceptable. Poverty will disappear. Improved standards of living and an increasingly well-educated population will raise the level of political debate, making the state more sensitive to the needs of the public.

Those in the Centre of politics commonly anticipate a future of this kind. Change will come in the form of a gradual evolution based on what is seen as a long-term and firmly based tendency for progress to continue.

The superoptimists share the belief of the guarded optimists in a future which builds on the desirable features of the present. Where they differ is in their estimation of the pace and extent of the changes that will take place. While this view again rests on new developments in science and technology, it suggests that the changes in this area now beginning to take place are of a qualitatively new kind. These changes have been said to amount to a 'new industrial revolution'. They involve the application of computing and microprocessor technology to automate a wide range of productive activities. As a result, the whole nature of the economic and social system will be dramatically transformed.

The 'tertiary' sector of the economy will expand rapidly while the decline of the industrial sector will accelerate. The attractive conditions now found only in a small minority of workplaces will become the norm. The amount of work required to produce the goods and services needed will be so far reduced that leisure and not work will become the main business of life.

Change will also take place in the way that society is governed. Scientists and professionals will play an increasingly important role in a society based on the possession of knowledge. Those in jobs requiring higher education may become a new 'technocratic' elite.

Society will move to a 'postcapitalist' or 'postindustrial' form where the major problems of scarcity of goods, and the class conflict arising from this, have disappeared. Possession of knowledge rather than ownership of property will become the basis of status and authority. Political conflict will dwindle and become confined to technical disagreements about the best means to reach agreed ends.

It should be noted that there are also pessimistic interpretations of the 'postindustrial' society. A right-wing approach sees the progressive erosion of support for the *laissez-faire* values of self-help and private property. This will result from continuing increases in state intervention in industry and the provision of social services. At the same time it sees the trade union movement as becoming more and more powerful, and economic decline as accelerating. Unless there is a strenuous opposition to existing trends, the future will involve a form of bureaucratic socialism which will stifle initiative and bring a reduction in political freedom. The left-wing version envisages an oppressive future whereby the masses are lulled into passive acceptance of their inferior position. This will occur because the increased standard of living will result in more leisure and greater consumption. People will withdraw from any concern with the wider society, into a 'privatized' life based on high consumption. Improvements in technology, particularly in communications, will give the elite greater power to prevent opposition from arising. These are both, however, minority views. Most depictions of a future based on high technology see it much more as an opportunity for liberation from the constraints arising from scarcity.

12.3.2 Conflict approaches

The common thread running through the conceptions of the future dealt with here is the belief that the working-out of existing trends will result in social breakdown. These views are generally held by radicals. The most common version of the radical approach identifies the major trend as the intensification of class conflict. They believe that the concentration of the ownership and control of productive assets will continue. British industry will increasingly come under the control of foreign MNCs. International competition will intensify and imported raw materials will continue to rise in price. Economic inequalities will persist and the economy will become more and more unstable as inflation and unemployment increase. Social services will be cut back and relative economic decline will turn into an accelerating reduction in living standards. As a result, there will be growing working class opposition to the system and a mass political movement supporting a radical ideology will grow up. Eventually economic collapse will result in a change in the form of government, bringing to power either a left-wing government or a dictatorship of the Right.

The other Conflict viewpoint sees social breakdown as likely to result from the consequences of the pursuit of economic growth. This approach to the future rests on the belief that continued economic growth, even if it is achieved, can no longer bring about improvements in living standards. In its depiction of the future this view concentrates on the trends involved in the way in which resources are used to produce goods. It is suggested that reserves of raw materials, such as oil, are rapidly being used up, while the demand for them is ever expanding. Nuclear energy, increasingly used as a substitute, is both inefficient and dangerous. At the same time, the consumer goods on which the modern capitalist economy is based are becoming more and more wasteful, because of 'built-in obsolescence' and over-elaborate packaging. The processes by which goods are produced create ever greater pollution and destruction of the environment, which will increasingly negate the benefits of further growth. This view anticipates growing revulsion against these trends and the growth of a social movement which will eventually lead to a completely new approach to the production of goods and services. This new approach will involve simpler goods and a non-polluting 'alternative' technology. Renewable energy resources such as solar power will be developed. The trend towards gigantism will be reversed and organizations and human settlements will be reduced in scale.

12.4 Conclusion

The previous section outlined a number of different directions which change might take in the future. It is difficult to assign probabilities to the likelihood of one or other of these possible futures coming into existence. Indeed, it is conceivable that the future will take on some form quite different from those discussed here.

The different images of the future outlined above rest on different assessments of the likely patterns of development in the following areas of life.

- Scientific knowledge and its technological application.
- The productiveness of the economic system.
- The political values and aspirations held by the population.
- The economic and social role played by the state.
- The impact of the international economic and political environment.

These are all areas where changes are both possible and likely. It is up to organizations of all kinds to make assessments about the likely direction of change and its impact on them.

This book began by highlighting the issue of change and its effects and it is appropriate to end in the same way. The important thing is to be sensitive to the likelihood of change and its possible directions. No one can draw up a plan of what the future will be like. For this very reason it is necessary to try to understand the tendencies at work which shape the future. To identify these tendencies involves an attempt to understand the present and the past. Throughout this book it has been emphasized how the perspective that is adopted colours the way society is viewed. The same is true of how the future is seen. All that can be predicted with certainty is that change will continue. Understanding the present, and the factors in it which are shaping the future, is more important than trying to forecast the detailed form it will take.

Guide to further reading
General

Freeman, Christopher and Jahoda, Marie (1978). *World Futures*, Martin Robertson, London. Chapters 8 and 9 contain a detailed analysis of a wide variety of alternative futures.

Subsections
2.1–2.4

Halsey, A. H. (Ed.) (1972). *Trends in British Society since 1900*, Macmillan, London. Contains much relevant material on trends of change.

3.1

Kumar, Krishan (1978). *Prophecy and Progress*, Penguin, London. Part 6 offers a powerful critique of theories of postindustrial society.

3.2

Dickson, D. (1974). *Alternative Technology and the Politics of Technical Change*, Collins/Fontana, Glasgow.
Schumacher, E. F. (1973). *Small is Beautiful*, Blond and Briggs, London. A classic critique of large-scale production.

Exercises
Review questions

1. What have been the past trends in the tertiary sector?
2. How have organizations changed in the last 100 years?
3. Why is the proportion of scientific and technical jobs increasing?
4. What changes have been taking place this century in Britain's international position?
5. What do the 'superoptimists' have to say about the impact of technology on work?
6. Why do some Conflict theories predict an intensification of class conflict?
7. Why do some people question the benefits of more economic growth?

Application and investigation

1. Identify the main features of the 'alternative technology' and discuss its implications for business.
2. Examine the impact of microprocessors and evaluate their likely economic effect over the next 10 years. Two useful references to start with are:

   Forester, Tom (1978). 'The micro-electronic revolution,' *New Society*, 9 November.
   Forester, Tom (1978). 'Society with chips and without jobs,' *New Society*, 16 November.

Project

Using SIC data, find out the proportion of GNP devoted over the last 10 years to the four sectors of business discussed in this book. Describe what you think life would be like at the end of the century if past trends were to be continued.

Appendix

Guide to official sources of data

There are a number of principal sources of information published by the government. Unless stated otherwise, the publications are produced annually by the Central Statistical Office. They can usually be found in college libraries and public reference libraries. In some cases they are accompanied by supplements explaining the definitions used, and these can often be of assistance.

Annual Abstract of Statistics is a basic source of data on many subjects: population, social services, the distribution of labour (using the SIC system), unemployment, production, the balance of payments, National Income, taxation, money and finance.

Monthly Digest of Statistics gives more recent information on many of the series in *Annual Abstract of Statistics*. It goes into some detail on the production and distribution of many specific commodities.

National Income and Expenditure (the 'Blue Book') gives information on the income and expenditure of the national economy and the various sectors, over a 10-year period.

Economic Trends (monthly) goes into greater detail on items such as consumer spending, industrial production and inflation. It also contains a diary of recent economic development. Its *Annual Supplement* gives long statistical series on these topics, going back to the 1940s in many cases.

Financial Statistics (monthly) describes the transactions of the financial sector, showing the assets and liabilities and the borrowing and lending of the many types of financial institution. It also shows security prices and interest rates.

The Department of Employment Gazette (Department of Employment monthly) contains many statistical series on employment, unemployment and pay, together with articles on aspects of employment.

The UK Balance of Payments (the 'Pink Book') gives details of Britain's overseas transactions and external assets and liabilities.

Social Trends contains information on many aspects of social life, such as family size, education, income and wealth, health, housing, patterns of leisure, law enforcement and political participation.

The General Household Survey covers some of the same topics as *Social Trends*, but goes into greater detail.

The Family Expenditure Survey (Department of Employment) gives details of consumer spending patterns, showing how they vary between income groups and through time.

The Guide to Official Statistics aims to cover all official and some important non-official sources of statistics. It can be of use when more specific information is sought.

Index